BEAR GRYLLS
MAN VS. WILD

BEAR GRYLLS
MAN VS. WILD

Survival Techniques from the Most Dangerous Places on Earth

HYPERION

NEW YORK

contents

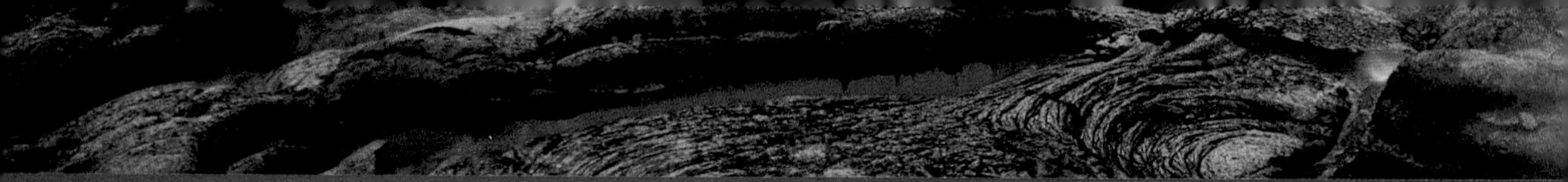

To my two boys, Jesse and Marmaduke. Whenever a situation has gone to the wire, it is you and your mama who have been the lights at the end of the tunnel guiding me home.

I love you so much.

Bear.

Wisdom may be much admired. But what really inspires mankind, what quickens the pulse and lifts the spirits, is its opposite: a display of magnificent, reckless impetuosity.

Just think about it. It's not wisdom that wins the Victoria Cross. It's the insane dash against impossible odds. It's not wisdom that paints the *Mona Lisa* or composes the *Eroica* Symphony. Wise people would never go into the arts in the first place. It's not wisdom that compels people to push themselves to the limits of endurance in order to realize some mad dream. It's a glorious perversity deep in their souls. And it's not wisdom that inspires people to risk everything in pursuit of a seemingly hopeless love affair. It's uncontrollable passion, and the existential urge to taste danger before you die.

Richard Morrison, *The Times*

Introduction

DID YOU KNOW THAT THE ARCTIC GROUND
SQUIRREL IS THE ONLY KNOWN MAMMAL
CAPABLE OF LOWERING ITS BODY TEMPERATURE
TO BELOW FREEZING? OR THAT A LADYBUG'S
BRIGHT COLORS ARE A POTENT WARNING, AND
THAT WHEN DISTURBED IT SECRETES OILY FOUL-
SMELLING YELLOW BLOOD FROM ITS LEGS TO
DETER PREDATORS?

Nowadays people refer to the natural world as
"wilderness," as if nature is somehow wild and
unkempt, out of control and confused. But it is
not. In fact the more I learn about the natural
world, the more I realize that nature is the one
part of life that actually has order; when you take
time to look under the surface of the plant or
animal kingdom or at bugs, you see a silent
world, forever moving, growing, changing, all
together and in unison.

The irony is that our man-made world is the
real "wilderness"; only in nature is there any sense
of genuine harmony. Wherever you look in man's
domain there is disunity and a lack of purpose:
on the big scale as nation is pitted against nation,
race against creed; and on the small, as companies
pollute rivers and individuals dump rubbish on
roadsides. This is the real "wilderness" and
disharmony in our lives. Wilderness is what we
have made and abused all around us. In nature,
however, there is none of this; there is no greed,
no waste, no envy. And it is in this nature that
the real miracles of life occur.

The snowdrops survive because the snow insulates them against the frost. Naked man would die in such snow in a matter of minutes. I have seen puffins flapping awkwardly among icebergs and gale-force-nine Arctic waves during a torrential storm, but apparently loving every minute of it. We were over 500 miles from land. My team and I were in a little rigid inflatable boat with all the latest equipment and technology and dry suits, but it was we who were about to die of cold and terror, not them. The natural world is, in every way, bigger, better, cleverer, and stronger than us.

It is only when I return to these so-called "wilds" of nature that I find my own spirit comes alive. I begin to feel that rhythm within me, my senses become attuned to what is all around; I start to see in the dark, to distinguish the smells of the forest, to discern the east wind from the westerly. I am simply becoming a man again; becoming how nature made us. These "wildernesses" help me lose all those synthetic robes that society has draped over us, all that pent-up aggression we see on the streets or that numbness of people without hope or a dream.

Nowadays so many people walk with their eyes down, fixed on the pavement. To them, survival is about surviving the day, the boss, the interview. These are all important things, but we lose out on so much if we limit our lives to that pavement in front of us.

If only we could make some time to look up – maybe in our lunch break on a bench in the park. Why is it that when we do these things we feel better, our imagination fires up, our ambitions and dreams awaken? Nature made us

like that. We are meant for more than pavement-staring. We have one life and there is one extraordinary world created for us to enjoy.

Despite man's best efforts to destroy it, the natural world is still the most advanced and remarkable combination of eco-phenomena ever known. Our finest technology cannot come close to the simple workings of a caterpillar becoming a butterfly, a marvel I bet you have rarely even thought about since you were a kid.

The more I see of our world from all my expeditions, the more I am amazed. People often say the world is so small. Yet, time and time again, I am surprised at just how huge and diverse and powerful it is. And you know what I think is one of nature's greatest indulgences? The lone, hidden flower in the middle of a jungle, which no man or eye will ever see. The bloom

is so clean and crisp and beautiful; it is as if such concealed wonders are God's indulgence. Made just for His pleasure.

The world is overflowing with such delicacies, and in return we have two responsibilities: one is to understand and protect them, the other is to enjoy them. It's worth saying once more: we do only have one life. There is a world of magic to be discovered, and the more I learn the more I realize there is still so much to know.

I hope this book could not only save your life one day, but might also encourage you to explore, and begin to understand and enjoy the indulgences nature has provided for us. Nature isn't something to be feared, but relished. As humans we have been given dominance over every animal and plant. I have

seen a tiny wizened desert nomad control eleven of the world's most lethal snakes simultaneously as they crawled around his toes. What knowledge.

Over the centuries our ancestors invented many remarkable "tricks of the trade" to keep us alive, fed, and watered in some of the harshest habitats. We mustn't let those skills die. Wouldn't you be proud if you were stranded on a desert island with your friends but no supplies, yet you knew how to collect water from a sapling, make fire without matches, and catch and skin a snake? Of course, because it is tapping into a part of you that has taken millennia to evolve. Your survival instinct.

Is our life better for all the wonders of modern existence? Maybe life is easier or faster, but is it better? Why, then, is depression so rife? Have we become so divorced from the real us inside?

I don't know. All I do know is that nature brings out the real me; when I need space or time, when I am grieving or in pain, where do I run to? I run to the mountains. I find quiet and solace there. It feels like home. I have time to shout and cry and breathe. That is natural.

Use the tools in this book to help you out of any trouble you might get yourself into on this road of high adventure. But, above all, use your God-given natural spirit. It might need some dusting off, having not been visited for a while, but it will always be there for you, and life is richer when we spend some time in its company.

So don't be scared to come alive . . . oh, and don't give the pavement more attention than it deserves.

Please Remember What's First ...

THE PRIORITIES OF SURVIVAL

I LOVE SUMMARIES! IF YOU'RE SHORT OF TIME OR HAVE A VERY SMALL MEMORY, THIS IS THE PAGE TO REMEMBER. MANY PEOPLE MAKE THE MISTAKE IN LIFE-OR-DEATH SITUATIONS OF GETTING THEIR PRIORITIES WRONG, SO THE LOGICAL PLACE TO START THIS BOOK, BEFORE WE GET TO THE HEART OF SURVIVAL, IS TO GRASP THESE SIMPLE LIFE-SAVING PRIORITIES.

PROTECTION

Priority number one in a survival situation is the protection of yourself – whether from extreme conditions (sub-zero temperatures and wet clothing, for example, will kill you in a few hours, as will extreme heat with no shade), dangerous animals, or an airplane about to explode. You must protect yourself first – there is no point getting water but becoming hypothermic in the process!

RESCUE

The next priority is to set yourself up to be rescued – lay out objects, stones, or whatever material is at hand, in a large SOS near your shelter. Rescue services will start their search as soon as they know you are in trouble, so don't miss those early opportunities to be saved; be prepared. As long as it is safe to do so, you should wait where you are. Stay put. If you are in a vehicle, don't stray from it. Stay nearby. I know too many stories of people breaking down in the Australian outback in extreme heat, wandering off to look for help only to be found days later, a few miles from their car, dead from dehydration. Be smart; make yourself safe, make yourself visible, and then wait to be rescued. (It's no good being in a snow hole that no one can spot!)

If the rescue services are not going to come, or days have passed with no sign of searches, then you need to think about planning self-rescue: getting yourself out of there on your own two feet. This should be a last resort, but ultimately rescue must be the main goal of survival and you must do whatever it takes to save yourself. Leave a signal, either on the ground with stones or anything you can find, to indicate the direction you are taking and when you left, then prepare yourself and go for it.

WATER

Once you are protected from the elements, and prepared for rescue, you must stay alive long enough for rescue to come! Water now becomes your top priority. Think in 3s: you can live three hours without decent protection from extreme heat or cold; three days without water; but you can survive for three weeks without food. Get your priorities straight. You *must* find water.

FOOD

Energy is needed even more so if your plan involves self-rescue. But remember, you can survive much longer without food than without water, and your body has plenty of reserves of both muscle and fat to work through. If water is in short supply, restrict your eating, especially of too much protein, which requires more water to digest. Learn to scavenge as early man did. Find berries, maggots, or grubs before you chase the big game! This is how you really stay alive.

So that's it: PRWF . . . Protection, Rescue, Water, Food . . . or Please Remember What's First!

"Strong people are formed by opposition,
like kites that rise against the wind."

NELSON MANDELA

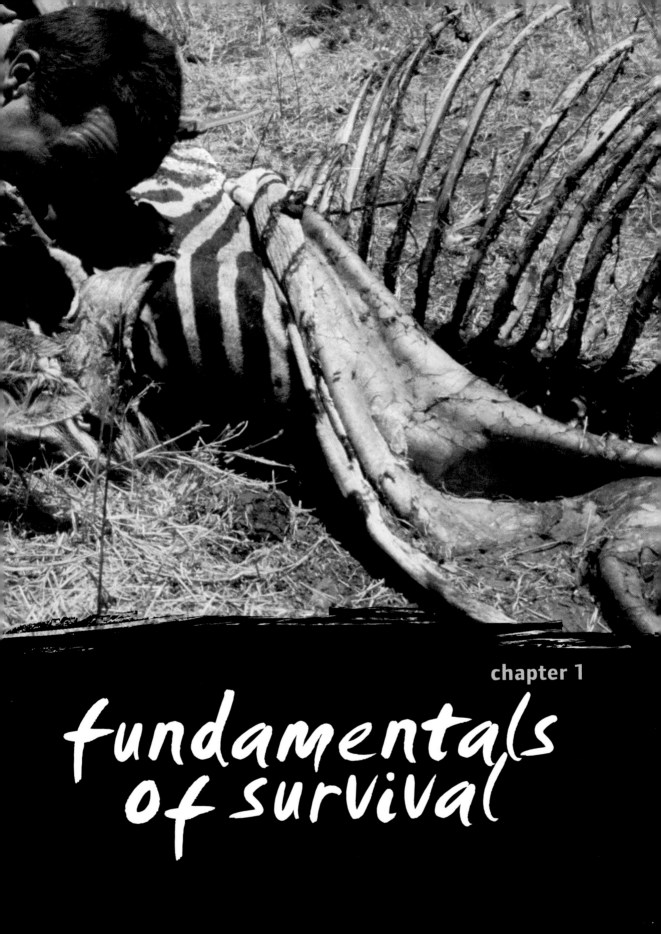

fundamentals of survival

The irony is that while we may have reached a stage in human development where we have more technology at our disposal than ever before, we have also forgotten many of the skills that our ancestors depended on for their own survival.

Today we take it for granted that we can talk to each other and see each other in an instant on opposite sides of the earth. Apart from the deepest reaches of the oceans, there is virtually nowhere on the planet that is inaccessible. Technology can tell us where we are to within a few feet; it can send an SOS message across continents so that the necessary rescue services can move into action; it can help us resuscitate people whose life force has been almost totally extinguished; it can produce at the touch of a button light, fire, warmth, hot water, and food.

What happens, however, when all of this is suddenly, and unexpectedly, stripped away?

Wading through the Everglades in the swamps of Florida – one unforgiving place!

When electricity is cut off, we are suddenly plunged into darkness and silence; our computer and television screens go blank and we are unable to communicate with the rest of the world. Our heating fails and we can't wash or feed ourselves.

For a while, for just a few hours, it all seems quite a novelty. We discover we have neighbors and talk to strangers and help each other out: things we don't do as much as we should in normal life. Then suddenly the lights come back on and we all revert to business as usual, confident that it was just a blip and we don't need to worry about it happening again for a long time.

Our growing dependence on technologies of all forms is a double-edged sword. The fact that our modern cosseted world has, at least on the face of it, become increasingly reliable and plain clever has, paradoxically, made us more and more vulnerable. People are no longer able to cope for more than a very short time when these "systems" fail.

And when technology does fail, at even the most basic level, we often feel peculiarly helpless. This book is really about redressing that balance. Reteaching us some of the skills that our ancestors would have taken for granted. Those skills, they would be horrified to discover, which we have lost so quickly. It is a "how-to" book on how to survive when the lights go out . . . and stay out.

About what happens when the technology on which we depend is entirely stripped away. When suddenly we have no means to communicate. When we find ourselves alone in a strange new world – maybe a desert, a jungle, or a mountain glacier.

How this has come about in the first place is unimportant. Your light plane may have crashed on a short hop over the mountains to a remote lodge. You may have become separated from a trekking party in a barren wilderness, or found yourself in a whiteout on a mountain trail. To your disbelief, you find yourself with nothing other than the clothes you stand up in. You are lost and alone, maybe presumed dead, and no one is looking for you anymore.

No cell phone or GPS can help you now. They have all been left behind on that faraway planet called civilization. You have no shelter, no water, no fire, and no idea where you are – and evening is falling. There are unknown creatures and dangers all around you and it is beginning to get very cold. What you wouldn't give for seemingly mundane and low-tech items, such as a lighter or a water bottle, or a sleeping bag to keep you warm. Even a simple compass out of a Christmas cracker would be nice. But no matter how much you may want them, they all remain locked firmly away in that distant land you have allowed yourself to become so dependent on.

From now on, until you get yourself out of there, you have to survive alone . . . or die.

This is the situation that the information in this book is designed to help you overcome. In the chapters that follow, I shall be looking at almost every terrain imaginable so I can let you in on some of the skills I know. Along the way I will be sharing the survival skills I learned during my time with the SAS, and telling some anecdotes from my experiences of climbing some of the world's highest and most dangerous peaks, plus many of the inspiring true stories of men and women who have, often against the odds, survived some of the world's most extreme environments and lived to tell the tale.

Many of the particular skills and techniques I will be covering relate to specific terrain types – a shelter in the mountains in winter, for example, will be very different to the one you build in a humid, sweltering jungle – but in this chapter I want to deal first with the skills that are, in general, common to all the different terrain types and situations you may find yourself in.

The Psychology of Survival

When disaster strikes and we find ourselves alone in an unknown and hostile environment, why do some people survive and others perish? Common sense tells us that the answer must surely lie in Darwinian evolutionary theory: namely that the "fittest," in the sense of the physically strongest and most knowledgeable, are the most likely to come through a survival situation in one piece.

It is certainly true that both these attributes will play a major part in any man vs. the wild equation. Astronauts and explorers, members of mountain rescue teams, and lifeboatmen all possess an invaluable store of knowledge and have conditioned themselves to be physically able to deal with the rigors of the environment they know they will have to face.

But it is still far from being the whole story. Almost all of the most extraordinary tales of survival seem to involve an indefinable Ingredient X, which can only be understood as having its source in that mysterious entity, the "human spirit."

Almost all of the most extraordinary tales of survival seem to involve an indefinable Ingredient X

And there are, indeed, some extraordinary stories to be told. They range from epic and famous examples of expeditions that went wrong to those of random individuals being suddenly and unexpectedly pitched into a battle with nature that they could not reasonably have been expected to survive.

The first category includes Shackleton's 1914–17 Antarctic expedition when he, his crew and their ship *Endurance* became trapped in pack ice. In an incredible feat of survival, a small group succeeded in crossing more than 800 miles of the most hostile waters on earth in an open boat to find help. In a very different environment, it also includes the crew of *Apollo 13* who piloted their stricken craft back to Earth after the near fatal explosion of two of its three fuel tanks.

The second category includes the story of two Americans, Helen Klaben and Ralph Flores, who survived the crash of their light plane during a winter snowstorm on the border of British Columbia and the Yukon in February 1963. Despite being severely injured and with no bushcraft or wilderness experience and very little food, they managed to survive for seven weeks in temperatures that frequently approached -45°C (-49°F).

These two categories highlight two very different sets of circumstances where survival was achieved against all the odds. The first category is made up of a very unusual set of people. The crew members of both expeditions would not have found themselves in such dire circumstances unless they possessed what the writer Tom Wolfe dubbed the "right stuff."

Just by being picked for the expedition in the first place, they had already demonstrated their physical strength and conditioning, and a mental toughness which would give them the best possible chance of survival in an extreme environment. They also had, particularly in the case of *Apollo 13,* considerable training and experience to fall back on.

The other category is far harder to tie down. It contains people without the specialist skills, but with the hidden X factor that is characterized by the will to stay alive. Klaben and Flores were just regular guys who had already demonstrated bad judgment by their decision to fly in the first place, given the predicted weather conditions. Owing to lack of knowledge, they failed to take advantage of almost all the survival techniques described in this book. Nonetheless, they too survived. Why? The answer to that question is at the very heart of survival. If I had the choice between knowledge and spirit, I would pick spirit any day. I use the same criteria when picking expedition colleagues, and the SAS (the Special Air Service of the British Army) picks its soldiers this way as well. Anyone can be taught skills, not everyone has the fire inside.

But before grappling with the source of this "fire," this elusive survival ingredient at the heart of all these stories, I want to try to distill some of the most important mental attributes demonstrated time and again by those who ultimately survive catastrophe. These "rules" will help you come through your battle with the wild: they are the all-important elements of what can only be described as the "will to survive."

Your first priority on finding yourself alone and coming to terms with what has happened is not to panic and to avoid doing anything that will make a bad situation worse. Everything, particularly physical energy, will be in short supply and must be carefully preserved like the dwindling charge in a battery.

It is now that you must try to achieve as objective a view of your situation as you can. Denial of your predicament is a common reaction to extreme stress, but it will achieve nothing of any worth, apart from reducing your chances of survival. At the same time, convincing yourself that you will be rescued tomorrow is more than likely to end in disappointment and add a serious blow to your dwindling morale.

The remains of Shackleton's ship, *Endurance*.

People might look at your survival situation and say: "Come on, be realistic, what options have you got here?" I say instead, as do so many of the survivors of disasters: "Be an optimist." In my experience, when someone says they are a "realist," it is generally just a lousy excuse for being a pessimist! Those who survive need to see opportunities not problems, hope not hopelessness, possibilities not impossibilities.

Remember that the difference between life and death often boils down to a matter of choice. The "reality" of your situation will be what you believe it to be. If you decide that the odds are so heavily stacked against you that you have no chance of survival, the battle is already as good as lost.

If, on the other hand, you choose to be inspired by the stories of those who have survived with no wilderness skills to fall back on, you will know that the seemingly impossible is indeed possible. No one is more likely to survive than those who can convince themselves they can.

Instead of dwelling on your bad luck, focus on the one-in-a-million chance that you survived in the first place. That you are, in fact, leading a charmed life and are incredibly lucky to be alive. Statistics say that most people are rescued from survival situations within five days – take heart from that. Keep a positive attitude, and you will always have hope. All survivors keep a tight grip on hope. It's a God-given gift.

In this situation, focus on how lucky you are to be alive!

It is also now that you will find yourself confronted starkly with both your strengths and your weaknesses. But be careful not to undermine yourself from within. Nobody is without their faults. Some of us have an irrational fear of the dark, while others have an exaggerated fear of spiders and snakes. Some feel they are cowards by nature, while still more have an over-exaggerated sense of their own abilities. (The latter make the worst survivors.)

Remember that courage and fearfulness are two sides of the same coin. Without feeling fear in the first place, you can never be truly courageous. Likewise, no one can really be said to be strong who has not confronted their weaknesses and overcome them. And that is exactly what you will have to do in the wild. Your confidence will gradually build and strengthen your resolve as you face and overcome each hurdle in turn, be it making a shelter, finding food, or crossing a river.

Your thoughts will also be assaulted by sudden shifts in mood. The knowledge that you might never again see your loved ones will at times seem utterly overwhelming. But don't make the mistake of trying to block "negative" emotions. If you do, you may well find they overwhelm you anyway. Far better to accept the power that these thoughts have and turn them to your advantage. Use them to strengthen your determination to survive. Don't feel sorry for yourself when actually it is your loved ones who will have to live without you if you fail to come through. So, for their sakes, keep going. Never give up. Let their faces be your guide, memories of them be your strength.

The blisters and pain and fatigue will always be temporary, maybe they will last a week, maybe a month, maybe a year, but the joy of survival, the reuniting, the looking back with pride at what you came through: those things will last for ever.

Many of those who live to tell the epic tale of how they survived relate how they were able to achieve a feat of mental gymnastics. On the one hand they were able to think decisively and clearly, to keep focused on the task in hand, breaking it down into small, achievable goals. On the other, they were also able to keep in mind some higher thoughts, whether of their faith or family, that helped them overcome the seemingly insurmountable.

The mind is our most powerful tool. Listen to the stories of those who have endured and survived torture and solitary confinement in captivity: often they talk of their minds being their escape, their strength, their anesthetic to the pain, and even ultimately their joy.

Look at the truly extraordinary case of Beck Weathers, a New Zealander on the infamous 1996 expedition to Everest when more than ten climbers died in a few days alone. After a severe storm near the summit, Beck lay motionless, severely frostbitten, dehydrated, and apparently dead for two days and a night before hauling himself to his feet and climbing down to safety.

Dr. Kamler, in his remarkable book, *Extreme Survival,* describes in great detail how the body responds to acute stress on the brink of death. He demonstrates how, in the most extreme circumstances, an area deep in our brainstem called the cingulate gyrus is capable of overriding every sensory, emotional, and rational input that our brain receives, in order to "create" its own reality. The cingulate seems to be the source of some miraculous returns from "near death" experiences.

But, as Dr. Kamler writes, despite the ability of science to pin down the brain waves emanating from the cingulate, "there will always be an impenetrable, mystical barrier to understanding ourselves. The fundamental nature of the human will must remain unknowable. Ultimately, our explanations for surviving the extremes will require not just science, but faith."

So how do we find that fire, that spirit? Is it in all of us, or just a precious few? I believe that each of us has it in spades; it is sometimes well hidden though, maybe by the fluff that has built up over us from a lifetime chasing the wrong things. Money, possessions, status: they are all shallow masters, and none will bring out the inner man.

All too often it is only when we are in this nightmare survival situation, and all the fluff has been stripped from us, that we stop long enough to let our spirit grow within us again. And that fire is irrepressible. However long it may have been extinguished, just like those birthday candles that forever relight themselves, the human fire

or will can never be put out completely. Just ask those SS soldiers who tried to kill the spirit of so many Resistance fighters in the Second World War. You can beat and suppress but you will never prevail where there is will and a spirit.

So often those who have depended on that will and spirit in their lives talk about a faith. Sometimes it is hard to draw out of them, but it is so often the reason for their survival. We all need hope; more than you might realize. And that hope needs a home, which for me is my Christian faith. Where you find your faith is personal to you, but Jesus Christ is the source of my survival fire. And who better to have beside you when you are alone, scared and cold, and a long way from home? It takes a proud man to say he needs nothing.

So it is my belief that we all have this ability to survive against the odds. In fact, it is at the very core of what it is to be human, and without it our species would never have been able to come as far as it has. But in our modern world, the more we find ourselves cosseted by technology and the idea that we can insure ourselves against anything, even death, the more another side of our humanity tries to break free.

At a time when we have never before been more safety conscious, we also yearn to take risks. Surely this is why so many adventurers record that the only way they can feel "truly alive" is when they are facing extreme hazards, the paradox being that when they look death in the face they are the most in touch with life.

Perhaps, finally, we need to acknowledge that man and the wild are actually entwined, part of a wonderfully made creation. The source of this creation is ultimately, I believe, a matter of faith not science. Without our faith – whatever it may be – we risk losing our rudder. We risk losing all the navigational charts the human species has ever had. And that's a kind of "lost" we never want to experience.

Fire: Gift of the Gods

The discovery of how to create fire at will was one of early man's greatest discoveries. The invention of the proverbial wheel was pretty amazing too, but if pushed I know which I would choose in a tight corner. In fact, there are still remote parts of the world where man lives without the wheel. Not so, without fire.

When, suddenly, you find yourself on your own in an alien and hostile wilderness, especially when it's dark and cold, fire will seem like your only true friend. Hardly surprising then that since time immemorial, fire has been seen as the gift of the gods, the earthly manifestation of the divine spark.

But you will need to treat your divine friend with the love and respect it deserves. While the gifts of fire are many – light, warmth, somewhere to cook and dry off, keeping wild animals and pests at bay – it can be notoriously difficult to coax into life when modern methods and equipment have been stripped away.

Safety matches, cigarette lighters and easily combustible fuels from gasoline to firelighters are items most of us take for granted. But the ready availability of fire-making materials is a relatively modern phenomenon. Friction matches, much as we have today, have been around since the early nineteenth century when Samuel Jones

Fire will provide you with heat, light, comfort, and protection.

patented the "Lucifer," but before that the technology for producing the all-important spark to start the fire had hardly changed since the earliest times.

Modern methods have dispensed with the need for the single most important ingredient when coaxing fire into life: patience. The chemistry has remained unaltered since the earth was young – that critical mix of the right amounts of air, heat and fuel – but the state of mind necessary to create the right environment for fire when modern chemicals are missing has somehow gone astray.

In the wilderness, patience will not just be the optional extra it has become at home. In fact, without it, you are almost certain to find your situation becoming progressively worse. Time, the commodity that most of us seem to have so little of in our daily lives, is something that suddenly you will have in excess. So any tendency to rush into everything with breakneck speed should be kept firmly under control because it is the enemy of fire. And fire, potentially, may be your savior.

While a number of environmental factors – not least, rain or damp – will be either with you or against you, if you have the determination, you should be able to produce fire under all but the most extreme circumstances. The secret is preparation, for which you will need that all-important patience. A fire that takes two hours to produce will be far better than one that smolders into lifelessness after one.

Always remember that your resources are finite: energy, morale, fuel, and spark may all be in short supply. But while time may be the only resource you can afford to squander, even that needs to be managed carefully. Always try to start your fire well before nightfall. Finding the right materials in the dark will be much harder.

Making a fire requires a logical set of actions: finding a location; finding and preparing the best materials to make tinder, kindling, and fuel;

Since time immemorial, fire has been seen as the gift of the gods.

producing a spark; nurturing the flame; and laying the fire. Each requires planning and methodical attention to detail. Different terrain types will require modifications on this basic model, but the principles will remain the same.

CHOOSING A LOCATION

Choose the site for your fire carefully. Wind and its relative proximity to your shelter are probably the most important aspects to consider. Wind, as anyone who has ever sat round a campfire knows, can be notoriously changeable, but small amounts of smoke can easily be tolerated and will have the added benefit of keeping biting insects at bay.

If the wind is strong, however, consider building your fire in the lee of a windbreak, like a boulder, embankment, or tree trunk, or in the V

Using a "smoker" to calm a bees' nest and get the honey.

of two logs. Another option is to dig a trench which will also reduce the wind's effect. It will help if the ground is as flat as possible so water doesn't run through your shelter when it rains. Avoid building it next to a tree or ice wall, or anywhere where melting snow can drop from above.

If, because the ambient temperature is so cold, keeping you warm at night is a major consideration, build it within arm's reach of your shelter. This will make maximum use of the heat and you will be able to attend to it during the night with the minimum of effort. The use of a simply constructed heat reflector will increase the warmth considerably. This can be a naturally occurring fallen tree trunk or even just a pile of small stones built the other side of your fire to reflect the heat back towards you. A more effective version is to pile up small branches between four sloping uprights staked in the

ground. This angled reflector, pointed back towards the fire, works most efficiently.

There are few things as lovely as reaching out lazily in the middle of the night to your woodpile and tossing another log on the fire, while still wrapped up warm in your shelter. So keep your wood supply close to you but not so close as to be a danger to you or your equipment.

Once you have decided on the location, clear an area of ground (about 6.5 feet square) down

Watching nature's TV – my fire.

to the soil or rock. Whatever the season and weather conditions, the ground will always tend to resist your efforts to produce fire, so always build a platform of small logs or stones on which the fire can be built. If a boggy area is absolutely unavoidable, build a raised platform from uprights and cross pieces and add a base of logs covered in several inches of earth. Choose green wood if you can so it will not burn through too quickly.

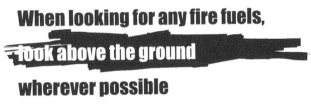

THE VITAL INGREDIENTS

There are three distinct ingredients that your fire will need if it is not to die before it has even started. These are tinder, kindling, and fuel. The difference between them is simple: their relative tendency to easy and rapid combustion. But one without the correct amounts of the other two combined with the right quantities of heat and oxygen will be absolutely useless.

TINDER

Tinder is the element in the fire-making hierarchy that modern methods have made largely redundant. Before the dawn of the safety match, it was common to carry in your pocket a "tinderbox," which contained a flint and steel and some tinder, often in the form of charred cotton material that could be ignited by a spark. It is a naturally occurring version of this which you will urgently need to find.

Nature, as ever, will often be obliging. As a rule of thumb, when looking for any fire fuels, look above the ground wherever possible. The earth itself holds the damp, whereas small twigs extracted from a bush or still attached to a dead tree will usually be much drier. Your tinder will need to ignite at the slightest provocation, so fine and fluffy fibrous material like the lining of a bird's or mouse's nest, dry moss, dry grasses, pine needles, cat's-tails, dried palm or bracken will all serve the purpose. These must be pulled apart, shredded, and teased so they will combust at a low temperature and be fed by a healthy supply of oxygen. Sticks of dry wood should be no thicker than a toothpick.

You will need to improvise. Once you know what makes good tinder, you will often have no problem finding it. Plants which have downy seed heads like clematis will ignite easily, and when mixed with dead, dry grasses, can be fluffed up into a ball which will smolder and burn when sparks land on it. If you are using grasses they will need to be fluffed up to about the size of a grapefruit at minimum.

The fibrous interiors of many mushrooms, like the bracket variety you see on many woodland trees, known as amadou, are also fertile sources of tinder, as is dry, soft, decaying wood or "punk," which can be crumbled up into a combustible heap.

When it is rainy and cold, lighting a fire will always be more difficult, but with a little application, there is no reason why it should not be possible. Keeping yourself, the fire, and all your materials well sheltered is a common-sense

When looking for any fire fuels, look above the ground wherever possible

precaution, and keeping your tinder dry is vital. To achieve this, always make sure that if you find some suitable material, you pick it up and put it in your pockets or next to your body. Then it will dry out as you go and you will be able to use it later.

It will also help to choose resinous materials like tree barks for your tinder. Birch, juniper, cedar and spruce, for example, all resist dampness better than most plant sources. Fluffing up small sticks with a knife into "fire sticks" (see diagram below) will expose the drier interior and provide more surface area for a spark to take. These can then be added to the kindling like improvised matches.

Some man-made items that you may be able to salvage will also work very well: cotton wool, tampons, or a roll of film cut into strips. Again preparation is all. Fuzz up tampons so they are not too dense and air is able to circulate.

Finally, remember to collect double the amount of tinder you think you need in case you have to start again from scratch in the morning.

KINDLING

Kindling is the middleman between the tinder and the fire's main fuel source, so it needs to burn long enough to perform this function. As the flame from the tinder will be short-lived and at a relatively low temperature, kindling needs to be small enough to ignite easily, so softwoods like pine cut up into pieces the size of pencils are perfect.

The size of the kindling can then be built up as the fire catches, until the main fuel ignites. The branches of dead evergreens make excellent kindling as they are full of resin, but they burn up very quickly.

FUEL

Fuel wood needs to keep the blaze going long enough to fulfill its purpose. Ideally, it should burn slowly enough to conserve the woodpile, make plenty of heat and leave an ample supply of long-lasting "coals."

The type of fuel you use will determine how the fire burns and whether it is best suited to cooking or heating. Softwoods (evergreens like conifers, cedar, spruce, and pine) burn more intensely, quicker, and with more smoke and less heat than hardwoods (broad-leaf trees like hickory, beech, and oak). These hardwoods are harder to ignite in the first place, but will leave smoldering coals which can be kept that way by covering them in earth and ash so they can be reignited in the morning. Again, when gathering fuel, look for sources above the ground, which will be drier, the best being branches from a dead tree. The more vertical its position when you find it, the drier it will be, as the rain will have had less surface area to fall on. Also remember that animal dung makes excellent fuel. In parts of India, some people still make their living following elephants, collecting their dung, drying it out, and selling it as a heating fuel. I have often used elephant dung as fuel in the wild – it smells but it works!

THE VITAL SPARK

Now that you have so carefully prepared all the materials for making a fire, you will have to find a way of producing enough heat to make a spark, as without this vital ingredient all your efforts will have been in vain. You might be lucky and be carrying some matches in your pocket. If you are, well and good. Protect them from damp with your life, and never use two when one would do.

But just because you have found some matches, it doesn't necessarily mean that you have instant access to fire. The problem with most available modern fire-lighting materials is that they are not designed to be used in testing conditions. They are also very susceptible to damp. And sooner or later you will find yourself having to fall back on methods used by our forefathers.

FIRE BY FRICTION

The most primitive methods for making a fire revolve around generating heat from friction. The principle involves rubbing wood together to create fine scorched wood dust, which can form embers that will ignite the tinder and start the whole process that results in a blazing fire.

DRILL-AND-BOW METHOD

One of the most ancient, and effective, ways of producing fire from friction is to use the drill and bow, a method which is still used by many indigenous peoples around the world.

The principle is to rotate a spindle, rather like a drill bit, into a base plate of wood until friction generates enough heat to produce embers. The drill is rotated with a bow driven by elbow grease. Of the friction methods considered here, it is the most effective as the bow produces the most efficient rotation. Significant downward pressure can also be applied through the drill and on to the base plate by the use of a pressure plate ideally made of hardwood (see diagram).

The three primary elements are the drill, bow and base plate. Ensuring that these elements are sturdy, the right size and made of the correct type of woods is crucial. Ideally the drill should be made of the same wood as the base plate. Birch, alder, sycamore and willow are all good candidates.

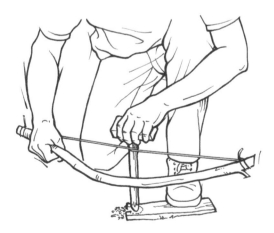

BASE PLATE
Ideally the base plate will be a board of seasoned wood about 3/4 inch thick, 4 inches wide and 8–10 inches long. The board needs to be kept

in place by your foot as you rotate the drill with the bow and needs to stay still, so any size that sits snugly under your boot is fine. Next, cut a depression a centimeter from the edge on one side. (It is into this depression that the spindle will fit and rotate.) Then cut a small notch from the edge of the base plate into this depression. When embers are formed in the depression, they will fall through this notch onto the ember tray, ready to ignite the tinder.

DRILL AND PRESSURE PLATE

The top end of the drill should taper to a blunt point that will reduce friction with the pressure plate. Conversely, the business end at the bottom can be rougher and wider and fit snugly into the depression on the base plate so as to maximize friction. The pressure plate can be a smooth stone or piece of hardwood that fits into the palm of your hand with a slight depression in one side for the drill to sit in. Try plugging grass into the depression to reduce friction.

Better to build two smaller fires, one for cooking and the other for warmth and light, than build one big one that does neither efficiently

BOW

The bow should be made of a resilient piece of live wood with plenty of play. It should be about 1.5 centimeters in diameter and up to a metre in length. If possible, cut this piece of wood so natural indentations at both ends provide grip points for the cord, which should then be tied from one end of the bow to the other under tension.

EMBER TRAY AND TINDER

The ember tray is made from anything thin that will slide under the base-plate notch and catch the embers. Thin, dry bark is fine. Then fluff up a "bird's nest" of tinder into the cupped palms of your hands and push the drill halfway into the ball to form a partial cylinder. This is where the ember will be placed.

MAKING FIRE

And now the good part! Take a turn with the bow cord around the drill. Place the tip of the drill into the base plate's depression, the pressure plate onto the top of the drill, and the ember tray under the notch. Kneel down with one foot on the board as near to the depression as possible without getting in the way of the drill. Then with a smooth sawing motion and with consistent downward pressure, move the bow back and forth to spin the drill. Once you have established a smooth constant motion, smoke will begin to appear. When it does, apply more downward pressure and saw the bow faster. When a thick layer of smoke has accumulated around the depression, stop at once and coax the embers through the notch and onto the ember tray. Slowly fan the glowing powder and then carefully transfer them into the cylinder in the bird's nest tinder you prepared earlier and blow gently but positively until it ignites.

HAND-DRILL METHOD

The hand-drill method is very similar in principle to the drill and bow, producing embers from the friction between a drill and base plate. The main difference is that the drill is controlled by spinning it back and forth between the hands. It is less dependable in wet weather as the friction is harder to maintain. Make sure the drill is very straight and with no nodules to give you blisters, and spit on your hands to improve grip. Don't press your hands together too hard. Start with an easy backwards and forwards movement and steadily speed up. Work the drill from top to bottom.

FIRE-THONG AND FIRE-SAW METHODS

Both these methods are popular with indigenous peoples living in the tropics. The fire-thong method uses a thin strip of rattan cane pulled back and forth vigorously between a split stick, while the saw method produces heat by rubbing two bamboos together.

MORE MODERN METHODS

Flame, sparks, or heat capable of lighting tinder can also be produced by more modern inventions such as flints and steels, magnesium blocks, magnifying glasses, binoculars, and camera lenses. Car and ordinary flashlight batteries will also produce sparks if the terminals are crossed with a wire.

While matches can sometimes be dried out in the sun, a good method of waterproofing is to rub them against your hair or dip them in candle wax. A flint and steel scraped together will produce sparks whatever the weather. Shavings from a magnesium block mixed with the tinder will also improve your chances no end. Other designs have magnesium mixed into the flint to produce a higher quality of spark.

Chemicals like potassium permanganate mixed with a glycol-based antifreeze or sugar will also produce fire.

TYPES OF FIRE

There are many methods of laying and feeding a fire, so you should decide the primary function of your fire before you build it, so that you can economize on fuel. Better to build two smaller fires, one for cooking and the other for warmth and light, than build one big one that does neither efficiently. A fire for cooking will need to burn down reasonably flat so that a cooking implement can easily be laid on top. A cross-lay design is usually the best.

All fires benefit from a platform of small logs to keep the dampness of the ground at bay. In very cold weather, snow should be completely cleared down to the ground or a bough platform built on top of the snow.

CRISSCROSS FIRE

Layers of small logs at right angles to one another throw out a lot of heat and settle well into a deep layer of embers that are perfect for cooking. This is my favorite choice of fire to use.

STAR FIRE

Thick logs are slowly fed into the central area in a star shape. This method also avoids the problem of breaking up unwieldy logs and provides a stable platform for a cooking utensil.

TEPEE FIRE

Shaped like an Indian tepee, flames lick up through the central chamber as they would draw up a well-ventilated chimney. This provides more light, but the downside is that the fire tends to burn more quickly and is less stable.

LONG-LOG FIRE

Long logs laid parallel to each other are the perfect answer for warming open-fronted shelters in winter. They also provide plenty of space and a stable platform for a number of cooking utensils.

TRENCH FIRE

Great for getting a fire started in high winds. As the name implies, you need to dig a trench about a foot deep and wide and 3 feet long, which should be lined with stones. These can then be buried later and will provide a source of ground heat all night long. Always be careful of wet, porous rocks, like sandstone, which can explode. On one occasion a fire-bed like this saved my bacon after I almost became hypothermic in a glacial river!

You can keep a fire smoldering overnight by covering it with ash or dry mineral soil; and a smoldering log can be transported in a bark tube

Fire is a life saver, especially if you find yourself cold and wet.

SNAKE-HOLE FIRE

Dig a hole into the lee side of a bank and push a stick or other implement into the cavity from above, creating, in effect, a chimney. Starting the fire underground will provide a focused heat source with which to cook and will also preserve fuel. Such a fire also sucks in a large amount of air draft, reducing the amount of smoke, and is easy to light in a high wind.

Whatever the type of fire, the key to keeping it burning efficiently is to regulate the flow of air carefully and make sure the pieces of wood are kept close together so that heat is not lost unnecessarily. The hottest part of any fire is not the flames themselves but the red-hot coals that form when a fire has been built up and then allowed to bed down. The best cooking fire for roasting and grilling has an even bed of coals, with heat reflected back in from the rocks around it.

TRANSPORTING FIRE

Once you have successfully created fire, the effort may well persuade you that it is worthwhile preserving the spark that fed the flame. Finding dry tinder is often the most difficult problem, so make some charcloth from partially burning any spare cloth you may have, or carry some "fire-dogs" – pieces of charcoal from a previous fire. These light easily even months after they were first burned.

You can also keep a fire smoldering overnight by covering it with ash or dry mineral soil; and a smoldering log can be transported in a bark tube.

The Preparation of Food

Perhaps it should go without saying that hygiene should be uppermost in your mind in even the most desperate situations, particularly when it comes to cooking arrangements. If you do let standards slip – handling food with soiled hands for example – you will almost certainly pay the price and that price may be the ability to go on. Even a minor stomach bug will leave you dehydrated and fatigued.

So try to establish a routine. Remember to wash your face, hands, feet, and teeth twice daily and your hands again every time you prepare food. If the availability of running water is a problem, you will have to do the best you can. Try rubbing your hands through some dew-wet bushes, or even dry dirt will be better than nothing.

It's better to hunt smaller game, like rabbits, snakes, lizards, and birds

GAME

Hunting big game on your own is likely to be time-consuming, energy-consuming, and dangerous. And anyway, most of the meat is likely to go to waste as you will be unable to carry more than a few portions at most. Better then to hunt smaller game, like rabbits, snakes, lizards, and birds.

RABBITS

Gut first, then skin and remove the head and feet. Spit roast them on a sharp stick, turning them over hot coals.

SNAKES

Remove the head, skin, and stomach and cut the meat into slices. Tastes best grilled over hot coals. Alternatively you can wrap the whole snake around and around a stick and secure the flesh top and bottom with some strands of vine or plant. This works well and is less time-consuming.

LIZARDS

Only the head and guts need be removed, before grilling over hot coals with the skin still on.

BIRDS

Can fester very quickly if the head, feathers, and guts are not removed immediately. They should also be bled as soon as possible. Don't waste the blood, drink it: it is packed full of ready nutrients. Most palatable when drunk warm. Cook them wrapped in leaves or thin bark directly on the coals.

FISH

Gut them but cook wrapped in leaves or bark with the scales still on. This will then peel off when you remove the covering, exposing the perfectly cooked flesh within. A good tip to know whether the fish is cooked is to wait until the white of the eye has popped out of its socket.

PRESERVING MEAT

If you do manage to kill a larger animal like a deer and know that food is likely to be in short supply, you can try drying or smoking the meat – as long as you do this when it is still fresh. You will also need two or three days in the same location to complete the process, so don't try this if you are moving daily.

The water content of any animal (including us) accounts for 70 percent of its weight, so after this has been removed the meat will also be a lot easier to carry. Remove, cook, and eat all the fat from the meat – fat doesn't dry out and attracts bacteria – and cut the carcass into strips, the thinner the better to increase surface area and aid drying.

Stick some spikes in the ground at 45 degrees and hang the raw strips so that all the meat is exposed evenly to the sun and air. If there are a lot of flies around, it may be better to smoke the meat with smoke from a slow-burning fire. Bark is often a good fuel for this purpose but do not use fir or pine as they produce soot which will spoil the meat.

STORING FOOD

Whenever possible, make sure you keep all your food out of smelling distance of insects and

Also, NEVER store food in your shelter or your camp area as it  will attract unwanted guests who may not distinguish between you and the food they're after

predatory animals. Soft fruits and berries will be best preserved wrapped in leaves or moss and if you're on the coast, keep seafood moist by wrapping it in seaweed. Also, NEVER store food in your shelter or your camp area as it will attract unwanted guests who may not distinguish between you and the food they're after. In the Rockies, where grizzlies and brown bears were a significant threat, I would keep all my leftover food in a can which I would suspend on a rope over a tree branch at least 100 yards from my camp.

Roasting my catch over an open fire in California's Sierra Nevada mountains.

Navigation and Weather

Unless there is an obvious chance of rescue by staying where you are, at some stage the time will come to move on. Having orientated yourself psychologically and come to grips with your situation, orientating yourself geographically will now be your most important task.

Almost all of the different terrains I have worked in required a different set of knowledge and skills. Much can be observed on the ground from signs of nature, which can give a very strong indication of direction, but these vary between different terrain types (desert, jungle, polar, etc.), and I shall be dealing with them in their specific chapters as they arise.

Here, however, I want to get to grips with some principles of survival navigation that will come in useful wherever you are in the world if you are ever unlucky enough to find yourself alone without a GPS, map, compass, or other navigational aid.

Before you abandon your first location, you will need to have a clear direction and purpose in mind. You will need to be sure that every chance of rescue from your current location has gone, and you must decide what equipment and supplies, if any, can be salvaged and carried. You will also need to have at least an idea of what the weather is likely to have in store for you.

If you are on high ground or can easily gain a vantage point to survey the topography of the land around, it will certainly help to make some sort of mental or physical sketch map, noting obvious landmarks that will help to reorientate you when you are moving. The "grain" of the land in terms of the orientation of the ridges and the rivers should be looked for and noted.

MAKESHIFT NAVIGATIONAL AIDS

Knowing the general direction of the four cardinal points of the compass will be an invaluable aid when you decide to move. In some featureless terrain types – in the desert or at sea for example – it will not just be invaluable, it will be vital. Movement without the knowledge of your N, E, S, and W will be futile as you are more than likely to end up going around in circles, and use up dwindling reserves of energy and water.

Here are a few very simple, but very useful, makeshift navigational aids that I have used many times to help confirm my position.

THE SHADOW STICK

Find a straight stick about a metre long and as thick as your thumb. Break off any twigs and push it down vertically into some flat, soft ground. Carefully mark where the tip of the shadow falls and wait fifteen minutes before marking the shadow tip again. The line between your two marks will denote an axis running approximately east–west. A line drawn at 90 degrees to this will be directly north–south.

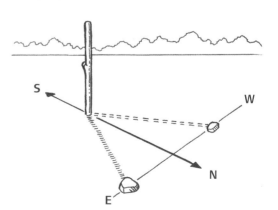

In the northern hemisphere, put your left foot on the first marker and your right foot on the second marker and you will be facing due north. Do the reverse in the southern hemisphere.

USING A WRISTWATCH

If you are in the northern hemisphere and your watch is still on your wrist (and still works!), the cardinal points can easily be deduced. Point the hour hand at the sun. Then form an imaginary line directly through the center of the "wedge" that is created between the hour hand and twelve o'clock. This is your south–north line.

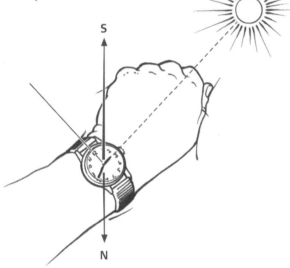

The height of the sun in the sky and the time of day will then show you which end of the line is north and which way is south, remembering that the sun sets in the west and rises in the east.

In the southern hemisphere, point the twelve o'clock mark at the sun and bisect that with the hour hand for the north–south line.

If you have a digital watch, just draw out a watch face in the ground with either the hour hand or twelve o'clock orientated at the sun, dependent on your hemisphere.

IMPROVISED COMPASS

Any thin piece of metal (make sure it's the type that rusts rather than aluminium, silver, or gold) can be easily magnetized to make a compass. A needle or razor blade is perfect for the purpose, but a straightened paper clip or even a piece of barbed wire will do. If you can salvage a magnet (all loudspeakers and headphones have them), so much the better, but a piece of silk or synthetic material (like a parachute) or even the back of your hand will produce a weak magnetic charge.

Rub the metal object along its length for about thirty strokes in the same direction. If you are using material, be careful to lift the needle at the end of each stroke and start again at the same point as before. Then float the needle on a thin piece of leaf or bark. If you are using a razor blade, suspend it on the end of some thread. The needle or razor blade will now slowly orientate itself north–south.

A needle can also be magnetized using a battery. Coil some insulated wire around a needle. If the wire is non-insulated, wrap the needle with a leaf. Attach the ends to the battery terminals (minimum two volts) and wait five minutes.

Remember that magnetism using both these methods will be quickly lost and you will need to "recharge" your needle frequently. Remember also that in extreme northern latitudes, magnetic variation will pull the needle a long way from true north.

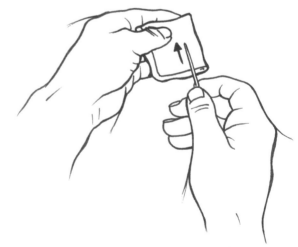

PRINCIPLES OF CELESTIAL NAVIGATION

Particularly in featureless terrain like deserts and at sea, a rudimentary knowledge of the solar system and how the celestial bodies move about the sky in relation to our home planet could be a life-saver.

When we look up at the stars on a clear night, it is sometimes difficult to grasp the immensity of what we are looking at. For our ancestors, it was easier to understand the heavens in terms of a soap opera. Clusters of stars that moved across the night sky appeared to be grouped into the familiar patterns of the creatures they saw around them during the day. Lions, horses, dogs, fish, and men played out a strange ritual dance as they moved across the sky.

It is only in the last few hundred years that we have discovered that the light band of cloud that vaults the heavens is in fact made up of millions of suns just like our own in a galaxy we call the Milky Way. Our own sun and the planets which orbit around it are just one solar system among billions located in an obscure corner of just one galaxy among billions. (Stay with me!)

The stars that we see most clearly in the night sky are our nearest galactic neighbors and move according to a fixed set of rules. The earth rotates on its own axis once every twenty-four hours and circumnavigates the sun once every 365 days. The tilt of the earth's axis at 23.5 degrees means that the northern and southern hemispheres move closer and farther away from the sun depending on their position during the annual circumnavigation. The resulting changes in temperature give rise to the seasons.

As all this goes on its merry way, the moon circumnavigates the earth every 29.5 days and the reflection of the sun's rays off the moon reaches us as moonlight with the moon waxing

and waning depending on the angle at which the sunlight strikes it. Observations of these phenomena led to a method of navigation which we can still use today when we become separated from the navigational instruments we take so much for granted.

Our ancestors realized that the sun, moon, and stars rise roughly in the east and move across the sky to set roughly in the west. This fact, combined with the observation of the North Star (Polaris) in the northern hemisphere and a constellation called the Southern Cross in the southern hemisphere, became the basis of navigation over long distances for hundreds of years until the advent of the compass and reliable maps.

The stars that we see most clearly in the night sky are our nearest galactic neighbors and move according to a fixed set of rules

NAVIGATION BY DAY

During the hours of daylight, simply observing the path of the sun across the sky – coupled with some astute observations of what nature is up to on the ground – will give you a good idea of the cardinal points of the compass.

As we have seen, the sun rises in the east and sets in the west. In fact, due to the earth's tilt, it is not quite as exact as that. At the equinoxes (March 21 and September 21), the sun does indeed rise due east, but on Midsummer's Day

(June 21) in the northern hemisphere it will rise up to 50 degrees north of east and at the winter solstice (December 21) it will rise up to 50 degrees south of east. The same applies for sunsets. In the southern hemisphere, this phenomenon works in reverse; and the nearer the observer gets to the equator, the less the variation will be.

NAVIGATION BY NIGHT

While traveling by night may, or may not, be desirable, depending on the terrain, if a clear view of the skies is attainable at least some of the time, some valuable direction pointers are always available.

USING THE MOON
Like the sun, the moon rises in the east and sets in the west, so if there is a full moon, the same shadow-stick method (see pages 32–33) can be used at night as used with the sun during the day.

Tip: Remember that the illuminated side of the moon is, by definition, always closest to the sun. If the moon rises before sunset, the illuminated side will be in the west, and if the moon rises after sunset, the illuminated side will be in the east. If the two events coincide . . . it will be a full moon!

Remember too that the line connecting the two points of a quarter (crescent) moon in the northern hemisphere will point roughly due south. Vice versa in the southern hemisphere. If there is a full moon, north can be found by locating the rabbit's head and two ears that are visible in the moon when you squint. Extend the line of the ear nearest the center through the moon for a line pointing roughly north.

NORTHERN HEMISPHERE: LOCATING POLARIS (THE NORTH STAR)
As we have seen, the sun and the moon move across the sky in an east–west direction. By and large, so do the stars, including familiar constellations like Orion and the Plow. In the northern hemisphere, there is one very bright exception to this rule: Polaris, aka the North or Pole Star. This star is the northern point of the axis around which the constellations rotate. When you know how, it is easy to locate and will always be pointing due north. Remember, though, that the higher the latitude you find yourself in, the less useful it will be, and at the North Pole, it will be directly overhead.

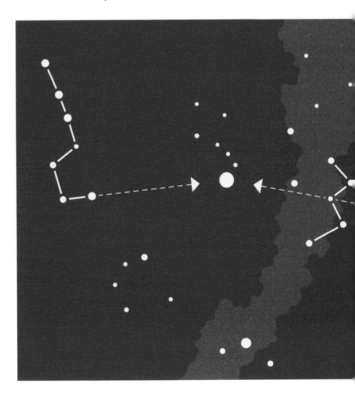

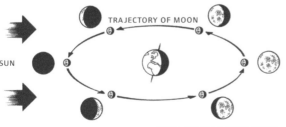

SUN

TRAJECTORY OF MOON

VIEWS OF MOON FROM EARTH

There are two ways to locate the North Star. The first is to find the Plow (aka the Big Dipper or Ursa Major). The Plow is easily distinguished because of its resemblance to an old-fashioned ox-pulled plow or, more familiarly, to a saucepan with a long handle. It is also one of the brightest constellations in the northern hemisphere. The two stars at the outer edge of the saucepan point directly at the North Star. Measure the distance between them in your mind's eye and then extend it outwards about four times. This will lead to the North Star.

If the Plow is obscured because of cloud, you will need to use the constellation of Cassiopeia, which looks like a big M or W and, like the Plow, appears to rotate around the North Star. A line drawn straight through the apex of the W leads roughly to the Pole Star, which is always distinguishable because of its brightness.

SOUTHERN HEMISPHERE: LOCATING THE SOUTHERN CROSS

In the southern hemisphere, there is no star bright enough to act as an equivalent to the northern hemisphere's Pole Star. Instead it is best to use the Southern Cross, which is just as distinctive and arguably more charismatic.

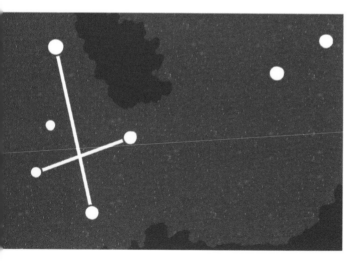

The Southern Cross is easily recognizable from its distinctive crosslike shape. Locate it by following the cloudy band of the Milky Way until you find a cloud of darkness like a blob of ink blacking out the sky. Near this blob (known as the Coal Sack) is the Southern Cross, which is made up of four stars, two of which are among the brightest in the night sky. Don't confuse it with the False Cross, which has five stars that are less bright and more widely spaced.

If the Southern Cross is upright, due south can be found by dropping a line straight down to the horizon from its central arm. If it is tilted, extend the central arm in a straight line towards the horizon by about five times its own length. Drop a plumb line from this point and you will be looking directly south.

STAR SIGNS

On nights when the sky is partially obscured, pick any bright star and monitor its movement through the sky using two sticks set up like the sights of a gun barrel. In the northern hemisphere, the following can be deduced:
- Movement left: star is in the north
- Movement right: star is in south
- Movement up: star is in the east
- Movement down: star is in the west

Reverse these rules for the southern hemisphere:
- If a star is rising, you are looking east.
- If a star is falling, you are looking west.
- If you can locate Orion's belt, the three prominent stars across the northern sky, then roughly perpendicular to the belt are three fainter stars, Orion's sword. The sword points through the belt in a northerly direction.

On the equator, a star that passes directly overhead will have risen directly east and will set directly west.

Once you have found your direction, you can pick a point on the night horizon or even a star and follow it. But beware: don't navigate by following a star for more than twenty minutes – stars move across the sky. The exception, as we have seen, is the North Star, which is a constant and can always be followed.

PREDICTING WEATHER

Reading the likely changes in the weather will help you decide when it is best to move and when it is best to stay put. The types of weather that you decide are best for moving will depend on the terrain you find yourself in. In the desert, another baking day will definitely not be the time to move but rather to hole up, whereas in the mountains it may well be the time to go. On the other hand, a distant storm in the desert may be a source of water, or if the signs change while you are on the move in the mountains, it may be best to find shelter sooner rather than later.

Predicting bad weather in the short term is not rocket science. When the omens look bad (dark clouds, thunder in the distance, gusting wind in advance of rain), they usually mean just that and you should take precautionary measures. A good tip I was told while with the SAS was that clouds tend to behave as they look – in other words if they look bad or benign they probably are.

Some weather signs, however, particularly clouds, can be very useful in predicting a long-term (more than six hours off) change in the weather, so being able to recognize different cloud types and what they mean is extremely useful.

Clouds form when air cools beyond its saturation point (100 percent relative humidity). For the purposes of identification, clouds fall into three categories of height:
- High clouds: 16,000–45,000 feet
- Medium clouds: 6,500–16,000 feet
- Low clouds: below 6,500 feet

And three categories of shape:
- Heap clouds: cumuliform
- Layer clouds: stratiform
- Feathery clouds: cirriform

Weather prediction, as any honest TV weatherman will tell you, is as much an art as a science. But observations of the cloud types (overleaf) and the likely future weather patterns associated with them are worth knowing. Nothing, however, is certain when it comes to the weather . . .

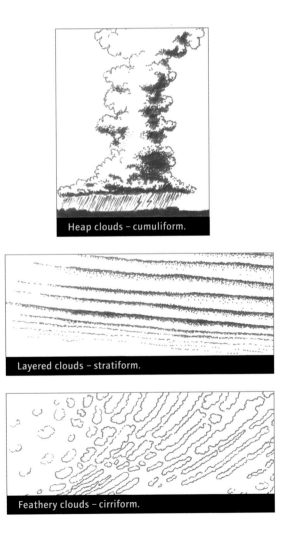

Heap clouds – cumuliform.

Layered clouds – stratiform.

Feathery clouds – cirriform.

	CLOUD TYPE	DESCRIPTION	LIKELY WEATHER
HIGH CLOUDS	Cirrus	Thin, wispy streaks/"mare's tails" (NB Cirrus are difficult to interpret. Some denser types of cirrus denote no change.)	Fine weather, then rain
	Cirrocumulus	"Mackerel sky"/"rippled sand"	Showers
	Cirrostratus	Amorphous cloud/halo effects	Rain
MEDIUM CLOUDS	Altocumulus	Dimpled heap cloud	Showers
	Altostratus	"Watery sun"	Rain
LOW CLOUDS	Stratocumulus	Heaped layer cloud	No Change
	Stratus	Amorphous layer cloud	Drizzle
	Nimbostratus	Layered cloud stacked high	Storm
	Cumulus	Heaped fluffy cloud	Good Weather
	Cumulonimbus	Fluffy cloud heaped very high	Thunderstorm

CROSSED WINDS RULE

Another useful guide to likely changes in the weather can be gained from the behavior of the wind. This is all to do with fronts passing through which produce changes in atmospheric pressure which in turn produce changes in wind direction. The following only applies when the clouds are medium to high in the sky.

Stand with your back to the wind:

- If the high clouds are coming from the left, the weather is likely to get worse.
- If the high clouds are coming from the right, the weather is likely to improve.

Reverse this rule in the southern hemisphere.

LIGHTNING

The approach of a thunderstorm in the wilderness should not be taken lightly. At the very least it will mean an unwelcome soaking.

More significantly, though, lightning is present in all thunderstorms and is the mechanism that causes the noise of thunder when the air around the bolt of lightning expands and contracts with incredible force. A massive release of electrical energy occurs when the lightning bolt makes contact with the ground and passes an electric current through everything in the immediate vicinity – including you if you happen to be in the wrong place at the wrong time. (Remember that lightning does not only affect one point of impact. The current can spread downwards and outwards.) If you have time, find shelter on lower ground at once and keep well away from open ground, single trees, or large rocks, which may attract the strike.

Find something dry to sit on that will not easily conduct the current (a climber's rope or wood will be far better than nothing) and sit in the fetus position with arms around your legs and your feet off the ground. This will ensure the minimum contact with the ground and give the smallest possible target for a lightning bolt. Keep away from or take off any metal implements like an ice axe or trekking poles or even jewelry and watches.

A cave will provide the best protection against lightning, but do not stand near the entrance under any circumstances as the current may spark across the opening. This also applies to rocky overhangs, which may well turn into death traps. Depressions in flat, featureless ground can also conduct ground current.

In the jungle, living with such ferocious lightning storms can be a daily occurrence, and at times the strikes have felt so close, so loud and so violent that I have fallen to the ground. I spent one night with a local jungle expert who described to me during one such storm how a bolt had struck within feet of him. Instinctively he had gone to cover his face, but he described then seeing the bones of his hands through closed eyes as he was thrown backwards in midair. What a great line to be able to say! He was lucky to be alive. I maintained that he was unlikely to be hit by lightning twice, so stuck pretty close to him during the thunderstorm that night in the jungle!

High in the Atlas Mountains of Ecuador, bad weather approaches.

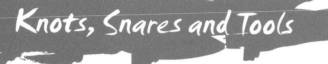

Knots, Snares and Tools

There is no secret to the art of tying knots. They simply require practice and, yet again, the survival key: patience. Being alone in an unfamiliar wilderness is not really the place to start putting in the hours required to instinctively know the right knot for the right use and, more importantly, how to tie it.

So my advice to anyone who loves the outdoors is to take two pieces of string with you when you go for a walk, and while everyone else dozes off on the riverbank in the sun, practice some of the knots I describe below until they become second nature. Good knot-tying is a hugely satisfying skill. Learn to tie your favorite knots with your eyes closed: you never know when you might need to do them fast and in the dark.

Knowing how and why to use a particular knot is an incredibly useful tool. At sea in a wind-powered vessel of any kind, knot lore is indispensable. It is under these conditions, when the forces acting upon sail, sheet (rope), and knot are changing all the time, that it is easiest to understand why any old granny knot will simply not do.

At the most basic level, knots hold two different objects together. These can be two pieces of rope tied together so they don't slip; a rope tied to another object that acts as an anchor; or a rope used to lash two different objects together (the upright and cross-pole of a raised jungle bed, for example).

Sometimes, as at sea or on a cliff edge, a well-tied, appropriate knot can, quite literally, mean the difference between life and death. On other occasions, in camp for example, a badly tied, inappropriate one can simply be a matter of extreme inconvenience. (Struggling to untie wet granny knots when moving camp in a storm is a waste of time, warmth, and energy.) But of one thing you can be certain: the failure of any knot can have unforeseen consequences, especially in the wilderness, and not being able to undo one at the crucial moment has often resulted in a fatal outcome.

Knots have evolved for different purposes. Some need to be fail-safe when they are suddenly required to bear weight; some need to be strong but release easily under load; some need to make a loop that will tighten when it is pulled; others need to hold slippery materials of different sizes together. The intention of anyone tying a knot should be to ensure that the type of knot used is the best one available for the purpose – although there are often a number of options – and that the knot itself is not the weakest part of the combined structure.

BASIC KNOTS

OVERHAND KNOT AND LOOP

Uses: among the simplest of knots, these form a part of many others. Often used to tie off the end of a rope to prevent it slipping or fraying or to throw over some sort of projection to take strain. Under load, it can be hard to untie.

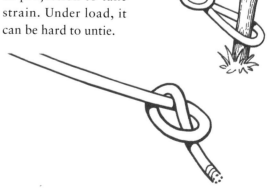

FIGURE OF EIGHT KNOT AND LOOP

Uses: more reliable than the overhand knot, it is also easier to untie. It is popular among climbers and mountaineers because if tied incorrectly it ends up as an overhand knot and will still be secure. The loop is used all the time with climbing harnesses and over spike anchors for belay ropes. Half hitch the free end for safety. (See reef knot below.)

KNOTS FOR TYING ROPES TOGETHER

REEF KNOT

Uses: one of the most widely used knots there is. Most useful for tying together rope of equal size but will slip if they are of different diameters (or made of nylon!). Can be untied easily if the rope is of reasonable thickness and not under great strain. Remember: right over left, left over right. Can be secured further by putting in a half hitch on the two loose ends.

DOUBLE KNOTTED OVERHAND BEND

Uses: primarily used for tying rope or cord together. Reasonably secure but best not to use under great tension.

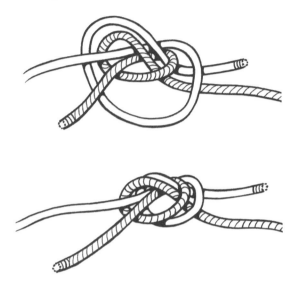

SHEET AND DOUBLE SHEET BEND

Uses: better than either of the above for joining ropes and is ideal for joining ropes or cords of different thickness or different material. Can be undone easily unless under great tension. The double is best for wet ropes and will not slip when strains are constantly shifting.

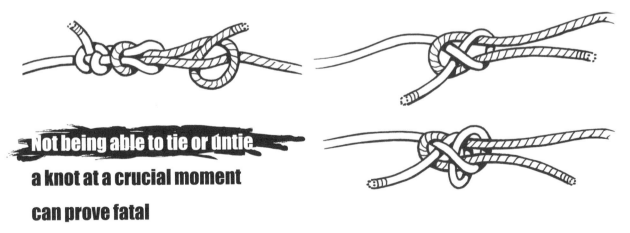

Not being able to tie or untie a knot at a crucial moment can prove fatal

FISHERMAN'S AND DOUBLE FISHERMAN'S KNOT

Uses: in the mountains, climbers use these knots to join slippery ropes and make secure strops or loops to place round trees or rocks. Fishermen use these knots for joining pieces of fishing tackle. In the jungle they are best for springy vine-like materials. Very difficult to untie but hold thin lines together well.

LOOP KNOTS

SLIP KNOT

Uses: the most basic loop knot, often used in tandem with others. Should be secured with a half hitch.

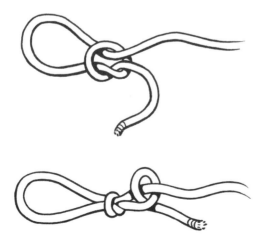

BOWLINE (MY PERSONAL FAVORITE)

Uses: a very useful and widely used knot that should be top of your repertoire. Used extensively at sea and in the mountains, it can be tied very quickly and is very strong and reliable. One of the most effective ways of creating a lifeline around the midriff that won't slip – or tighten! – under strain. Best remembered with that old scouting aide-mémoire: "A rabbit comes out of the hole, goes around the tree, and back down the hole." If your life depends on it, secure the free end in a half hitch to avoid it ever working loose.

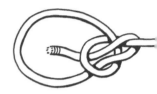

RUNNING BOWLINE

Uses: particularly useful for snares, its key attribute is that it WILL tighten when holding something in the loop. So this potential hangman's noose should NOT be used around human limbs.

TRIPLE BOWLINE

Uses: this type of bowline is invaluable when it comes to lifting or hauling heavy objects with its three loops. In the mountains it is particularly useful as a lifting harness with one loop around each thigh and another around the chest.

Learn to tie your favorite knots with your eyes closed: you never know when you might need to do them fast and in the dark

PRUSIK KNOT

Uses: also known as a wagoner's knot, this is a sliding loop that can be attached to a branch or another rope to make foot- or handholds that won't slip under tension, but which can be moved backwards or forwards when the tension is released. Vital to know when ascending in mountainous terrain.

Alternatively there is the French prusik where the loop is wrapped around the line seven or eight times, then the bottom end is passed through the loop at the top end. This knot frees more easily than a traditional prusik.

I used this French prusik to claw my way out of a crevasse in the Alps. Without that prusik, which formed a long foot strap for me to stand up on and slowly ascend the thin rope, I would probably still be in that crevasse!

KNOTS FOR LASHING

DIAGONAL AND ROUND LASHING

Uses: lashing together pieces of logs, branches, poles, or bamboo to make shelters, platforms, walls, or rafts is a basic requirement in a survival situation. Diagonal lashing can be used for joining X-shaped structures where two beams cross at right angles.

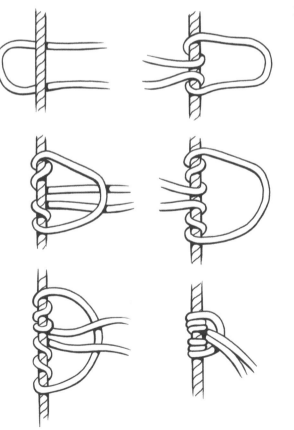

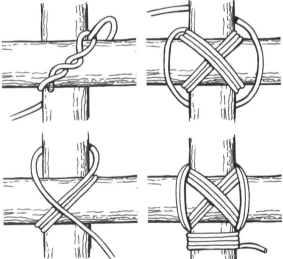

Round lashing is for joining two poles that extend in the same direction to lengthen the structure in question.

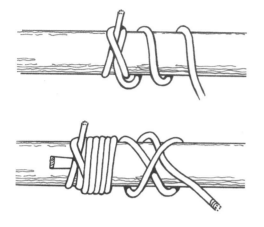

CLOVE HITCH
Uses: hitches are primarily used for attaching rope to a fixed point. The clove hitch is most useful when the pole or post is horizontal. If at an angle to the ground, it may well slip.

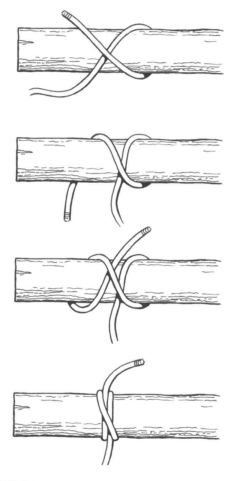

WHIP KNOT
Uses: a simple but effective knot – if tied correctly. Its main purpose is for joining handles to blades, or prongs to the end of a spear. Tension is everything here.

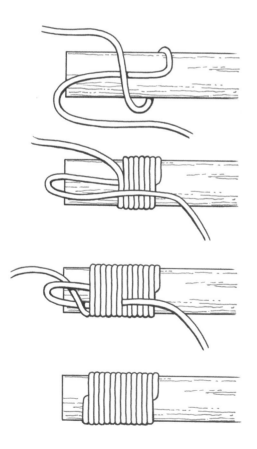

ROUND TURN AND TWO HALF HITCHES
Uses: commonly used for attaching a rope to a branch or post and can be made to untie easily with a slipped version. It is reasonably slip-proof and can take uneven strain from any direction.

SNARES

Hunting wild animals should not be your first thought when looking for food. It will often be easier and use up less energy finding plant foods. But snaring, once you have made the tools, should always be tried; it takes little time and energy to set them up, and should be done before you sleep each night. Find shelter; collect wood; make fire; set snares. That's the motto. Then let them work while you rest. Catching fish is often easier than catching mammals and I shall be dealing with the best techniques for catching fish in later chapters.

Owing to the suffering of the animals caught in snares – a quick and painless end is by no means guaranteed – most types are, quite rightly, illegal in many countries (including the UK and the USA). Having said this, in a survival situation a snare that produces a rabbit for the pot when your morale is low will raise your spirits no end.

A snare is a piece of wire, rope, or cord with a loop at one end which tightens round an animal's neck as it struggles to free itself having been caught in the noose. It then strangles itself to death. It's not a very nice way to go, but if it is your life or the animal's, then the snare is worth it.

Most animals can be snared with a wire noose placed in the right position, like near the entrance to a den or above an animal path between two trees. (Beware: don't place snares right outside animal holes – they are most suspicious when first emerging from their dens. Place it one or two bounds away instead.) The noose should slide freely, and the other end of the wire should be anchored securely to a tree or post. Snares are most useful at night when the animal cannot see them.

Successful snaring is based on three main principles: choosing the right type of animal to hunt and understanding its behavioral habits; making a simple, but effective, snare to trap and kill the animal; placing it in the right location and keeping it camouflaged.

Let's deal with each of these elements in turn.

UNDERSTANDING ANIMAL BEHAVIOR

Depending on the terrain, you will first need to decide what type of animal you hope to catch. Be modest in your ambitions. Some venison may seem a tasty idea, but killing a deer may well be a more difficult proposition than you imagine. It will also produce a huge quantity of meat that you will not be able to eat and will rapidly go off. Unless dried, it will also be too heavy for you to take with you and will attract other wild animals (like bears) that may put your own life at risk.

Much more fruitful will be to consider smaller mammals like rabbits, squirrels, foxes, and even badgers or weasels. When surviving for real, leave your preferences and prejudices back home. You need food.

Find shelter; collect wood; make fire; set snares.

That's the motto

Setting snares while stranded in the Alps.

Look for ample evidence that there is a reasonable population in your area. Once you know what creature it is you are hunting, it will certainly help to know something about its behavior in terms of where it sleeps, eats and drinks, as this will be vital when it comes to positioning the snare.

MAKING A SNARE

Now that you have decided which type of animal you are hunting, you must build the right sort of snare for the job. Certain snares work better for certain animals, depending on their size and weight. Here are the elements of a snare:

MATERIALS

Although snares can be used with rope or cord, wire is much the best if you have been able to salvage any. Think laterally. I have used wire unraveled from the metal housing of the ripcord on my parachute. The animal may chew through the rope if it has not been killed quickly. Use the smallest diameter capable of holding the animal that won't break under the strain.

LOOP

Snares are designed to trap your prey around the neck, and the size of your loop will depend on the size of the animal. If the loop is too large, the animal may be able to break free; and if too small the loop may miss the animal altogether. Make the noose opening slightly larger than the animal's head (three-fingers width for squirrels, fist-sized for rabbits). Your intention should be to place the loop clear of the ground so that the bottom curve of the loop hits the animal at chest height. This can be achieved by supporting it with twigs.

TENSION SNARES

A sapling bent over under tension can be attached by a cord to a pole fixed in the ground to which the snare itself is then attached. When the snare is sprung, it releases the trigger pole and the sapling lifts the prey clear off the ground. The advantage of this is that no other prey can then help itself to your hard-earned meal!

There are countless varieties of tension or spring snares. They are limited only by your imagination. For example, one trigger can have multiple snares running off it, meaning less work (i.e. only one spring and trigger pole needed), but more snares can be set, and hence there's a greater chance of a catch.

LURES AND DEADFALLS

Adding a lure to your snare will significantly improve your chances of trapping some dinner for the pot. These can be anything from parts of dead carcasses and rodents to pieces of fur that will attract curiosity.

These lures work especially well with deadfall traps, where the prey is lured by the bait and in the process knocks a trigger that drops a heavy rock or branch down, trapping the animal. These deadfalls can be easy and quick to set using any available dead logs or small rocks.

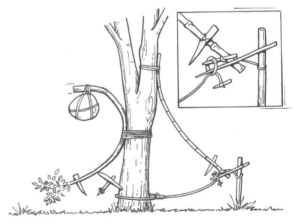

I always work on setting eight to ten traps, hoping for one kill. But there is no hard-and-fast rule. The bottom line is, make and set as many snares as you can, be consistent, be patient, be careful in your positioning and setting, and you will get lucky eventually – your brain is bigger than a rabbit's!

LOCATION

The final consideration in the successful use of a snare is to position it in the optimum location. Look for fur that has been rubbed from an animal's back in the undergrowth. This will often indicate a frequently used pathway. Animals move along and stop in the same places, so observing their habits will reveal important details: where their den is located and where they eat and drink. Their pathways to and from these locations will be the best position to place the snare.

Fencing or bottlenecks which guide the animal towards the snare should be subtle and well camouflaged. Make sure both they and the snare itself blend in with the surrounding undergrowth

and all newly broken bits of wood are covered in mud. When you are setting the snare, disturb the area as little as possible and try to avoid leaving a scent trail by covering your skin. If you have a source of smoke – smoldering leaves for example – this can be used to disguise your scent. Or simply rub the wire down with wet grass or mud.

TOOLS

Imagination and lateral thinking are again the primary requisites for making tools in the wilderness, and you will instinctively discover the tools that will be the most useful to you – knives, clubs, spears, bows, and cooking utensils for example. There is no great secret to their design, other than having the patience to search long enough for the right materials and effectively fashioning them into usable implements.

I remember on open days for SAS selection, wannabe recruits would be known to turn up with all manner of Rambo-style knives hidden on their persons! It was as if they imagined they would straightaway be diving through embassy

Primitive man survived mainly due to his ability to make tools.

windows. Often the most useful and practical of knives and tools are the simplest Swiss-army-style penknives – light to carry but sharp enough to splice wood and gut animals. Most experts I have met only carry the smallest of knives – though they are always well sharpened!

Tools can be made from stone, bone, and wood.

STONES
Useful for striking and chopping, while flints can be fashioned into very fine edges for cutting. I have used just such a flint disc knife to sever the head of a rattlesnake.

BONE
Has many uses, including fishing hooks, spear-tips, and handles. Shatter with a stone and fashion the splinters from there.

WOOD
The uses of wood are only limited by your imagination. For the purposes of tool-making, there are basically two types of wood: hardwood and softwood. While softwood can be good for kindling, it is best avoided for tools. Use your fingernail to tell the difference. If you press it into the bark and it leaves a mark, it is a softwood; if not, it's a hardwood.

Remember that if wood is to be used for striking or as a sharpened point, it pays to fire-harden it first. Hold the tip over a mature fire-bed and rotate it until it starts to hiss and steam. This will enlarge the cells and thicken the sap, which will in turn make the wood far more resistant to striking.

COOKING UTENSILS

BOWLS AND POTS
Use wood, bone, horn, bark, or other similar material to make bowls. If you want to make a depression in wood for a bowl or pot, don't try to carve it out with a sharp object like a knife, as this will just leave you with a mess and lots of splinters. Instead, use red hot "coals" from a fire and place them on top of the wood where you want the cavity to be. Feed the smoldering wood by judicious blowing and it will gradually turn to charcoal as you add more coals. The resulting charcoal cavity can later be dug out and smoothed down.

FORKS, KNIVES, AND SPOONS
Carve forks, knives, and spoons from non-resinous woods so that you do not get a wood resin aftertaste; nor do you taint the food. Non-resinous woods include oak, birch, and other hardwood trees.

WATER BOTTLES
Make water bottles from the stomachs of larger animals. Thoroughly flush the stomach out with water, then tie off the bottom. Leave the top open with some cord attached for closure.

WEAPONS

CLUB
Images of Fred Flintstone come to mind, but a club made of wood, or a stone lashed to the end of a strong pole, can be very useful as a weapon to protect yourself against wild animals, to kill a snake, or to finish off an animal struggling in a trap.

SPEARS AND THROWING STICKS
Spears and sharpened sticks can be used to kill wild animals but are best used in defense against them rather than offense. They can also be used for fishing. Attach sharpened bone with a whip

When surviving for real, leave your preferences and prejudices back home. You need food

knot (see page 44) to the end of a long, very straight sapling with the bark removed. Harden and straighten it over a fire first. Beech hibiscus is the perfect wood for this purpose.

BOWS AND ARROWS

Effective bows are all down to choosing the right wood for the flexing stave of the bow itself. This should be strong, long, very flexible, and without the nodules caused by branching. Yew, oak, hickory, and birch are the best woods for the job. The bow stave needs to be dried for several days over a fire. Notch the ends and tension the cord. Birch saplings make the best arrows and should be about 2 feet long and about half an inch in diameter. Make sure they are straight and true. This will ensure greater accuracy and power.

I have made a bow and arrow in the Amazon before and used it to catch piranha successfully. The key was a long arrow (6 feet) so I could fire at point-blank range while keeping my shadow off the water.

OTHER USEFUL ITEMS

DIGGING STICKS

Many chores, including digging worms or grubs out of the ground for eating, will be made considerably easier by making yourself a digging stick. Find a hardwood stick that is 3 feet long, 3/4 inch in diameter, and as straight as possible. Remove the bark. Form the end into a chisel shape and fire-harden as above.

I often make a longer version of this and double its use as a walking stick – this is very useful in the mountains, helping me move through snow, test frozen ice on lakes and dense forest undergrowth, as well as dig for worms and spruce roots.

PINE GLUE

Fresh sap from pine trees makes excellent glue. Collect it by severing the bark and allowing it to drip down a twig into a container. Heat on a fire and coat a stick with the resulting resin. Then light the stick and let it drip onto whatever surfaces need to be glued. Sprinkle some ash over the result, which will activate the gluing process. This is very useful but relatively simple to do.

SCAVENGING

Early man was above all a scavenger. He survived by letting other animals do the hard work of the hunt before moving in afterwards and scaring the predator away. I came across a lion kill in Kenya, where a zebra had been taken down hours earlier. It was still warm and the lions had eaten the blood and soft organs and most of the meat before vultures swarmed all over it. Once I had frightened them off, the carcass was all mine. I fed on raw zebra meat from its neck muscles and took some more to eat as I walked. Beware eating a lot of meat, though, if water is in short supply. Protein needs water to digest it. But if you have water, don't be afraid to scavenge. It can be the most efficient way to find food. Birds' eggs are a good example of this, and in the Moab desert I have scavenged several ravens' eggs that made scrambled eggs when cooked on the piping hot rocks that had been baked from the sun's heat.

Feeding off maggots I found in the rotting corpse of a small deer.

Keeping physically healthy in a survival situation will hugely improve your overall chances of holding out. And keeping a positive mental attitude is made much easier when you know your body is working well. If you are lucky enough to find yourself relatively unscathed in the first place, your priority should be to stay that way. If not, knowledge of some simple procedures that can be carried out without medical equipment will be of enormous use.

Many of the basic techniques of first aid (such as the recovery position and mouth-to-mouth resuscitation) assume the presence of both a patient and a rescuer. In your case, this will not be possible because you are a sole survivor, so I shall only deal here with self-medication techniques that are useful in all terrain types. In later chapters I shall deal with the problems that are specific to individual terrain types, such as hypothermia in the mountains during winter, snakebite in the jungle, and heat stroke in the desert.

The basics of first aid depend on clear thinking, common sense, some basic medical knowledge, and an ability to improvise. The most important is the ability to improvise – one of my best paragliding buddies, Gilo, was told there was a month-long waiting list for his swollen tooth that needed removing. The pain was so great, though, that that same night he went into his workshop and drilled the tooth himself, relieving the pressure at once!

We are often capable of doing much more than we ever imagine, and a white coat might feel reassuring, but in a life-or-death situation you can probably do just as well without the coat. Remember the story of Aron Ralston who, after being trapped with his arm under a rock for five days, decided that if he did not get free he would die. Using his pocketknife, he amputated his arm below the elbow, put on a tourniquet and administered first aid. He then rigged up anchors and fixed a rope to rappel to the floor of Blue John Canyon in Utah, and escaped to safety.

The old mantra of prevention being better than cure is even more true in the wilderness than it is at home. If we are careless at home with our health, we can always book an appointment with the doctor. In the wilderness, you can do the same, but this time the doctor will be you. (At least, while your resources will be limited, there is never any waiting list!)

STAYING HEALTHY

On a physical level, the secret of staying healthy will be largely bound up with your ability to avoid dehydration; taking in more energy in food than you give out; and maintaining a high level of personal hygiene.

WATER

Our bodies are 70 percent water. While it is possible to survive without food for several weeks, without water most people will die within days, maybe sooner, depending on the terrain. Large quantities of water are used up by the body

The basics of first aid depend on clear thinking, common sense, some basic medical knowledge, and an ability to improvise

going about its normal functions in order to maintain life. These include processing food, sweating, urinating, defecating, and breathing.

At a temperature that places no added stress on the body (68°F), our kidneys expel over 2 quarts of water a day, and more than another quart is evaporated in sweat which we will probably not even notice. Environmental factors like intense heat, cold, activity, altitude, burns, or illness will mean these figures are magnified still further. All this water must be replaced. If it is not, the body becomes dehydrated, which will decrease both your ability to think straight and to work efficiently.

When you lose more water than you are taking in, your blood becomes thicker and unable to carry oxygen to the muscles or move heat through the body and out through the skin. The loss of as little as 5 percent of your body fluids causes thirst, irritability, nausea, and weakness; 10 percent causes dizziness, headache, inability to walk and a tingling sensation in the limbs; 15 percent causes a loss of vision, pain when you pee, swelling of the tongue, deafness, and a feeling of numbness in the skin. More than a 15 percent water loss and all your discomfort will magically disappear. Because you will almost certainly be dead.

The most common symptoms of dehydration which you should immediately take note of are: dark yellow urine with a foul smell; a reduced quantity of urine; skin being less elastic when pinched; draining of color from fingernails; tiredness. All of these symptoms may occur well before a raging thirst takes hold. Thirst is not a good indicator that you need to take on more water. If you're thirsty, you're already dehydrated!

I know what it's like from my time on Everest. When we were up at the south col at 26,000 feet, we would wait hours just to melt enough ice for a cupful of water. We were climbing up to sixteen-

It's easy to get dehydrated in the mountains, even in the cold.

hour stretches and were so dehydrated we were all hallucinating. Our pee became a foul dark brown color. It is not a good state to be in!

Avoiding fluid loss in the first place is always the best strategy, so keep out of direct sunlight and be absolutely sure that any activity which uses energy and produces sweat achieves something worthwhile. The best strategy is to drink small amounts of water at regular intervals. In an arid climate you can lose up to 3.5 quarts per hour.

FLUID LOSS (QUARTS)	PULSE RATE (PER MINUTE)	BREATHS (PER MINUTE)
0.5	Under 100	12–20
0.6–1.5	101–120	21–30
1.6–2	121–140	31–40

PULSE CHECK

A very handy way of estimating how much fluid you may have lost is to check your pulse and breathing rate as shown in the table above.

PURIFICATION

Avoid taking risks with water. You will lose far more water from illness than you will gain by drinking contaminated water. If in doubt, boil all water for at least five minutes.

FOOD

It is possible to survive up to three weeks without food, although your physical and mental state will rapidly deteriorate if you go without food for more than a few days. To stay healthy you will need to find a balanced diet of carbohydrates, protein, fats, vitamins, minerals, and fiber. You can die from a diet of only rabbit or fish. The protein is so lean that it doesn't have enough fat in it to sustain you. Your body needs a mix of carbohydrates and fats as well as just protein.

Understanding the basics of nutrition and why all these elements are important will help you make priorities when it comes to finding food in the wild. So . . .

PROTEINS

One of the body's most important building blocks. Our muscles, skin, and bones need them to grow. Common survival sources: meat, eggs, fish, dandelions, nuts, camel, goat or cow's milk, animal blood.

CARBOHYDRATES

The body's main energy source, which can be processed quickly. Carbohydrates produce lots of heat and are stored in the liver, but are quickly depleted. Common survival source: cat's-tails, nuts, fruit.

FATS

Good form of energy storage, but difficult to break down. Common survival sources: bone marrow, liver, fish stomachs, animal fat, camel, goat, or cow's milk.

MINERALS

Iron deficiency means the body will be unable to produce sufficient heat. Common survival sources: animal blood, fish, dandelions, nettles.

Avoid taking risks with contaminated water. If in doubt, boil all water for at least five minutes

VITAMINS

Essential to metabolic functioning of the body. Low amounts produce scurvy and countless other irritations. Common survival sources: pine and spruce needles, nettles, the under layer of bark on many trees, fish, most edible plants and berries.

FIBER

Necessary to help our intestines break down food. Too little can cause irritable bowel syndrome. Common survival sources: grasses and pine needles.

SURVIVAL PLANTS

In everyday life plants are one of our most important sources of food and nutrition, but when events conspire to plunge us into a survival scenario they take on added significance. All of today's cultivated food crops – from staples like corn, rice, and vegetables to fruits, nuts, herbs, and spices – once grew wild and many still do. Most of what we drink, from alcohol to tea, coffee and soft drinks, is also derived from plant materials.

While it may not always be in a form you instantly recognize, in most wildernesses there will be some form of plant material that is edible and nutritious. However, any list that is not hundreds strong and focused on the wilderness terrain of any one country or ecosystem is bound to be selective. In the UK, for example, there are numerous types of fruits, berries and nuts in our woods and hedgerows that can stave off starvation indefinitely.

So in this brief overview, I have kept to plants that I have either used effectively myself or which are found over wide swathes of the globe. I also include other rarer examples which are specific to more extreme desert or sub-zero terrain.

CAT'S-TAIL

Habitat: common throughout the world on the banks of rivers, lakes, streams, and in wetlands.

Appearance: three to ten feet tall, they are easily recognizable from the seed head which looks like a cork fishing float (some say a sausage on a stick). The rhizomes (root stems) spread horizontally beneath the surface. Uses: its edible roots contain about 46 percent starch and 11 percent sugar. These can be eaten raw or cooked over the embers of a fire. The starchy pulp removed from the resulting barbecued root tastes like sweet chestnut. The seed heads can also be used as tinder and insulating material.

DANDELION

Habitat: open areas of high sunlight throughout the temperate regions of the northern hemisphere.

Appearance: distinctive for its bright yellow flower which opens during the day and closes at night. The leaves, on average about 6 inches long, have a jagged edge and grow close to the ground. Uses: high in calcium and vitamins A and C, the leaves can be eaten raw or cooked. The roots can be eaten boiled or roasted and make a good substitute for coffee.

NETTLE
Habitat: moist areas along streams throughout the temperate regions of the northern hemisphere. Appearance: often growing 3 feet or so high,

nettles are distinctive for the fine stinging hairs on the edges and undersides of their leaves. Uses: the young shoots and leaves are edible and very nutritious, and the leaves at the top of the plant are high in protein. Boil in water for about fifteen minutes before eating.

ROSEHIP

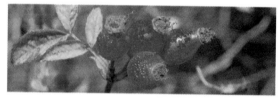

Habitat: hedgerows and woodland margins all over the northern hemisphere but not too far north. Appearance: rosehips are the fruit of the dogrose, a climbing rose thorn with arched stems and a pink flower. The fruit is usually bright red, 1/2–3/4 inches long and oval in shape. Uses: one of the richest plant sources of vitamin C, but also contains vitamins A, D, and E. Best taken as an infusion as the seeds can irritate the gut if eaten raw. Good for dizziness and headaches.

WATER LILY
Habitat: throughout the world's temperate and subtropical regions. Appearance: easily recognizable from its

large leaves floating on the surface of the water surrounding a large fragrant flower that is usually white or red. Uses: the flowers, seeds, and roots are edible raw or cooked but the roots should be peeled first. The liquid from the boiled roots can help ease diarrhea and soothe sore throats.

BAMBOO
Habitat: around a thousand species worldwide grow in a huge variety of habitats from steamy jungles to cold mountains. Appearance: instantly recognizable from its use

as a furniture material, bamboo can grow up to 50 feet tall. Uses: the young shoots are edible raw or cooked. Bamboo can also be used as a building material in a huge variety of survival structures, including shelters, beds, rafts, and cooking utensils. Very strong and hard to cut down. I have burned the base of bamboo trees in order to fell them.

AGAVE
Habitat: most prolific in Mexico, agaves are common throughout Central America, tropical South America, the Caribbean, and the southern and western USA. Appearance: thick, fleshy leaves with sharp points and edges appear to grow straight from the root and are colored yellow and green. They only flower once and produce a massive stalk. Uses: the leaves are very useful for making cordage, and the juice will lather like soap in water. The flowers and buds are

edible but should be boiled before eating. Used for making tequila in Mexico – excellent!

PRICKLY PEAR CACTUS

Habitat: desert and semi-desert areas of the USA and Central and South America but also in

other similar habitats throughout the world. Appearance: flat, padlike green leaves with pearlike fruits. Uses: all parts of the plant are edible and the pads are a good source of moisture, which can also help heal wounds. Be very careful to avoid the tiny, pointed hairs, which can be removed by rubbing the cactus in the sand. The seeds can be roasted and ground into flour.

ARCTIC WILLOW

Habitat: common in North America, Europe, Asia, sub-polar regions, and mountainous and rocky moorland areas in temperate regions. Appearance: tiny shrublike willow with round, shiny green leaves with silver hairs. It is a low-lying shrub that forms in dense mats and rarely reaches more than 18 inches off the ground. Uses: young willow leaves are very rich in vitamin C. New shoots both above and below the ground can be eaten raw after stripping off the outer bark.

REINDEER MOSS

Habitat: very resilient to cold, reindeer moss grows in both hot and cold conditions in northern Europe and the USA. Needs an open and well-drained environment. Appearance: a green, brittle lichen with bright red reproductive structures. Uses: the entire plant is edible but often bitter. Crush and boil in hot water. Can be used as medicine for diarrhea. Also can be eaten raw, if found in the stomach of a dead deer, as the moss is partially digested and therefore fine to eat. Norwegian Resistance fighters in the Second World War survived by using this technique.

SURVIVAL TREES

No other inhabitants of the world's wildernesses are as welcoming or useful to the sole survivor as trees. In an otherwise hostile environment, they often seem like the only real friends you have. Trees provide protection from the elements; shelters and rafts can be built from their trunks and branches; their bark, seeds, fruit, leaves, and needles are often edible and nutritious; and fluid from their roots, trunks, branches, or hollows can provide a life-giving drink. The only problem is knowing one from another and the help they can potentially offer.

Trees fall into three distinct categories: broadleaves, conifers, and palms. Broadleaves have wide, flat leaves and most are seasonal, losing their leaves in the winter months. Those that do not are known as evergreens. Conifers have needles and are evergreen (except for the larch) and their fruits are usually woody cones.

Palms have trunks without branches with leaves growing from a central point normally at the top of the trunk.

The following are among the most useful trees you will find in wilderness environments.

BEECH

Habitat: enjoys temperate latitudes and can be found all over the eastern USA, Europe,

temperate Asia, and North Africa. Appearance: a large, symmetrical tree with a smooth, light gray bark, dark green leaves, and spiky seedpods. Uses: the white meat of beechnuts is the perfect survival food as it is extremely nutritious.

JUNIPER (CEDAR)

Habitat: North America, Europe, the Middle East, Asia, and the mountains of North Africa. Likes open spaces and sunlight. Appearance: recognizable from its densely clustered, tiny leaves and distinctive smell. Uses: the berries are edible raw and the twigs can be soaked to make a nourishing tea.

SPRUCE

Habitat: temperate latitudes stretching into mountainous areas of extreme cold in both northern and southern hemispheres. Appearance: a pyramid- or column-shaped conifer with long, prickly needles that vary from dark green to silvery blue. Can grow to 100 feet tall. Uses: spruce needles soaked in hot water make an excellent tea rich in vitamin C.

PINE

Habitat: temperate latitudes of the northern hemisphere but likes the sun and can be found all over the USA, the Caribbean, the Middle East, and parts of Asia. Appearance: there are well over a hundred different species, all of which are evergreen with a resinous, sticky sap and distinctive smell. The bark of most

pines is thick and scaly with a trademark spiral growth of branches. Uses: the moist, white inner bark can be eaten raw or ground up, while the needles make a nutritious tea. Both are full of vitamins A and C. Pinecone seeds are edible too. The sap can be heated and used as glue or as an emergency tooth filling. The needles can also be crushed in the hands and the resin smeared on the skin as a mosquito repellent. Reapply every hour or so. Both spruce and pine burn hot and fast due to their resinous needles and make excellent kindling.

DATE PALM

Habitat: native to North Africa and the Middle East but grown in many other semitropical locations around the world. Appearance: tall and, like all palms, has no branches but a crown of leaves at the top of the trunk. Uses: fruit is yellow when ripe and can be dried and preserved for long periods. The leaves can be used to thatch roofs and walls while the trunk is excellent for shelter-building materials.

NIPA PALM

Habitat: coastal regions throughout Asia. Appearance: its short and large trunk grows mostly underground and has very large sticking-up leaves which are sometimes 15 feet tall. Uses: the juice of the flower stalk when young is rich in sugars and the fruit seeds are edible, while the leaves make excellent thatching material.

RATTAN PALM

Habitat: a rainforest tree that grows mainly in tropical regions of Africa, Asia, and Australia. Appearance: a climber that attaches itself to other rainforest trees by the hooks on its leaves. The stem can grow up to 200 feet long. Uses: the stems contain considerable quantities of drinkable water, while the stem tips and the trunk meat are edible raw or cooked. The stems can also be wound for making cordage.

SAGO PALM

Habitat: tropical rainforests of Asia. Found mainly in damp, watery inland terrain. Appearance: stout, short, spiky trunk with thick, hard bark and crown of leaves. Uses: the soft white inner part of the lower trunk can be pounded up, strained, and made into oatmeal. Highly nutritious and full of starchy sugars. Sago nuts are also edible.

BAOBAB

Habitat: savannah lands of Africa and Australia. Appearance: distinctive for its bulbous trunk which can sometimes grow up to 25 feet in diameter with short, stubby branches near the top of the trunk. Its fruit is gourd-shaped, up to 18 inches long and covered with short dense hair. Uses: the hollow of the trunk collects water while the roots, leaves, fruits and seeds are all edible. The bark is also very useful for making rope.

PERSONAL HYGIENE

BODY

Make a conscious effort to wash every day and pay special attention to hands (especially under your fingernails), armpits, crotch, teeth, feet, and hair. Remember that anywhere hidden, moist, and warm is a prime target for infestations.

White ashes, sand, or loamy soil can be used instead of soap, or you can have a go at making soap yourself from animal fat and ashes. Don't forget that in the absence of water, you will still benefit from an "air bath." Take off as much clothing as makes sense without compromising your well-being in other ways, and let fresh air wash over you for an hour. It'll do a world of good. Sunlight kills bacteria as well – leave dirty clothes out in the sun when appropriate.

TEETH

Try to keep your teeth and mouth clean. If you have no toothbrush, make a "chewing stick" from a twig by chewing on one end to break up the fibers, which can then be rubbed along your teeth and gums. If you're near a river, use cat's-tails. Pull apart the small stems, which leave a tooth-shaped end that fits snugly over your teeth, freshening them up. Then take the same stem and bend it in two and use the abrasive bent point to scrape off any plaque. After five minutes of this your teeth will feel fresher than ever before. It is amazing. No wonder local native Indians have such good teeth. Rinsing your mouth out with salt water (don't swallow!) or bark tea will help keep throat infections at bay.

FEET

Rule one for every soldier: look after your feet whenever you get the chance. Be kind to your tootsies: you depend on them to get you out of there. Wash, dry, and massage them and don't wait until a blister has developed. Prevention is always the key with feet. If in doubt or if you feel a "hot spot" looming, take five minutes out, air them, dry them, and refit socks and boots as best you can.

Strategically placed moss from the forest floor on the inside of the sock can sometimes prevent a blister developing, as long as it doesn't add to the pressure. If you do get a blister, leave it alone. If it bursts, treat it as an open wound.

Sunlight kills bacteria as well – leave dirty clothes out in the sun when appropriate

MEDICAL PROBLEMS

With only yourself to rely on in the face of a medical emergency, your options will inevitably be limited. However, if you stay as calm as possible and try to control feelings of panic, your chances of a good outcome will be greatly improved. Minor injuries should be attended to immediately, before they develop into life-threatening ones.

WOUNDS

Wounds occur when the skin is broken – they can be caused by anything from minor cuts, abrasions, and blisters through to burns and frostbite – and should be treated seriously, however trivial they may seem at first glance. As well as the danger of losing blood, a far more likely and potentially lethal possibility is infection. Bacteria from any number of sources that come in contact with the wound may lead to this.

The keywords for an actively bleeding wound are pressure and elevation (although the latter does not apply to snakebites – see in the chapter on Deserts, pages 213–214). If the wound is actively bleeding, apply pressure and sit down so that where possible the site of the wound is above your heart and blood will arrive at the wound site under less pressure. The pressure you put on must be firm enough to stop the bleeding and applied for long enough to allow the blood to start clotting. Release this pressure slightly every fifteen minutes.

Cleaning the wound with water and then keeping it clean should be your first priority. If fresh water is unavailable, use urine, especially if you need to flush out any debris. Urine is sterile. Unless it's a very serious wound, it's best left open to the air.

SHOCK

(See also the section on thin ice in Chapter 3, pages 136–137.) Shock comes about when the heart can no longer pump blood around the body at sufficient pressure to provide an adequate supply to the organs and tissues. This can be caused by injuries of all kinds but also by infection, heatstroke, fluid loss, salt loss, fatigue, and vomiting.

Severe blood loss should be stanched at all costs. A loss of more than 2 quarts of blood may well be fatal. Find shelter immediately, keep warm, keep your legs raised, and take small sips of water.

BLISTERS

Let them be! Don't try to burst them as this will allow bacteria under the skin. If they do burst,

treat them as for any other open wound: flush them out with fresh water whenever possible and allow air to circulate.

BURNS

A copious amount of cold, running water as soon as possible is the best treatment for any burn, large or small. Keep the burn under water for as long as it takes to cool the body tissue and stop further damage – the tissue will keep burning for much longer than you think. Drink extra water to compensate for increased fluid loss.

SUNBURN

Potentially a major problem anywhere in the world, from high mountain passes in winter to the middle of a blazing desert. While it may not win you a prize in a beauty contest, smear your face and exposed skin with earth. This will protect you against the sun's most damaging rays. It's not for nothing that pigs like wallowing in mud. I have used this very effectively in Alaska and the Himalayas, especially where the glacial burn can be intense.

BOILS

Apply heat to bring the boil to a head. Fabric on the end of a stick dipped in boiling water will do the trick. Drain the boil using a sharp (and sterile) instrument. Once the pus is drained, flush under running water. Keep covered to avoid reinfection.

FUNGAL INFECTIONS

Sunlight is the key here. Keep the skin exposed to the air and light and try hard not to scratch it, which will only make matters worse. Some natural antiseptics (see page 62) can help.

Cleaning the wound with water and then keeping it clean should be your first priority. If fresh water is unavailable, use urine

RASHES

Matron's rules still apply. If it's moist, keep it dry. If it's dry, keep it moist! Boiled acorns or the bark of a hardwood tree sometimes work on weeping rashes, while animal grease can keep dry rashes moist.

LICE AND TICKS

Both can give you typhus through their feces, so you should always be checking for them and remove them at once from your clothing, either by exposure to sunlight or by boiling if feasible. Don't scratch louse bites as this will make them vulnerable to infection, but wash them down in water. Ticks in your skin can sometimes be persuaded to let their jaws go when smoke is applied, but this leaves their vomit behind, which isn't ideal. Either way, try to remove them with their heads still attached, as leaving them behind will cause infection. The tip of a burning twig works well for removing ticks, as does alcohol or a cigarette end.

SPRAINS

If it's an ankle, it's best to keep your boot on in the first instance in case it's impossible to put it back on after the limb swells. Rest and stabilize the ankle, keeping it up. An ice pack will help immeasurably if available, or if not, cold water will help reduce swelling. Remember RICE: rest, ice/cool, compress, elevate.

FRACTURES

Immobilization is desirable, if not always possibile. A moving fracture can cause internal bleeding and is a major cause of shock. Splint very thoroughly if movement is essential.

DISLOCATIONS

Realigning the limb is best done sooner rather than later. You'll know what you need to do. Do it quickly and early on if you can. The short-term pain will be better than the long-term agony of leaving it and also not being able to use it. Rest immediately, keep warm, and drink water.

NATURAL ANTISEPTICS

SPHAGNUM MOSS
A natural source of iodine that can also be used as a dressing. I used this in the Alps after cutting myself with my knife while making snowshoes. It worked perfectly: cleaning and stemming the wound.

WILD GARLIC
Rub it on a wound or boil and then use the water to rub on the wound.

SALT WATER
Helps kill bacteria.

BEE HONEY
As is or dissolved in water, honey has powerful antiseptic properties.

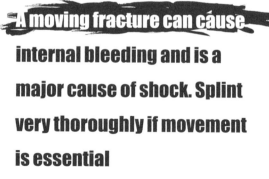
A moving fracture can cause internal bleeding and is a major cause of shock. Splint very thoroughly if movement is essential

MAGGOTS

Never mock a maggot! As well as being a useful source of protein, the humble maggot also has some useful medicinal properties in a tight corner. If an open wound does become badly infected and appears to be getting worse, treatment with maggots may be a sensible last resort.

Instead of avoiding flies, let them crawl on the wound and lay their eggs. When the maggots appear, cover the wound up and they will eat the dead tissue and pus. When fresh blood starts to appear, you know they have gone far enough and are starting on the healthy tissue. Flush the maggots away and check regularly to make sure they are all gone.

Keep your faith and decide to survive.

The Bear Necessities: Five Basic Rules of Survival

RULE 1: DECIDE TO SURVIVE

No matter how much you may know or not know about survival techniques, knowledge will always be secondary to spirit. Only you can decide whether to give up or go on. And in that decision is where you distinguish yourself. The pain will never last forever.

RULE 2: WATER IS LIFE

When pushed, the human body can survive extreme discomfort with little or no food for as long as three weeks. But without water, it will collapse after as little as three days. Always make it a top priority, before you are too thirsty.

RULE 3: HOME, SWEET HOME

Belonging is one of the deepest human instincts. Build yourself as comfortable and warm a shelter as is possible and things will immediately begin to look up. A warm, dry, comfy shelter brings pride and a smile, and suddenly everything will not seem so bad.

RULE 4: FIRE OF THE GODS

Nothing will improve your morale more than successfully conjuring a fire out of the resources around you. It will warm you, help feed you, and may ultimately save you. Become a master of fire-making: it is one of life's key skills.

RULE 5: KEEP THE FAITH

Don't be too proud to have a faith. Have it in yourself, in your God, and in one another. Time and time again, throughout the ages, having a faith has proved to be man's greatest ally and strength.

"Expect to have hope rekindled. Expect your prayers to be answered in wondrous ways. The dry seasons in life do not last. The spring rains will come again."

SARAH BAN BREATHNACH

mountains in summer

WHILE HIGH MOUNTAINS – WHEREVER THEY ARE IN THE WORLD AND WHATEVER THE SEASON – WILL BE VULNERABLE TO FREEZING TEMPERATURES, STRONG WINDS, AND DANGEROUS ICE, ON THE LOWER SLOPES AND IN THE VALLEYS NATURE WILL BE AT HER MOST ABUNDANT IN THE SUMMER MONTHS.

The great enemies of human survival – extremes of temperature and a lack of drinking water and food – will not be such major factors here as they are in many of the world's other terrains.

So count yourself lucky. After all, a positive mental attitude is a vital ingredient in any survival situation. That is not to say that making it back to civilization in one piece will be easy. For as well as the more obvious hazards, the mountain ranges of the earth cover the full range of climate zones from the Antarctic to the edges of the Sahara Desert and everything else between.

Some ranges, like the Urals, which run from the Arctic Ocean to the border between Russia and Kazakhstan, are covered in taiga: dense coniferous forest that makes navigation hard and brown bears a constant threat. In winter the ground is frozen solid with temperatures reaching as low as -60°C (-70°F), while during the short summer the snowmelt creates swamps, which makes movement extremely difficult.

And then there are the Andes. The world's longest mountain chain runs 4,500 miles down the western side of South America, from the Caribbean Sea to Cape Horn. Along its length lies Cotopaxi

A positive mental attitude is a vital ingredient in any survival situation

in Ecuador, the highest active volcano in the world; the Atacama Desert in Chile, one of the driest environments on earth; and Tierra del Fuego in Patagonia, which has glaciers at sea level.

But most of the mountain ranges in the temperate zones of the northern hemisphere – the Alps and the Pyrenees in Europe and the Rockies in North America – while remaining snowbound all summer long on their highest peaks can be relatively benign in the forests and valleys.

But in summer or in winter, while often of sublime beauty, the higher slopes of the world's mountain ranges are not a place to linger. So, assuming a speedy rescue is unlikely and there is no shelter available, it will often make sense to lose altitude quickly and descend into the valleys, where the air will be warmer and the chances of finding shelter, water, and food will be far greater.

Yet even this seemingly obvious decision can be fraught with danger if thought is not given to how you will go about it. While gravity may be working in your favor, rock-climbing on near-vertical terrain is inadvisable for anyone who has not had specialist training. At the best of times it can be difficult to see what the terrain is like below, and to find, after several hours of scrambling, that the only escape is back up again will drain your strength and morale in equal measure.

I have experienced this firsthand, while in New Zealand. I was descending a mountain by a different route from the one I had taken to the top. As I started down alone, the rock face steepened and began to bulge out in front of me into a hidden overhang of smooth rock. The drop until the next ledge was just 10 feet, so I hung over the edge and dropped down.

I continued down like this, dropping off ever increasing overhangs onto ever smaller ledges. Finally I came to a lip and peered over ready to drop down again, when I saw nothing but air beneath me. This drop was not just 10 feet down,

It will often make sense to lose altitude quickly and descend into the valleys, where the air will be warmer and the chances of finding shelter, water, and food will be far greater

but a sheer 500 feet. I had climbed myself into a trap with no way back up or down.

Above was overhanging bare rock, and below was now a drop far greater than any length of rope I might have. I had no choice but to attempt to climb back up those overhangs above me. If I could not climb those lips, I would be stuck; and on this precarious rock face I would eventually run out of the strength to hold on.

That vulnerable feeling of being alone and exposed was very frightening, and the climb back up was one of the more committed ones I can remember! So beware coming down where you can't see a clear route below. Climbing yourself into a trap where it is impossible to go up or down is a common cause of fatalities in the mountains.

There are also natural hazards that are particularly common in the mountains. Lightning can kill you anywhere, but is most dangerous in exposed areas where you are the only route to earth (see pages 38–39). River valleys may seem to spell safety but have their own fair share of danger. Flash floods caused by the runoff of heavy rain on to dry mountainsides can be triggered with unbelievable speed, while swamps, bogs, lakes, and unfordable rivers can make navigation a nightmare.

At least you're alive! But let's start at the beginning and try to get you out of this unholy mess . . .

Making a Shelter

Shelter should be a top priority in any survival situation. Even in summer when the elements are in a benign mood – for the moment at least – the importance of finding, or making, a shelter cannot be emphasized enough. Water and food will soon become necessities, but their beneficial effect will be significantly compromised if you are using up unnecessary energy keeping warm and dry because you have no shelter.

This will probably be the first assault of the mental battle I talked about in the first chapter. Can you really think calmly under such intense pressure? Will you be able to use what mental and physical energy you do have to your advantage without squandering it? Will you rediscover the real meaning and value of that instinctual "common sense" that most of us in our pampered modern lives have lost touch with?

Fatigue, through lack of rest, leads to bad decisions, which themselves result in a rapid physical and mental decline. As much as anything else, a place you can call "home," however humble, will be a major psychological boost.

But, as with every element of survival, you must think carefully before wasting precious energy on an inappropriate shelter. Ask yourself some key questions. Should I stay where I am? Would I have more chance of being rescued if I did? If not, where should I be looking for an alternative site for a shelter? How long am I likely to spend in this location and am I likely to return?

Remember to think. If you rush off and build an unstable, badly ventilated shelter in the wrong place – where water runoff from higher ground is going to soak you during the first downpour or a wild boar is going to come crashing through your lovingly constructed new bedroom – it will

Above all else, shelter building takes imagination and commor

Shelter should be a top priority in any survival situation

not only be useless, it will be worse than useless. Much precious energy will have been used up, not to mention that awful, parched feeling in your throat . . . and now it looks like it's about to rain and darkness is closing in and . . . "Ah no, no, no. Why didn't I just sit down and think about this when I had the chance?"

So let's get back to basic principles.

LOCATION, LOCATION, LOCATION

Even in the back of beyond, conventional real-estate-agent wisdom still applies when it comes to building a nest. Location is everything. And the best way of choosing the right location is to remember the key attributes of an effective shelter in the first place. So what are they? The first, and most vital, is protection from the elements. And in the mountains you will be faced with the full range of what nature can throw at you. The sun, the rain, the wind, and extremes of temperature will be constantly testing the ability of your shelter to keep them at bay. It needs to be sturdy and stable and well away from natural hazards like flooding, rockfall, or disturbance from wild animals or insect swarms.

So take time to study the terrain around you. If you are anywhere that is directly exposed to the wind and rain – high on a mountain ridge for example – consider an alternative location.

Also aim for south-facing slopes, where the rock and trees will keep their warmth from the sun for longer.

In general it makes sense to drop down into the valleys, but try to avoid the valley floor, where there may be rivers, marshy ground, or the risk of flooding, and where temperatures will drop rapidly at night as the cold air sinks.

The ideal place for a mountain camp is on flat ground about 100 feet above the valley bottom,

> ## Aim for south-facing slopes, where the rock and trees will ~~keep their warmth from the sun~~

preferably protected by heat-absorbing trees or rocks. Just those 100 feet up from the valley floor will add a good few degrees of warmth to your shelter.

Avoid any area where there are obvious animal tracks. It may well be in regular use and its users may not take kindly to your construction blocking their path to food or water. And before you start to build, look up. Trees with rotten branches have left many an unwary hiker with a sore head or worse. Make sure it's not your head.

TYPES OF SHELTER

The type of shelter you create will largely depend on how long you intend to stay in any one location. Sometimes, you will only be looking for a short-term overnight shelter, or even just somewhere to keep dry for a few hours in a rainstorm.

NATURAL SHELTERS

CAVES

May be a godsend in the short term if you happen to find one nearby. Longer term, though, their disadvantages tend to outweigh their advantages. They are often cold and damp and may be inhabited by bats, snakes, or other wild animals that may not welcome your presence and could spread disease.

TREES, HOLLOWS, AND BOULDERS

Any tree, rotten tree trunk, or natural formation that offers protection from the elements is a potential shelter. The addition of a protective structure around you, such as thick leafy branches to act as a windbreak, and some bushy insulation beneath you, is just as important.

If taking advantage of a hollow in the ground, a drainage ditch is vital to avoid being soaked when the inevitable rainstorm arrives.

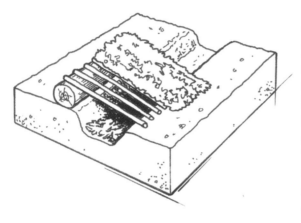

LOW-HANGING BRANCHES

The lower boughs of trees with thick, bushy branches (conifers are better than broad-leaved trees) are often an excellent source of makeshift protection against wind and rain, with the added advantage of the fallen pine needles, which cushion and insulate the ground.

The ideal place for a mountain camp is on flat ground about 100 feet above the valley bottom

TEMPORARY SHELTERS

90-DEGREE STRUCTURES

Naturally occurring features like boulders and tree trunks that are roughly at right angles to the ground can easily be adapted to make an effective shelter. Dig a shallow pit in front and line it with small branches and undergrowth. Then cover the resulting space with branches and foliage.

LEAN-TOS

Much the same principle as the right-angle structures (see above), except with an open front face where a campfire and a reflector can be built for added warmth. Lean branches and foliage at a 45-degree angle to a branch, pole, or rope connecting two trees of the same height. To be shower proof – in the absence of a tarpaulin or plastic sheeting – the foliage will need to be at least 4 inches thick and weighted down with branches on the top. Remember to angle the shelter away from the prevailing wind. Avoid branches poking down through the shelter as these will carry rainwater and drip onto you.

BENDERS

Young saplings can sometimes be found growing together in such a way that bending them towards each other and lashing them at the top will make a structure much like the typical dome tent you see at rock concerts and campsites the world over. If not conveniently placed, cut some down, dig a series of small holes in a circle, and push the saplings into the ground before lashing their tops together as above. Weave branches and foliage into the structure to insulate.

TRIPOD STRUCTURES

Tripod structures of varying shapes and sizes constructed from strong, straight branches can be used as the basic framework for a number of kennel-type structures that make excellent shelters. Lay logs and branches along the sides to create walls which can then be covered in layers of leaf and foliage.

The internal size needs to be worked out early on by lying under the basic framework and adjusting accordingly. Enough space should be left to provide for ventilation and to move around without compromising heat retention. Remember the overlying foliage will weigh down on the structure and reduce space during the building process.

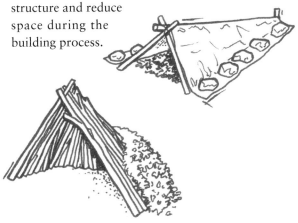

DEBRIS SHELTER

If you come across some natural debris, such as a small fallen tree, maybe caused by storm damage or bear movement, you can clear the underside of its branches and you will be left with a natural shelter. All you need to do is pad out the sides with foliage, moss, leaves, or dead branches and you have a very quick, easily made shelter.

I used this type in the Rockies when I was dropped into the mountains with

nothing but the clothes on my back, and it worked well for that first night when I didn't have much time to build an elaborate shelter. It was as much as 10 degrees warmer inside than out, especially when the ground and roof were well insulated with moss and pine needles.

WICKIUP

The wickiup is based on the Native American tepee-shaped structure using the basic lean-to construction technique. Success is based on choosing branches of similar size and length that can be put together in a cone or dome shape so that the structure is either freestanding or built around the trunk of a

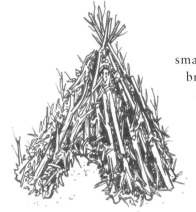

small tree. Again, the branches of the walls can be dug into the ground to make the structure more robust. Insulation can be added by weaving in layers of leaves and foliage.

A-FRAME

While it may take longer to build, an A-frame shelter will provide better and longer-term protection against the elements. Find a strong and straight cross-pole – the length will determine the overall size of your shelter – and lash each end to two further pairs of poles in an inverted V-shape at either end. Use the crook of a tree branch or otherwise elevated platform to support one end as you attach the frame at the other. Once you have one end up and running, the other will be easier.

Decide which end will be your door and weave a grid of branches and foliage on the walls and the back of the structure. After you have made a grid of branches, "thatch" the structure with leaves and foliage (see the Construction Masterclass, opposite). A second, or even third, layer can be added, depending on weather conditions. A fire can then be built at the open end with a boulder or heat-reflecting rock to push the heat back inside.

In the jungle (as we shall see), this structure can be adapted to include a raised bed on the cross-bar of the A-frame to keep unwelcome creepy-crawlies at bay.

Building a raised bed, clear of the water, in the Everglade swamps.

SURVIVAL SHELTERS
CONSTRUCTION MASTERCLASS

As my sergeant-major used to remind us with such concern for our well-being, "Being cold and uncomfortable is a mug's game." A sturdy, well-built shelter is your first step back towards the creature comforts you will now be missing. A little care at the construction stage is all that is required. So follow these tips and you won't go far wrong:

- Remove a layer of clothes before you start work. If it is humid or wet, this will mean you have something dry to wear when you are finished and everything won't be covered in sweat.

- Always make sure you start your construction at least two hours before it gets dark. It gets much harder at night.

- Work out the size of the structure before you start – it will be too late after it's already built.

- Remember that the underlying structure must be strong enough to take the layers of insulation to be added later and the inevitable excess rainwater which will soak into the upper layers.

- Orientate all shelters at 90 degrees to the prevailing wind. This will make the shelter a windbreak – as opposed to a windsock – and will blow smoke away from your campfire and not into your shelter.

- Make sure that the frame-ends of your shelter – the top of an A-frame for example – do not stick up above the main structure. If they do, they will collect water and drip onto your walls.

- Use any materials you may have such as plastic sheets, tarpaulins, ponchos, or pieces of canvas to help in your construction. Assuming they cannot be put to better use collecting water in very dry environments, they will be invaluable either as waterproofing above your head or as protection from the cold beneath.

- Remember many a life has been saved by the humble black trash can liner! Don't overlook their life-saving properties as a waterproof windbreak.

- If you do use a poncho or suchlike as a waterproof shelter, make sure you keep it taut and at an angle of more than 45 degrees to the ground. This will make sure the rain drains quickly and is less likely to penetrate the fibers.

- Layers of insulation – foliage, leaves, moss – used for thatching the walls of your shelter should be added to the frame from the ground up so that each successive layer overlaps the one below. It is better to have used too much insulation and roof foliage than too little – especially when the heavens open!

- A thatched lattice does not need to be particularly regular, so don't waste time and energy trying to make it so. Let the natural shape of the materials you are using dictate the shape and texture.

- Make sure you dig a drainage channel around any shelter where the rain might run down the hillside onto it.

- Even in summer, always make sure that the ground beneath you is well insulated, as this can be a major form of heat loss (and comfort!).

- Pine needles stuffed in plastic bags or spare jackets make great duvets, mattresses, and pillows.

- Before you sleep, stuff your jacket and trousers with moss, bracken, or cat's-tails, which will create pockets of air and help insulate you during the cold nights.

- Loosen your boots at night for the same reason.

"Any fool can be uncomfortable!"
EX–SAS SERGEANT MAJOR

Finding yourself alone in the mountains, and wet as well, makes the job of surviving much harder.

Finding Water

On the face of it, finding water in the mountains in summer should not be a major problem. Runoff from melting snows on the peaks will feed crystal-clear mountain streams, while the rivers in the valleys below will be of the seething, fast-running, well-oxygenated, white-water-rafting variety.

Well, maybe. If you're lucky. But the mountains you probably have in your mind's eye are the lush, Alpine *Sound of Music* type with the distant tinkle of cowbells gently floating up on the breeze from the valleys below. In fact – assuming you have arrived in your current predicament from the air – you are just as likely to find yourself cut off on a high and arid mountain ridge with very little vegetation and no obvious source of either food or water. Even then, after you have made your way down to warmer elevations, you can still find yourself in arid, semi-desert terrain.

Whatever your situation, finding a drinkable water source should be very high on your list of priorities. Trust me, I have seen more people collapse from dehydration than malnutrition! The French Foreign Legion didn't mind not feeding us very much, but they were rigorous in making us drink liter after liter of water. The desert is a terrain the Legion knows better than anywhere and they have learned that lesson well.

In desperate situations it actually pays to keep your mouth shut and breathe through your nose so that the saliva in your mouth doesn't evaporate unnecessarily. This is done by all the desert nomads of the Sahara – they will always have their mouths covered to avoid excessive loss of vapor through exhalation.

While you may be lucky enough at some stage to find an unlimited supply of purest, life-giving drinking water, it will be very hard to take it with you. Water is heavy and bulky in the quantities that you will need it, and even if you have containers, you will never be able to carry enough. Almost inevitably, you will be facing the possibility of severe dehydration at some stage.

This means jealously guarding every drop that you have inside you. Make every fluid ounce lost to the atmosphere count for something and lose as little of it as possible in the first place. Dehydration through vigorous and unnecessary activity with no positive result will not help. Manic activity brought on by surges of panic should be avoided at all costs. Anxiety itself causes dehydration.

Whatever your situation, finding a drinkable water source should be very high on your list of priorities

So while you are thinking about your water-finding strategy, keep calm and stay in the shade. When you do finally begin your search, always remember that water purity is as important as the water itself.

Generally, I always make sure wherever possible to try to boil any water for at least five minutes before drinking it. I also flavor it with vitamin-rich rosehip buds or pine needles and then let it cool to make it more refreshing.

In the absence of any means of purifying it (see page 79), it is far better to leave a suspect source of water well alone and search elsewhere.

SIGNS OF WATER

If you are observant, nature herself will give you many clues as to nearby sources of water.

- Grass-eating mammals feed at first and last light and their tracks will often lead to a water source, particularly where the tracks meet in a V indicating animals arriving from different directions.
- Birds often circle watering holes in the early morning or late afternoon and some, like finches and pigeons, fly low and slow when they have drunk their fill.
- Swarms of flies, ants, and bees all mean that a source of water is likely to be close by.

SOURCES OF WATER

SURFACE WATER

In the absence of rainwater, look for surface water such as mountain streams and the rivers they run into. Fast-flowing water and rocky bottoms are best, as this environment helps filter out potential nasties. One of the advantages of altitude is that water is apt to be near its source and so it is more likely to be drinkable than at lower levels. If no dead animals can be found in the water within about 1,500 feet upstream, you will probably be OK. My trick before drinking from streams is to walk along them downhill for five minutes to check they are clear of dead animals. The sound of running water also gets the thirst buds going first!

UNDERGROUND SOURCES

If no streams are nearby, don't forget to look in crevices and depressions in the rock. A clump of vegetation in an otherwise arid landscape is usually an indication of dampness near the surface. Drops licked from the damp rock face will taste like nectar if you are sufficiently thirsty.

On flatter, softer ground, dig into the damp soil and allow the muddy water to settle before collecting it. Dampness near the surface can also be condensed in a still (see opposite).

WATER FROM ANIMALS AND PLANTS

In the mountains, plants and vegetation as a possible water source may not be as numerous as in some other terrains, the jungle for example. Nonetheless, animals, perhaps even the remains of animals recently left behind by predators, can provide a source of fluid in a desperate situation. The thought of liquid squeezed out of an eyeball – a very reliable source of drinkable fluid – may not be too appetizing, but if it's the difference between life and death it can become surprisingly tasty. I ate the eyes of fish I caught on my raft once in the South Pacific, and even sucked the fluid out of the spine!

The thought of liquid squeezed out of an eyeball – a very reliable source of drinkable fluid – may not be too appetizing, but if it's the difference between life and death it can become surprisingly tasty

COLLECTING WATER

Even if sufficient quantities of surface water are not available, you can still collect water from plants and the atmosphere, using traps or ground stills.

TIP: Get up early before the sun steals away your precious source of water!

RAIN AND DEW TRAPS

Rainwater is always safe to drink and only needs collecting. If you have a waterproof sheet or tarpaulin available, stretch it over a wide area, preferably on a slope, and run the water off into clean containers. If you are on flat ground, dig a hole in the ground and spread the tarp over the top, remembering that water is heavy and that you will need to pin the tarp down with heavy boulders.

Dew comes about as a result of the basic principles of thermodynamics. As the ground rapidly cools overnight, warmer water vapor in the atmosphere condenses. The greater the temperature differential, as in many mountain environments, the more dew there will be. Remember the expression: "Dew on the grass, no rain will pass." (The dew is formed by colder, cloudless nights that signal good weather, so make use of the wetter morning ground.)

A dew trap uses this principle to collect water. Dig a hole about 18 inches deep and line with clay or a waterproof material. Fill with smooth stones to encourage condensation, which will then be trapped at the bottom of the hole.

Or, far easier, drag your T-shirt through the foliage to collect the morning dew or walk through the grass with rags tied around your legs, then wring out into your mouth. This technique has saved many a life and sustained survivors on the move through the most arid regions.

STILLS

If there is no sign of rain and you are in an arid area with little vegetation and you have waterproof material of any sort – polythene, plastic, canvas, whatever you can get your hands on will do – you can still collect dew in a solar still.

Suspend the material over a hole dug into flat ground as for a rain trap. But this time instead of collecting rainwater pooling on the top surface, collect it from the bottom surface as dampness in the ground rises in the heat of the day and condenses on the cooler bottom side of the tarpaulin.

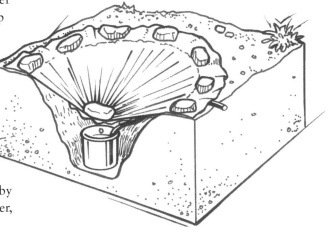

A small rock weighing down the middle of the tarp will attract the droplets to the center so that they can drip into a container.

This method will often produce as much as 16 ounces in twenty-four hours. Increase the amount of liquid produced by a still by adding vegetation to the hole and peeing in it as well!

Exhilaration at the summit of a rock face in California's Yosemite National Park.

PLANT CONDENSATION

Like us, trees and plants are made largely of water. This can be coaxed out of them by tying plastic bags around branches, succulent-looking leaves or bushes exposed directly to the sun. Try to make sure the bag is not in contact with the leaves, as this will hinder efficient condensation.

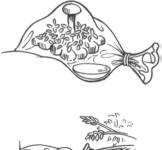

the small intestine and can cause chronic diarrhea, is often present even in apparently clear mountain water. In general, the farther water is from its source, the more likely it is to be contaminated.

Drinking contaminated water is even worse than drinking no water at all. In general, the farther water is from its source, the more likely it is to be contaminated

Water collected from the atmosphere, or from plants or ground stills, has the enormous advantage of always being pure. However, it should be possible in most situations to purify an otherwise dodgy water source. Many people carry water-purification tablets or iodine when they are traveling abroad in areas where bottled water is unavailable, so you may have some on you. Basic filtration can also be achieved through a shirt or bandanna or even a sock filled with sand.

The most effective way, bar none, however, assuming you have fire and enough fuel and are not at an altitude where water boils below 100°C (212°F), is to boil water for at least five minutes. This will kill 99.9 percent of the bugs that can harm you.

On Mount Everest at our high camp at 26,000 feet the air was so thin that water boiled at the dramatically lower temperature of 70°C (158°F), insufficient heat to kill any bacteria – but as all the fluids we were drinking were melted ice and snow that was very fresh and clean, we could get by with using a simpler rule: don't melt the snow that is yellow!

WATER PURIFICATION

Drinking contaminated water is even worse than drinking no water at all, so it is always better to assume the worst than take a risk. Even well-oxygenated running rivers can be full of tummy bugs, and meltwater from ice and glaciers can contain bacteria. Giardia, a parasite that infests

Finding Food

The potential for food in mountain terrain at this time of year is good. Nature is at her most bountiful, which means that a balanced diet made up of a healthy mix of carbohydrates, protein, vitamins, minerals, and fiber is, at least theoretically, possible. Remember that with relatively few exceptions, you can eat some parts of almost anything that crawls, swims, walks, or flies.

On the downside, your hunt for food will be constantly sapping your supply of energy. So never forget the two golden rules for finding food in a survival situation: don't use more energy finding food than it will give you back, and always take your opportunities when you find them. To massacre an old adage: one in the stomach is worth ten in the bush.

You might like the idea of running off through the woods hunting wild animals, but it is a very inefficient way of finding food. It is generally much better to set traps and sit back and let them do the hard work for you. When you have made a few traps or snares, you can reuse them over and over again. Remember the other saying: "Good enough, near enough." Traps don't have to be works of art, they just need to be functional and to work. Generally, if it is close enough, it is good enough!

Keeping these golden rules in mind, let's look at the possible food sources available in the mountains and weigh up their pros and cons.

With few exceptions, you can eat some parts of almost anything that crawls, swims, walks, or flies

TREES, PLANTS, NUTS, AND BERRIES

Most mountain ranges around the world, at least on their lower slopes, will have some type of edible vegetation. There are some 300,000 classified plants in the world, of which about 120,000 varieties are edible (of these, 10,000 can be found in Europe). The most energy-rich parts of the plant are the roots and its seeds, nuts, or fruits, while leaves are a good source of vitamins.

There's only one problem. The resident populations of everything from caribou and grizzly bears to birds, squirrels, and rodents have had plenty of time to work out which plants are edible and which give them a bad headache and a dose of the runs. While many of the food sources they eat will be edible for humans too, some will not.

So what to do? This is not the time for random experimentation; positive identification is vital. While your plight may be grim, a poisoned body will make it far worse. Better to stick to a few easily remembered rules concerning plants and berries and look for other sources of food to supplement your diet.

So, just remember this . . .

TREES, PLANTS, AND GRASSES

- Plants that grow in water or moist soil are often the most tasty and nutritious.
- Most roots, bulbs, and tubers are safe, but must be cooked to be digestible.
- All ferns are safe to eat if boiled.
- All parts of a fir tree are edible, as are most parts of a pine tree. Spruce trees have a sweet-

tasting inner bark at the bottom of the trunk. Peel off and scrape.

- Most tree leaves and many plant leaves are edible, but avoid any tree with a milky sap.
- Red and white plants and those covered with spines or fine hairs are likely to be poisonous.
- The tips and seeds of all grasses are edible and a valuable protein source, but the stems need boiling. Watch out for highly toxic (and easily recognizable) infestations of ergot, which grows like small black shafts in the seed-tip.
- Cat's-tail, a type of river rush, is found near fresh water all over the world and is easily recognizable from its seed head, which looks like a cork fishing float (some say a sausage on a stick). Its edible roots contain about 46 percent starch and 11 percent sugar. These can be eaten raw – wash off in fresh water first to avoid parasites – or cooked over the embers of a fire. The starchy pulp removed from the resulting barbecued root tastes like warm sweet chestnut.
- Beware of hemlock – if you eat it, it can kill you in a matter of hours, just ask Socrates! This biennial herb can grow up to 8 feet tall and has triangular, finely divided leaves with bases that sheathe the smooth purple-spotted stem. Its fresh leaves and roots have a rank, disagreeable, parsnip-like odor, and the small but attractive white flowers, arranged in umbrella-like clusters, open in early summer. The fruit of the hemlock is tiny, flattened, and ridged. Consumption will cause nervousness, trembling, loss of coordination, depression, coma, then death.

FRUITS AND BERRIES

- Single fruits on a stem are usually edible.
- Blue or black berries are usually edible, white and yellow are not, while red ones should be treated with caution. (Blueberries also contain the most antioxidants of almost any fruit—if you find them in the wild, eat them all!)
- Aggregated fruits and berries (think raspberries/blackberries) are always edible.
- All single fruits with five petals at the end of a single stem belong to the rose family. One excellent example is rosehip itself, which is a rich source of vitamin A and C and tastes great brewed up as tea.

NUTS AND SEEDS

- Observe other animals such as deer, who often spend much of their time rooting for nuts and seeds. Also notice where smaller animals such as wild pigs have been digging – copy their habits.
- All cone-bearing trees produce seeds which are edible. Pine needles are stuffed with vitamin C.

MUSHROOMS

- While some may look tempting, unless you are already an expert, it's best to leave fungi well alone. Cooking will not dissipate the poison of a toxic mushroom, and the penalty of picking the wrong type of mushroom, could well be fatal.
- If you have to eat them, a general rule of thumb is to avoid white gills and stick to brown-gilled ones. Test a tiny bit on your tongue and wait five minutes. Then taste a small part and leave thirty minutes. Continue very cautiously.

INSECTS, GRUBS, AND WORMS

Not many of us relish the prospect of a breakfast of maggots, beetles, and worms. But the tough reality is that the yuck! factor is not something we have the luxury to indulge when our lives are on the line. And as I have found on many occasions when my hunger has been intense,

If you have to resort to eating slugs, it may be best to swallow them whole!

suddenly the yuck! factor isn't the problem it is back home. And that comes from someone who's normally a finicky eater!

The great thing about creepy-crawlies is that they are the most abundant life form on earth and are easy to catch. They are also 80 percent protein, compared to beef's 20 percent – although I don't suppose the fast-food chains will be offering Beetle Burgers any time soon.

Maggots contain around 70 calories an ounce, which means if you are holed up and expending little energy, you could just about survive on a handful of maggots a day. Before you tuck in, though, remember to bite off their heads and spit them out—they taste a whole lot better that way.

Also, if you can collect enough, fry them up first before eating them, or cook them and dry

them before crushing them into powder for stews. Worms can get the same treatment.

Whenever I have eaten either maggots, slugs, or worms (and I have had some pretty horrible-looking and very long ones), I always tend to swallow them whole. Then I get the benefits without the disgusting sensation of pus squirting into my mouth, which is what you get if you bite them.

During the summer in the northern hemisphere there is a great way of collecting wood-ant larvae for a swift emergency meal. If you come across a large ants' nest, lay out a tarpaulin and break open the nest. Then throw the ants, nest material, and their larvae into the middle of the tarpaulin, and roll up the edges to create some shade. The ants will then all scurry about carrying the larvae to the protection of the shadow, where after a few minutes you can collect and eat them. The larvae look pretty unappetizing, like puffed rice, but are a nutritious, quick, high-protein meal.

INSECT LORE

- Larvae, grasshoppers, beetles, grubs, ants, termites, and worms (best dropped in water before eating, where they will expel any bacteria) are edible.
- Anything stinging, biting, hairy, brightly colored, or plain smelly will be inedible, as are caterpillars, spiders, ticks, flies, and mosquitoes.
- Most insects can be eaten raw. While the majority of them taste fairly vile, wood grubs are bland and some ant species are actually quite nice as they store honey in their bodies.

The great thing about creepy-crawlies is that they are the most abundant life form on earth and are easy to catch

- Insects like beetles and grasshoppers with a hard outer shell will have parasites, so remove any wings and barbed legs and cook them before eating.
- If you still feel like retching, grind some insects into a paste and mix with some plant roots. It may just make the difference.

FISH

Where there are mountains there are valleys; and where there are valleys there are rivers with fish swimming in them. Of all the available mountain food sources I have looked at so far, fish are by far the most palatable.

You can fashion hooks from thorns, bones, or feathers as our earliest ancestors did, and can make a fishing line from fibrous material like nettle stalks or from some strands of clothing or cord you may still have on you. But in the first instance, your best bet is to trap your prey and use your hands.

TRAPPING, SPEARING, AND TICKLING

Sometimes fish actually trap themselves – in pools, for example, that have been left behind when the river level has fallen in high summer – so you should look out for these first. If this is not an option, a basic understanding of fish behavior will help you work out where they can be found. Then you can drive them into a trap that, like all good cooks, you prepared earlier.

Fish, like us all, need to feed and breathe. For this they like clear, well-oxygenated water. They also usually feed – and are therefore easier to spot – in the early morning, late afternoon, or at night (when you'll need a torch).

The outside bend in a fast-flowing river where the water is shallower is usually fertile territory. Also like us, they tend to head for the shade when it is very hot and into the sun when it is cooler. So look under the banks in the heat of the day.

Using this knowledge, and having located a good spot, you can construct a simple funnel trap either of rocks, sticks, or if you have it, the decapitated remains of a plastic bottle (see diagram), into which the fish can be driven and from which they will have no means of escape. These can be very effective when fish are moving in large groups to spawn. Bait the bottle if you can with insects or the guts from previous catches.

Spearing is also an option, but fish will often hide under rocks, making spearing hard. Remember to aim behind where you actually see the fish to take into account the water's refraction.

You can consider "tickling" your prey by easing your hands gently into the water with your palms upwards and fingers and thumbs cupped. Then you will need to locate them, feel for them without frightening them off (difficult!), and then pounce with speed and luck. It's not easy. However, if you are patient it works.

Good tips are:
- Start downstream of them.
- Allow your hand time to cool to a similar temperature to the water.
- Approach them slowly from behind, keeping your shadow off them.

Bring your hand over the top of the fish then drive it down into the silt to get a grip on its slippery scales. Then pull it out of the water. Or slide your hand under the fish, "tickle" it by stroking its belly gently to imitate the flow of the water, then scoop it fast out of the water on to the bank.

I have used both methods successfully, and have even eaten the fish raw, seconds after catching it. Grab the fish in the gills and bite hard through the spine. It also might be worth flicking it a bit first to get any waterborne parasites off if this is a concern in the area.

Fish are most docile when they have swum up into small pools but have not been able to get out again with the dropping water levels. As oxygen gets used up in the stagnant pool, the fish's reactions slow down and that's when they are easiest to catch.

Or alternatively you can wade out into the middle of a stream, kick up a lot of silt and muck off the bottom, then move downriver. The silt will drive the fish to the banks to seek fresh oxygenated water. This is often a good place to tickle trout, downstream of where you have disturbed the riverbed.

Eating Alaskan salmon, raw and straight from the river.

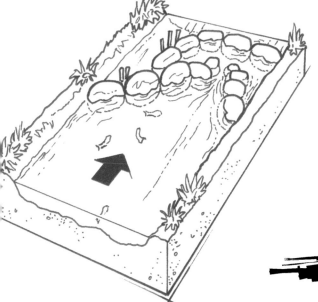

especially if there is little food around for the fish and they are inquisitive. You can set any number of these lines and I have caught many fish in this way. I advise you to work on a 20 percent catch rate— i.e., set five lines to get one fish. Night-lines make very effective and efficient fishing. Let the lines do the hard work, not you.

Night-lines make very effective and efficient fishing. Let the lines do the hard work, not you

NIGHT-LINES

Better still is to fashion a line from any threads from clothing or string you have, and hooks from thorns or pieces of wire you can salvage, and set out night-lines. Attach five or more hooks along the length of a line and weight it with a rock at one end in the river and to the bank at the other end. Bait with fish, game guts, worms or other insects, or if none of these are available use a bright lure made from any shiny metal object you can find. Set these before sunset and check them in the morning. One catch tends to attract others,

GAME, SNAKES, AND RODENTS

Although potentially abundant in many mountainous regions, large game like deer will be extremely hard to hunt unless you are carrying a gun. In the first instance, therefore, it will be best to concentrate your efforts on the smaller animal species like snakes and rodents, which are easier both to hunt and to prepare.

As we saw in Chapter 1 (see pages 45–48), snares can be relatively easily made, although these should only be used in a life-or-death situation, as they are illegal in many countries. Studying the habits and behavioral patterns of your prey will always pay off. Many animals use the same tracks regularly on their way to find water and food, which therefore make a sensible location for a snare.

Animals like rabbits can also be killed by spearing; the weapon can be relatively easily made by selecting a strong, thin sapling and sharpening the point with a knife or sharpened rock before hardening the end in a fire. Bait outside holes and sit and wait. This is less efficient than snaring, however, which allows you to sleep while the hard work is done for you.

You can also smoke animals out of their holes. Block up all but two entrances, start a small fire outside one and set a net or dig a little pit trap outside the other remaining hole. Have a spear at hand to kill the prey, or if it is caught in a net, catch it, hold it by the rear legs and neck, and twist and pull to break its neck. Remember: when slaughtering, act decisively. A halfhearted attempt at killing an animal doesn't help you or the poor beast!

You can also fasten four safety pins together to act like a mini anchor-shaped barb. This can be baited and dropped into rabbit holes, or left out for birds to take.

If you can find, locate, and kill a snake – as I have often done – it can easily be skinned and the meat skewered and barbecued over a campfire. Snakes make a very tasty source of energizing fat and protein.

Trap by pinning the head with a long stick and kill by smashing a rock on its head. Repeat to make sure it's dead . . . angry snakes are bad things to have slithering around!

Skin by severing the head, peeling back the skin, and pulling it downwards to separate it from the body. The guts will be pulled out along with it, leaving the meat ready to be cooked.

For cooking, the snake can be wrapped around a stick and tied at one end with some stalks, and at the other end by trapping it between a splice in the stick. It can also be laid out flat to bake on hot embers or coals.

Remember: cooking on open flame will dry the meat out and cause it to lose precious moisture and nutrients . . . but it does taste better. Judge the best way to cook or bake it based on the relative abundance or lack of food and water around you.

While I was with the SAS, I saw desert nomads carrying rattlesnakes in their backpacks with their mouths sewed shut. This ensured that when the nomads wanted the meat five days later it was fresh and alive rather than rotten and dead. A good trick!

Having gutted a rabbit at the site of the kill, it is now ready to carry back to my camp.

If you find yourself at a very high altitude, descending may be a critical necessity to avoid acute mountain sickness (AMS), more commonly known as altitude sickness

I hope that, by now, you will have established a camp and found reliable sources of food and water, plus had a chance to rest up and take stock. Eventually, though, the time will come to move on. If there seems no chance of being spotted from the air, and the food and water resources are thin, moving on may not be an option but a pressing requirement.

Indeed, if you find yourself at a very high altitude, descending may be a critical necessity to avoid acute mountain sickness (AMS), more commonly known as altitude sickness. Although the symptoms usually do not show up for thirty-six hours, almost everyone will be affected in some way over 1,200 feet above sea level.

Before you go, don't miss the chance to salvage anything that you can. Think laterally. Ask yourself: what can I find in the wreckage of my plane or parachute that will help me on my trail back to civilization? Many consumer items that are made for one purpose are fashioned from materials that can just as easily be used for another, quite different, purpose. A tin can for a cooking pot will be invaluable, as will plastic bags and a water container, while wire can be used to make snares, and the magnet you will find in any loudspeaker can be used to make a compass (see Chapter 1, page 33).

One of the most helpful items to have with you, particularly in the mountains, is rope. When I land in a parachute, as I have often done, the canopy material and cord that I salvage are invaluable during my escapes. Parachute canopies are made of ultra-strong rip-stop material and, while technically only showerproof, can be used for everything from a makeshift rucksack to constructing a shelter. The lines themselves are also invaluable. Cord or rope can be used for any

number of uses, including abseiling down a cliff or ravine to find food or water. (See Abseiling Techniques, pages 94–95.)

The basic rule is: be inventive, think laterally, and remember "necessity is the mother of invention." When it matters, people in survival situations have come up with some ingenious life-saving tricks from the most mundane of objects, such as discovering how good everyday

A soldier parachuting.

camera film is to use as tinder for a fire in an emergency. It will burn hot and bright with just a spark to ignite it.

Efficiency of movement when you are on the move is also crucial. Your energy is at a premium, and nothing will drain your morale quicker than being forced to retrace your footsteps, and maybe this time with gravity working against you. So as well as your head, use your eyes. If you are already high up, try to find an unrestricted view that will give you a few clues as to the overall lie of the land. If you can memorize the basic contours of the land ahead

Parachute canopies are made of ultra-strong rip-stop material and, while technically only showerproof, can be used for everything from a makeshift rucksack to constructing a shelter

and a few distinctive landmarks, so much the better. (Remember: don't make the mistake I did in New Zealand, by becoming trapped halfway down a cliff face!)

A rule of thumb for finding your way out if lost, which is told repeatedly to all SAS recruits before they begin the mountain phase of their selection, is: "If you are lost then head downhill until you find a stream, follow the stream until you hit a river, follow the river until you find civilization . . . then call us . . . here's a 10p piece—don't lose it!" It may be crude but it always seems to work!

ORIENTATION

Your most pressing task will be to get orientated. Without knowing the general directions of the cardinal points of the compass, there is no point in going anywhere. Going around in circles when you're hungry only makes sense if you're a vulture.

As we saw in the first chapter, learning the basics of navigating using the stars, the sun, and the moon is invaluable, and makeshift navigational aids like the shadow-stick method or creating a crude compass by magnetizing a needle are invaluable. But in the mountains you will rarely be able to continue moving in a straight line for long. The weather may well be cloudy and your makeshift compass temperamental. Whether you are able to utilize these methods or not, you will regularly need to confirm your direction as you pass through often inhospitable terrain. To do this, an understanding of some clues from nature will be invaluable.

USING NATURE'S SIGNS

Nature leaves many clues to your direction. If you know the direction of the prevailing wind, and the trees and bushes have been very obviously bent over, you already have a very useful directional pointer. North- and south-facing slopes will also often have dramatically different types of vegetation. The thicker and taller vegetation will be growing on the southern slopes while the branches of a tree that faces south – and therefore receives more sunlight – will often be horizontal. The branches on the north side, however, which have been straining to reach the sun on the other side, will have grown nearer to the vertical.

An isolated tree may also have more moss on its northern side (moss prefers shade), while saplings may be whiter on one side (a natural form of sunscreen) and darker on the other. The sun's rays also have a bleaching effect, so on an otherwise dark rock, the lighter side will be to the south. Likewise the rings of a fallen tree stump will be thicker towards the south.

On a glacier, rocks often topple forward towards the south. The shade from the rock means the ice melts around but not underneath it, often leaving rocks perched on little pillars of ice. As the sun from the south melts that pillar, the rocks tend to fall southwards. A lone rock is not good enough to judge this on, but if you see that a whole host of rocks have fallen in the same direction off the ice, then that is a good indicator of a southerly direction.

All these indicators should be used in reverse in the southern hemisphere, of course, and none should be used in isolation. They are all pieces in a jigsaw that will hopefully fit together to make up the overall picture.

NEGOTIATING RIVER VALLEYS

Before long, you will almost certainly descend into a river valley. Rivers are a conundrum. On the one hand they offer a limitless supply of water and a route to safety – they often lead to settlements, roads, bridges, and ultimately a lake or the sea – but they also hold potential danger. During sudden heavy rains, flash flooding can build with terrifying speed, especially during summer when the runoff from the dried-out hillsides can be much greater. While in the army in North Africa, I saw a wadi in the desert that was parched dry fill up in a matter of hours into a torrent. Luckily we had just moved our patrol camp an hour earlier.

Following a riverbank may not be that easy either. Bogs, swamps, or impassable ravines may mean that you have no choice but to climb all the way back from where you have just descended,

Attempting to swim under a logjam in an isolated slot canyon i

as building a raft or using a makeshift flotation device may be just too risky.

Your first task will be to assess the risk that a river poses. How cold is the water? How deep is it? How fast is the water running? What obstacles are there both upstream and downstream? Is the river straight or does it bend with fluky, unknown currents? Is this actually the best place to get into the water and where will I exit?

In general, rivers are narrower and shallower upstream, so that may be an option if crossing the river is your intention.

Rivers are a conundrum. On the one hand they offer a limitless supply of water and a route to safety – but they also hold potential danger

If you can avoid it, don't get into an unknown mountain river. They are lethal and you can easily get injured or end up hypothermic. In the Rockies I almost suffered both and only just made it out of the rapids in one piece, shivering and battered. It is smarter to keep clothes dry at all costs.

Rafts can be made by lashing logs together (see the diagram in the Jungles chapter, page 170), but they are of most use on slow-flowing jungle rivers. In the mountains they run the risk of being smashed apart by the rocks. Flotation devices that keep your head above water are usually a more viable option: sections of clothing – trouser legs, for example – filled with air and bracken

and tied off with string, or a backpack filled with empty plastic bottles. The secret is to hold your flotation device in front of you and not risk sinking it by putting all your weight on it. Also always go feet first down the river so you can use your feet to fend off any obstacles you hit.

Clothing will give you little or no protection against the cold, but it can be psychologically comforting and protect your skin against scrapes. So keep an underlayer on if you have the option, and do everything that you can to waterproof your remaining clothes and keep any tinder you have in plastic bags. Use these bags tied together as your flotation device. Keep any knife on your body close at hand in case you or your bags get snared by underwater roots or branches.

Take your socks off but keep your boots on to protect your vulnerable feet and ankles. (Dry socks to put on afterwards are very important for warmth and morale.)

Once you have decided to get into the water, you must make it count. There's no point in deciding the water's too cold or the current's too strong when you've just lost all that valuable body heat for no gain. Remember also that the glacial meltwater you often get in the mountains will be near freezing even on a hot summer's day. Your body's shock-response system will make you gasp as a reflex action, and you risk taking in a bellyful of water before you've even started. So don't dive in, but wade in surely but slowly.

In very cold water, you will have a maximum of ten minutes or less before suffering extreme hypothermia, so you must know before you get in where you are aiming for and how you will get out of the water.

Once you are in, keep as far as is possible to the most even flow of water and remember that on a bend the current will be flowing fastest on the outside. Do not attempt to shoot any rapids.

However, if you are unavoidably caught in rapids, aim for the "tongue" of the rapid, the area where the most volume of water flows. This will hopefully keep you away from protruding jagged rocks. Beware of "holes," where the water drops behind obstacles, creating a sucking whirlpool. If caught in one, swim positively out and to the side. Confident but controlled and calm movements are the key to surviving rapids.

ABSEILING TECHNIQUES

Abseiling is not something you should attempt lightly. If done properly, it should be perfectly safe, but if it goes wrong you are likely to find yourself in a far worse predicament than when you started. Once, in the Rockies, I was forced to abseil down a cliff in order to reach a road and a way out. I could see the bottom and the rock face itself looked solid, so I went for it. But you have to be very careful and have the correct training for large cliff faces. If your survival depends on it, here's what you need to do.

Make sure your rope is at least twice as long as the height of the cliff face. Loop it in half and put the looped end around a secure anchor – this might be a tree or a rock. Double up any anchor points for safety – i.e., put it round two or three trees.

Look very carefully for sharp edges that might fray or cut the rope just at the moment when it, and you, are under maximum tension. Pad out sharp edges with smaller, greener branches to protect the rope.

Facing your anchor point, pass the doubled rope between your legs and around the back of your right thigh. Pull around to the front of your body, up across your chest, and over your left shoulder, pulling it down across your back and in front of you again with your right hand. This hand will be used for paying out the rope as you descend.

Next, hold the rope connected to the anchor with your left hand, plant your feet about 18 inches apart on the edge of the cliff and lean back. Do not try to support your weight with your left hand but lean right back into your "harness." Step slowly and surely down the cliff, paying out the rope as you go.

There is no need to go at breakneck speed as if you are on a commando raid. A sure, steady descent is the best way. Once down, you can then retrieve the rope by pulling on one end.

MOVING MOUNTAINS

Efficiency of movement may be your goal, but how exactly do you achieve this in terrain which by its very nature is demanding on the human body? Observing, so far as is possible, the following rules will certainly help:

- Always pick what appears to be the easiest and safest route.

- Keep to a comfortable pace and take regular rest stops when needed. (I always take five minutes every hour and stick to it religiously. It provides a structure to work within. Don't wait longer or you'll stiffen up.) Shorten your stride going uphill.

- Go around obstacles, not over or through them. (But don't become "track-happy," where you end up following a track that leads in the wrong direction because it is easier to walk on! This is an easy mistake to make in rough terrain when exhausted.)

- Zigzag when climbing on steep slopes. When going down a steep slope, keep your knees bent.

- Don't climb scree slopes if at all possible. On the other hand descending a scree slope can be a fast way to lose height. Take big steps and keep your weight on your heels. If you begin to slip, go with it and turn into the slope as if stopping on skis. Keep a wary eye ahead: scree slopes often turn suddenly into sheer cliffs. Also look behind you when you stop for any falling rocks you might have dislodged. On the whole it is safer and better to move slowly and cautiously. Survival is not a sprint but a marathon.

- Use the spurs of hills to descend into the valley. They will give you a much better idea of the surrounding terrain.

- Take special care of feet and look after your socks as much as you can. When you take your boots off, keep your socks on for a few more minutes as your body heat will help to evaporate excess moisture. Keep them well clear of pine needles, which will give you blisters.

- Avoid overdressing and overheating.

- If moving by night, travel in bright moonlight. Remember it takes up to thirty minutes to acquire night sight, which will be instantly ruined by a bright light. If you need to use a flashlight to navigate by map, cover one eye to preserve your night vision. (In the SAS we used gaffer tape over our flashlight heads and just left a pinprick-sized gap to allow a thin beam of light through to map-read by.)

Natural Hazards

The thought of seeing one of the world's great predator species in the wild is a magical idea for many people. But you'll soon be praying that you don't when you're alone and lost in the mountains. That cuddly toy image of a bear will evaporate very quickly in grizzly bear country.

Nonetheless, your fear will almost certainly be exaggerated. Your chances of being attacked and killed by a wild animal are far smaller than the possibility of falling prey to dehydration and exhaustion. Many predators are so elusive and avoid human contact to such a degree – the Himalayan snow leopard for example – that you would be more likely to win the lottery on consecutive Saturdays than be killed by one.

Some, however, like grizzly bears, can be a significant threat. While they may not be specifically targeting you, they may take a shine to your food and grab a bite out of you along the way. You can never be too cautious in preparing and storing your food and bait in the wild.

But unless food is involved, animals usually only attack if they are surprised or threatened. If you do surprise a large animal, quietly back away.

Remember it is not just large animals that are deadly. The venom from a funnel-web spider will kill you just as surely as being mauled by a lion. So with some knowledge of how dangerous animals of all kinds behave, and knowing how to avoid them in the first place, you should be able to avoid this fate.

Bears generally only attack if surprised or threatened.

GRIZZLY BEARS

In general, even large animals like grizzlies fear humans and prefer to steer clear unless you stumble into their territory or they are very hungry. They will only attack as a last resort and usually only if you invade their personal space. It's very important to make your presence known before you get near, so if you suspect you are in bear territory, shout and bang a stick against a tree as you move along.

If you suspect you are in bear territory, shout and bang a stick against a tree as you move along

Avoidance, as ever, is the best strategy:

- When in camp, store all food (in a plastic bag if possible) at least 300 feet from your shelter, preferably up a tree. Burn all rubbish that might have an odor.
- Disturbing a mother bear and its young is definitely not a good idea. Retreat immediately if you see a baby bear; its mother will almost certainly be nearby.
- If you do come face-to-face with a bear, your best chance is to avoid eye contact and adopt a submissive posture. Back away slowly, turning your body slightly side on, as a full-frontal posture could be seen as aggressive.
- DO NOT TURN AND RUN, as the bear will immediately see you as prey and charge. You have no chance of outrunning a bear.
- If attacked, throw yourself to the ground, keeping your fingers locked tightly together around your neck, which along with your throat you should protect at any cost. Play dead – if your heart hasn't stopped already – while the bear sniffs you.

- If the attack continues and you have a knife, stab at the eyes and mouth.
- If the bear leaves you, stay still until you are absolutely sure it has left the area.

SNAKES

- Snakes are cold-blooded. They like shade in summer and sun in winter, so never put your hands (or feet!) into dark spaces or under rocks, logs or undergrowth without probing with a stick first. (This includes your boots – shake them out first thing every morning!)
- Snakes will not attack unless they are disturbed, so in snake territory where you cannot see the path ahead clearly, walk with a firm footfall, feeling the way in front of you with a long stick. They are very sensitive to vibration and will usually move away unless cornered.
- If you do see a snake, freeze until you work out exactly where it is. Do not turn your back on it as this may well cause it to strike. Walk backwards slowly.
- Snakes are best killed by beating with a heavy stick or stone, breaking their back as near to the neck as possible. Pin them first with a forked stick if possible.

BEES

- If you disturb a nest but are still more than five yards away, sit still. Bees look for movement and may ignore you.
- If you are being attacked, run towards thick undergrowth or dive into a river or lake.
- Do not swat at them. This will annoy them still further and attract others to the fray.

The thought of seeing one of the world's great predator species in the wild is a magical idea for many people. But you'll soon be praying that you don't when you're alone and lost in the mountains

In the mountains the changing weather is one of the most unpredictable natural hazards. It can change with alarming speed, and if it catches you out in challenging terrain when you are at your most vulnerable, the consequences could be serious. Your decisions on when to travel and when to look for shelter should take into account the likely changes in the weather. Predicting these changes is not easy, but nature, as ever, drops some heavy hints:

- **Spiders' Webs**
  When the weather is looking good, spiders' webs have long, open filaments and their owners patrol energetically. When rain is on the way, the web will be shorter and tighter and the spider will remain lethargically at its center.

- **Biting Insects**
  Especially annoying two to four hours before a storm.

- **Feeding Game**
  Large game such as deer, elk, and caribou feed heavily four to six hours before a storm.

- **Smoke Signals**
  Steadily rising smoke from a campfire indicates good weather ahead. When it rises and then falls again, pressure is falling and a storm is in the air.

- **Rainbow Magic**
  A rainbow in the morning is a sign of foul weather ahead. In the late afternoon, things look set fair.

- **Large Corona**
  The circle (corona) that can sometimes be seen around the sun or the moon gets larger when the weather is likely to be good and smaller when rain is imminent.

- **Green is the Color**
  A hint of green above the sun as it sinks below the horizon in a clear sky indicates fine weather ahead.

- **Wind from the South**
  In the northern hemisphere, remember the old adage: "Wind from the south brings rain in its mouth." Reverse that down under.

- **Lull before the Storm**
  Most creatures stop what they are doing just before a storm breaks, which accounts for that eerie silence before the rains come.

- **Smell**
  There is often a distinct smell of the forest before rain as nature opens up ready to receive the moisture.

- **Sound**
  Tends to carry further before rain as the moisture-laden atmosphere acts like an amplifier.

- **Heavy Morning Dew**
  The sign of a good day ahead. Dew forms from the lower temperatures of a cloudless night, indicating stable weather.

- **Lenticulars**
  These lens-shaped clouds indicate high winds at altitude and moisture in the air in advance of a cold front, when winds and clouds will steadily descend.

- **Jet Trails Lingering**
  Airplane trails that linger for more than two hours indicate low pressure (and bad weather) on the way.

- **Red Sky at Night, Shepherds' Delight, Red Sky in the Morning, Shepherds' Warning**
  Applies to the northern hemisphere, where the red sky is formed by sunlight shining through particles of dust suspended in the steady high-pressure atmosphere. Seen in the evening, it signals high pressure coming from the prevailing westerly weather, but in the morning it is a sign that the high pressure has moved over you – hence change is afoot.

Lenticular clouds often indicate the advance of a cold front.

The Bear Necessities: Surviving the Mountains

RULE 1: THINK FIRST – ACT LATER
Preserving your energy in the mountains is half the battle. Consider all your options, then act decisively. If you fail to have a plan, you plan to fail. So make a plan and stick to it.

RULE 2: SHELTER FROM THE STORM
Mountain terrain can be very exposed to the elements, but at the same time a good shelter is perhaps easier to build than in any other wilderness terrain. Use the abundance of nature around you. She has given you all you need.

RULE 3: USE HEIGHT EFFECTIVELY
Always use height to survey and orientate yourself to the surrounding terrain before you descend. Make a mental map. It will pay dividends later.

RULE 4: WATCH THE WEATHER
Weather changes quickly and dramatically in the mountains. Always keep an eye on the sky. Use good weather to your advantage, but prepare early if things look likely to change. Tune in your instinct to bad weather; learn from the animals.

RULE 5: RIVER LORE
Rivers are often a route to salvation, but they can also be very dangerous. Don't get wet and cold unless there is no other option. But learn to use the river and live off it. Follow it downstream – it will eventually take you to safety.

"It's a good thing occasionally to have all the props pulled out from under us. It gives us some sense of what is rock under our feet, and what is sand."

MADELEINE L'ENGLE

sub-zero terrain

Crossing a crevasse on Everest – treading carefully!

The long evolution of *Homo sapiens* has taken place almost exclusively in the temperate zones of our planet. Hardly surprising, perhaps, when you consider that in order to keep the vital organs functioning, the human body must keep its core heat within a very narrow temperature band around 37°C (98.6°F). If this falls to 95°F, hypothermia will begin to set in and death will rapidly follow if the process is not reversed.

True, there are some notable exceptions to the rule. The Inuit of northern Canada and the Nenets, one of a number of reindeer herder tribes from Siberia, are among an exclusive band of indigenous peoples who have found ways of surviving life in nature's freezer. But this has only been achieved through adaptation over many centuries combined with all the ingenuity our species can muster. Whether ancient or modern, it is only "technology" – from clothes made of reindeer hides to twenty-first-century GPS navigational instruments – that keeps us alive in these sub-zero conditions.

The world's most extreme winter environments exist at the physical extremities of our planet: the most southerly, the most northerly, and the most elevated. The Arctic and the Antarctic, encompassed by latitudes 66° 33´ N and 66° 33´ S respectively, both cover areas larger than Europe and the USA combined.

In the Arctic, half of this area of roughly 9 million square miles is a gigantic mass of pack ice floating on the Arctic Ocean surrounded by frozen landmasses, which include parts of Alaska, Canada, Greenland, Iceland, Norway, and Russia. In winter the sea ice is typically around 10–12 feet thick, but the diameter of the area covered in ice shrinks from around 2,500 miles in winter to around 1,900 miles in summer – an area which is now shrinking dramatically due to global warming.

The human body must keep its core heat within a very narrow temperature band around 37°C (98.6°F)

Antarctica, on the other hand, accounts for 10 percent of the world's land surface, 95 percent of which remains covered in ice even during the summer. It is the coldest (and, paradoxically, the driest) place on earth, where temperatures reaching nearly -90°C (-130°F) have been recorded.

Finally, high-altitude peaks on the world's mountain ranges, even near the equator, can produce conditions where snow and ice are present all year round.

But all these statistics disguise a huge variation in the conditions present in sub-zero environments. Whether north or south, high or low, winter or summer, a survivor stranded in sub-zero ice and snow needs to be able to cope with the hazards produced by three very different types of cold-weather environment: wet, windy, and high.

Antarctica covers 10 percent of the world's land surface.

Sub-Zero Weather

WET: THE ARCTIC

Sub-zero environments that create a predominantly wet and damp climate largely exist when "freeze then thaw" follow each other in the daily cycle. This happens when the average twenty-four-hour temperature is above -10°C (14°F). These conditions are much more common in the Arctic than the Antarctic. During the Arctic (northern hemisphere) summer, slush and wet snow may be very common during the long daylight hours, with the ice becoming thin and very treacherous towards the edges of the melting ice floes and leaving gaps of icy water known as "leads."

The battle you must fight and win, in order to survive in the Arctic, is to keep yourself and your equipment dry

Despite its warmer temperatures, this is why survival in the Arctic can, for different reasons, be just as difficult as in the Antarctic. In 2001 when the explorer Børge Ousland made his epic 1,000-mile solo journey across the Arctic from Russia to Canada, his biggest problems were related more to the ever-changing state of the thin ice than to the temperature. For the entire eighty-two days of his journey, he was walking on frozen seawater, and while he had skis to spread his weight and help stop him falling through the weakest ice, he often found himself clambering over mountains of jagged ice where winds and currents had smashed ice floes together with such force that the blocks were sometimes pushed more than 50 feet into the air. Surviving in the Arctic can be a treacherous, bone-crunching process.

The battle you must fight and win, in order to survive in the Arctic, is to keep yourself and your equipment dry, and avoid the dramatically colder temperatures that come when wind chill combines with the wet.

WINDY: THE ANTARCTIC

"Great God! this is an awful place!" wrote Robert Falcon Scott about Antarctica in 1912. As well he might. After all, the continent is the coldest, highest, windiest, and iciest continent on earth. It is also – a seeming paradox – the driest. Although it receives slightly more rainfall than the Sahara (around 2 inches a year), Antarctica is officially the largest desert on the planet.

Vast quantities of water are locked up in the ice, and most of it has been there a very long time indeed. In 2002, scientists extracted core samples from the East Antarctic ice sheet thought to be more than half a million years old, while the thickest ice in the interior measures more than 1,500 feet.

This lack of rainfall and average daily temperatures below -10°C (14°F) means the ice on the landmass remains frozen day and night, summer and winter (although the ice shelves over the surrounding sea are shrinking fast).

Rather than wet, a survivor's main problem is extreme cold exacerbated by high winds, blizzards, and a life-threatening wind-chill effect. (The "wind-

Børge Ousland, right, is one of the world's leading polar explorers.

chill index" is a measurement that combines wind speed and ambient temperature to arrive at what the equivalent temperature would be if there was no wind at all.) Wind amplifies the problems of sub-zero temperatures and seriously increases the rate at which the body loses heat. Antarctic winds of 190 miles per hour have been recorded as well as the world's lowest recorded temperature: -99°C (-146°F) at Vostok on 21 July 1983.

Travel in winter in Antarctica is virtually impossible during the months of complete darkness. Temperatures vary according to latitude, height, and distance from the sea, and there are three distinct climatic regions: the interior, the coastal regions, and the Antarctic Peninsula, which stretches up like a crooked finger towards South America. The coast is by far the windiest region, with super-cold air funneling down off the ridges producing blizzards which at times reduce visibility to a few inches.

Even with the best modern equipment, snow blindness, hypothermia, and frostbite are a constant threat.

HIGH: MOUNTAINS IN WINTER

All the extreme hazards of both polar regions combine to differing degrees during the winter months in the world's highest mountain ranges. Glaciers and lethal crevasses, along with the threat of avalanche, are an ever-present danger in the mountains during winter. The problems of wet, cold, and high winds, plus the many dangers of thin air and altitude, make a lethal combination for the sole survivor in high mountains.

The key here is to act early, prevent the cold taking effect (once you are freezing cold, it is much harder to get warm), listen to your body's signals, and if in doubt: descend, descend, descend.

Making a Shelter

Shelter will be your first priority if you find yourself alone in sub-zero terrain. If the weather looks good, it will inevitably get worse. And anyway night will soon fall and the temperature will drop dramatically. So prepare at once for the inevitable while you still have the chance. Darkness can come very fast, especially when the sun drops behind high ridges – and it is an awful lot easier to find or make a safe shelter when you can see.

Hypothermia (see pages 139–141) can take a grip very quickly, so retaining your body heat must be uppermost in your mind. First look for natural features which can act as a windbreak. If there are trees or rocks in the near vicinity, get out of the wind, but always beware of the possibility of avalanche or snow falling from above. If you are in a featureless landscape, dig a trench in the snow or build a windbreak in the form of a snow wall.

It is an awful lot easier to find or make a safe shelter when you can see

The survivors of the infamous Andes air crash in 1972, when sixteen of the original forty-five passengers and crew on board survived seventy-two days in the snow and ice, now acknowledge that if one of their number had not suggested building a wall against the wind, they would almost certainly have frozen to death during their first night on the mountain. Always make shelter from the wind priority number one – it is the main killer in sub-zero environments.

Now that you have a measure of protection, consider what type of shelter you need. When weighing up your options, consider the terrain, your available building materials, the weather, and whether you intend to stay put or move on. Any shelter will take a lot of energy to build, draining precious body heat, so think rationally while you still can and decide what type of shelter is best under the prevailing conditions.

GENERAL PRINCIPLES

CHOOSING A LOCATION

In the mountains, wooded areas are best, as you will be able to combine excellent building materials with a source of fuel as well. If there is tree cover, a tree-pit shelter or lean-to snow tent is fast to make and very effective at retaining heat, but if you have no natural protection against the elements, you will have to dig a snow trench or snow cave.

Avoid any natural hazards like hillsides that may be in danger of avalanche and watch out for a heavy buildup of snow on rocks, cliff faces, or trees. On the other hand such natural windbreaks as these can also make the perfect shelter site. Use your judgment but always err on the side of caution.

One night while on location in the Alps I was too drained to make a full snow cave. Instead I dug a small snow scrape in the lee of a bank of drift snow. It was soft and easy to dig out and protected me really well from the prevailing wind. In under ten minutes I had a protected shelter, out of the wind, with some heat retention coming from the small snow roof over me. This emergency trench was only slightly less effective than the snow cave that took me two hours to make!

INSULATING QUALITIES OF SNOW

It seems counterintuitive that cold, fluffy, damp snow should make a good building material and can even protect us from the cold. But such are the miraculous, life-giving qualities of frozen H_2O. Snow can save your life and will insulate you far better than the metal of a broken-down car, for example. Snow's extraordinary insulating qualities can be demonstrated by the fact that a single candle can raise the temperature by as much as 4°C (7°F) in an igloo, and a well-built snow shelter can be as much as 30°C (54°F) warmer inside than it is outside. A snow shelter can be built from snow no more than 6 inches deep, although deeper snow will be far easier to work with.

Also be aware that dug-out snow will always compact and shrink a little after a few hours. Whatever type of shelter you make, creating warmth will often depend on creating the right balance of not having too much space around you to heat up, while ensuring you are not making your own grave with a shelter that is too small and shrinks on top of you.

Struggling to keep warm in a snow shelter I made in the Alps, wrapped in my salvaged parachute.

VENTILATION

Easy to forget but absolutely vital in any snow shelter is a decent source of ventilation. Stranded survivors have been known to make a snow cave and escape the wind, only to be killed by the asphyxiating buildup of carbon monoxide from their fire. They fall asleep, get cold, simply fail to wake up, and freeze to death.

When you are in your shelter, you will want to keep the entrance closed to trap the heat inside, but you must ensure good ventilation to avoid this asphyxiation. Even without a fire, make sure fresh air is circulating. Exhaled breath contains carbon dioxide, which is also toxic.

To achieve this, keep two holes open in the roof, each around 2 inches wide, as you build the shelter, and keep a stick handy inside to poke up through them during the night when they start to freeze over or are blocked by fresh snowfall. A ski-pole, if you have one, works well, left permanently protruding from the snow roof.

Snow will insulate you far better than the metal of a broken-down car

TOOLS

Your bare hands must be protected in the cold and you must find some insulated implement to help you dig. Anything that can act as a spade, ice saw, or ice axe is ideal. Improvise. Paracord can cut through snow like a saw. I have used the back protector from a parachute harness to dig before, and the parachute stuff sack to protect my hands. When your hands are cold, you tend not to feel the damage and cuts that can come from the often sharp ice and compacted snow.

TYPES OF SHELTER: SHORT TERM

SNOW TRENCH

In open ground when the snow is frozen hard or conversely in an emergency when speed is of the essence, dig a snow trench. The simplest and quickest type is a shallow scrape deep enough to give protection from the wind and wide enough to allow a small space for air to circulate around your body. The snow you dig out of the trench can be piled on the sides and compacted, and then covered with a tarpaulin or parachute canopy for a roof which can then be covered in more snow. Remember to pin it down effectively or it may collapse with the weight. Leave one end of the trench open as an entrance and block the other with a rucksack or more snow.

If the snow is compact enough or you hit an ice sheet, a deeper, more elaborate construction can be made by carving blocks of snow like thick paving slabs (they will need to be about 2 feet thick). Either lay them flat over the top of the trench or lean them against each other in an A-frame shape for a roof which will give more headroom.

If no tarpaulin or covering is available and the snow is of the wrong consistency for snow blocks, make a 3-foot-diameter snowball, cut it in half,

and lay both halves over a narrow trench, giving you a ready-made roof. Then burrow in from one end and dig the trench wider the deeper you go.

TREE PIT

Using whatever protection the natural environment has to offer is often the quickest and most efficient way to build a shelter. Below the tree line in a conifer forest, for example, you will have many potential shelters all around you. As snowshoers and cross-country skiers know to their cost, the area around the trunk of a conifer is likely to conceal a hole where the snow has been prevented from falling by the dense upper branches. This, with a little bit of extra excavation and some careful reinforcement of the covering branches, makes the perfect shelter.

Some trees will make better shelters than others. Choose one with a generous "skirt" of branches on higher ground where the air will be warmer. Then clear away a suitable space for yourself and a fire on the lee side. Dig down and expand any natural "well" and clear away some of the lower boughs so you have an entrance. You can then reinforce the area around the entrance by laying branches around like a tepee and covering in more packed snow for insulation.

I have used this style of tree shelter in the Alps. It was such a relief to descend off the glacier into the wood line. The forest of dense spruce trees allowed me to make a shelter that gave me one of my best rests ever in the wild! I piled about 2 feet of soft spruce branches on top of the snowy ground to really insulate the shelter. These branches should be laid with their natural blow upwards, giving a warm springy mattress to lie on. Remember: survival is about making yourself as comfortable as the world around you will allow.

If the snow is deep and firm, you may be able to tunnel back a bit away from the tree to create an underground nest. If the snow is shallow, build it up to create a snow wall for protection. When you've done all this, build a long log fire (see Chapter 1, page 28) and a reflector and settle down to watch nature's TV flickering in front of you as it warms your soft, spruce-lined nest!

TYPES OF SHELTER: LONGER TERM

QUINZEE AND SNOW MOUND

A snow version of a dome tent can be constructed by making a large mound of snow and hollowing out the center. The quickest version is the "quinzee," which is made by piling snow on top of a pile of stores, rucksacks, or anything with bulk that you have to hand. Build on the deepest snow you can find so you can lower the floor later, and build the mound as compactly as possible, or ideally cover with a tarpaulin or parachute so the snow doesn't penetrate. The mound should be a bit bigger than the size you will comfortably be able to move about in.

Then cover the interior mound with liberal piles of powdered snow to form the outer shell. This should be at least 2 feet thick but will compact down later to about half that. It is important to leave plenty of sticks embedded in the outer shell. Before you start, lay the sticks next to each other on the ground and mark a notch on the same point in each so that when you are hollowing the structure out from inside, you will be able to ensure that the thickness of the snow roof is the same across the entire dome. This gives the shelter its porcupine appearance but ensures you avoid digging too far out and breaking through the roof when clearing the snow from inside.

You should try to find several sources of snow from different places round about and remember to keep it fluffy and powdered rather than trying to compact it. This mixing of snow at slightly different temperatures creates a reaction called "sintering," which causes powdered snow to freeze solid and harden. It does take time, though, and you will need to leave the structure to solidify for several hours. Be patient – this structure is very effective – but don't leave it too late in the day to start building.

When it has hardened, decide where the entrance will be (remembering to make it at right angles to the prevailing wind) and dig down to create it. It is most effective to dig a curved entrance that tunnels underneath the wall of your quinzee, which will not only stop drafts from getting in but will also trap cold air at the bottom of the curve (remember, cold air always sinks). Think of this entrance as being like a toilet's U-bend! Then hollow out the inside and remove the contents of your pile. To speed things up a bit, make another temporary entrance on the other side to haul out the mound of gear, then reclose it later.

A snow mound is exactly the same as a "quinzee" except the structure is dug out of a huge mound of powdered snow when you have no equipment or other materials to make a mound. It takes longer and requires considerably more snow and energy.

SNOW CAVE AND SNOW HOLE

In drift snow or on a hillside above the tree line, digging a snow cave is as intuitive (and effective) as a rabbit digging a hole or a badger making a sett. In fact, many mountaineers have been saved by simply digging into the snow when caught out in a storm.

The best choice of location is not quite so intuitive, however, because, unlike all other shelters, it will be best located facing into the wind and not away from it. The reason for this is that snowdrifts build up on the lee side of a slope which can bury you if you get caught in prolonged, heavy snowfall. To protect yourself from the wind when climbing in and out, build a snow wall outside the entrance as protection.

It is most effective to dig a curved entrance that tunnels underneath the wall of your quinzee, which will not only stop drafts from getting in but will also trap cold air at the bottom of the curve

Inside an ice tube, under a glacier in Northern Alaska.

A snow cave requires a sloping snow surface and snow that is well compacted, but soft enough to shovel. Before you start digging, probe with a stick to make sure there is not a rock or tree stump just under the surface that will mean all your initial efforts are wasted. When you are satisfied there is deep snow beneath, dig in at an upwards slant so that your entrance (and the colder air) will be below the level of the floor and sleeping platform. This platform can then be insulated with a parachute or rucksack well above the cold air in the door-well.

Remember: this cold-well is vital in snow caves, and can mean the difference between a snug cave and a frozen grave. Cold air will always sink; just a simple hole dug into the floor of your cave will be enough to trap this, and only takes seconds to make.

A fire, if you have one, should be small and up high with an effective source of ventilation.

Make the roof inside arched and dig a small trench around the whole area to catch meltwater running down the walls. This will then run towards the colder area at the entrance, where it may well refreeze. Finally, cut yourself a thin block of compacted snow to act as a door and keep it on the inside, where it is less likely to freeze shut.

Remember also to smooth off the ceiling of your cave with your hand to avoid jagged little ice pinnacles where drops of melted ice water can collect and drip onto you all night. Again, this takes seconds but can be easy to forget. I once built and used a snow cave in the Alps. It was getting dark by the time I finished, and I failed to smooth off the inside of my roof sufficiently; the subsequent dripping made all my clothes wet. If the sun hadn't come out the next morning I might have been facing a much worse survival situation than I was currently in. This sort of mistake is one you generally make only once. Learn from my errors!

The sleeping platform should be raised off the cold floor and built like a shelf in the side of the cave. Again, allow for shrinkage when the snow settles, but keep this platform quite snug to avoid heat loss.

A snow hole is basically a snow cave but built on flat ground. This can be made by digging a hole 5 or 6 feet in diameter which can then be covered. Dig a tunnel entrance starting from about 5 or 6 feet away. The same principles then apply for ventilation, cold-well, roof, and sleeping platform.

IGLOO

Igloos are extremely efficient at protecting their inhabitants from the elements, but are definitely best left to the experts: otherwise known as the Inuit of northern Canada. Making snow blocks can take a long time and will almost certainly be beyond your immediate scope in a survival situation. The snow must be of the correct type and you will need an ice saw to cut the blocks. Powdered snow is useless for building igloos, and it will not be practical to compact it given all the other problems you will be facing.

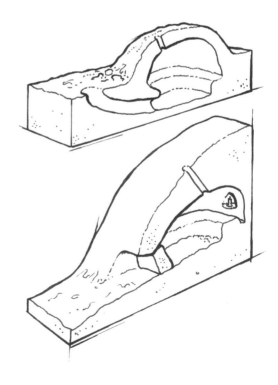

REMEMBER, REMEMBER . . .

While the different types of shelter all have different characteristics, the following rules apply to them all:

NO SWEAT
Keep cool while you're working and avoid soaking your clothes with sweat – it will only freeze later and further dehydrate you. Hypothermia is your greatest enemy. Strip off some layers while you work.

SMALL IS BEAUTIFUL
Construct a shelter no larger than you need – about three times your own size is best. This will reduce the amount of space to heat. Be aware of the common error in cold-weather-shelter construction in making the shelter too large, so that it steals body heat rather than saves it.

SHRINKING SNOW
Snow compacts, so remember that the roof of a snow cave may well get lower, but this does not usually mean it is going to collapse. It is just your shelter becoming effective and settling. Allow a small margin, though, for this snow shrinkage, to avoid getting entombed!

MAKE A GOOD ENTRANCE
Orientate your entrance into the wind to avoid it being blocked by drifting snow. But build it as small as is practically possible and keep it covered up when you're inside. Both will help conserve heat.

INSULATE, THEN HIBERNATE
When sleeping, always keep a layer of insulation between yourself and the snow. Use whatever comes to hand. Branches and foliage are perfect, and if you have a rucksack or parachute canopy, so much the better. Never sleep directly on the ground. It is where you lose the majority of your heat.

BREATH TEST
The last thing you want is for the interior of your shelter to melt and drip all over you, so make sure the interior temperature stays below zero. If you can't see your own breath, it's too warm.

DON'T BE A DRIP
By design, the air inside your shelter will be far warmer than outside. Smooth down the snow roof inside so any drips run down the walls. Then dig a channel around the walls to collect meltwater and keep dampness away from you.

ESCAPE METHODS
Any shelter made of snow is vulnerable to collapse, so keep your digging tool close by or have some other method of forcing your way out if the worst happens.

PEEING
If you need to pee during the night, don't go outside in the cold. Just go on the floor inside the shelter. The urine will dissipate down through the snow. Remember, survival is what matters here. Once you are getting warm don't go and waste it by venturing outside and losing that buildup of heat just to have a pee!

Smooth off the ceiling of your cave with your hand to avoid jagged little ice pinnacles where drops of melted ice water can collect and drip onto you all night

Finding Water

On the face of it, avoiding dehydration in an environment covered by snow and ice would seem a lot easier than among the parched dunes of a desert. No problem, you may think, surveying the barren wastes: water, albeit frozen, is everywhere. This may be true, but don't be complacent. Taking on fluids will not be as easy as it may at first seem, and when you are cold the symptoms of dehydration mask themselves very effectively. You must keep drinking, and preferably before you need to rather than after.

While water loss may not be as acute as in a desert, you will still need to replace at least a quart of fluid a day. Don't forget that you will still be losing large quantities of water to the atmosphere through your skin. Even more fluid will be lost through stress hormones triggered by the cold that will make you pee more. Some of the techniques for finding water we looked at in Chapter 2 (see pages 75–79) still apply in a sub-zero environment, but in general it is not the source of water that is the problem. Instead, getting it into a form that is drinkable – pure and at body temperature – will be the real challenge.

Eating snow and ice "raw" is rarely a good idea. The heat sucked away by your body in order to melt the water will often outweigh the benefit gained. The only exception might be when you are working hard, moving through snow terrain, when having a little snow in your mouth keeps you cool, avoids excessive sweating, and provides some added hydration.

Look for alternative sources of water before trying to melt ice or snow. There may well be trickles of running water in hidden fissures or buried streams, and there is no point in wasting body heat or fuel if there is a ready supply of natural meltwater.

Water sources in Arctic and sub-Arctic regions are generally cleaner than elsewhere, owing to the cold and smaller amounts of rotting organic material that can pollute them. Nonetheless, always be careful. Snow and ice are no purer than the water from which they are made.

If you do find yourself forced to eat snow and cannot melt it first (see page 118), melt it in your mouth before you swallow it. Think of this as a last resort, as over time it will produce sores in your mouth. Also note that snow and ice are just frozen rainwater. They don't have any of the minerals or salts found in stream water. This will make rehydration less effective. If available, try to add some spruce leaves, roots, or berries to the melted water, to give the fluid some nutrients.

SNOW AND ICE

Snow is seventeen parts air and one part water, which makes it a fantastic insulator but one of the least efficient sources of fresh water in sub-zero terrain. Ice, assuming it's not seawater, will always be a better source of water than snow. In fact, it takes 50 percent more energy to turn an ounce of snow into water than it does ice.

When you have no choice and must melt either one or the other, always remember that there are many different types of both. For instance, snow that is slightly buried – more granular and less powdery – will produce a lot more water than surface snow. Likewise, ice that has frozen from seawater – recognizable from its rough texture, its tendency to shatter, and its milky/grayish color – will be completely undrinkable unless it is more than two years old. By then the salt will have largely disappeared.

Melting snowballs into my cup in an Alpine tree shelter.

While water loss may not be as acute as in a desert, you will still need to replace at least a quart of fluid a day

Older sea ice has a much smoother texture and a pronounced bluishness to it and can be drunk when melted, although you should make sure it has not been contaminated by more recent salt water on the surface.

USING FIRE TO MELT WATER

If you manage to make a fire, drinking water will not be a problem. Melt the snow inside a makeshift pot but make sure you don't just cram it in and expect it to melt. Snow that has been too closely packed will simply evaporate, leaving a space at the bottom and scorching your precious pot. Instead, heat bite-sized chunks slowly until they melt, and progressively add more. The process can be speeded up by adding hot rocks or pebbles.

Another method is to make a large snowball – often referred to as a "marshmallow" or a "snowman's head" – and spear it on the end of a stick so that it can be warmed gently above a fire. Its meltwater will then drip into a well-placed pot or even into your boot if nothing else can be found. Make sure it is not too close to the fire and simply collapses into a snowy mush. I used this method very effectively in the Alps with several sticks poked into large snowballs which were then placed protruding from my snow heat reflector around my fire. The snowballs slowly dripped into my cup, giving me effortless supplies of water.

Another similar method is to wrap powdery snow too cold to be compressed into a ball inside some porous material like a shirt or sock and suspend it near a fire so that the meltwater drips through into a container. The downside of this is that the cloth is then wet at the end of the process.

OTHER SOURCES OF HEAT

In the absence of fire, you can use excess heat from your body when you are on the move or working, although it's a much slower process. Collect snow or ice in a bag and place it between layers of clothing (but not next to the skin). The best places are where the blood supply is greatest and nearest to the surface (your head, groin, and armpits, for example), but don't do this when sleeping or resting.

During cold weather, avoid drinking a lot of liquid before going to bed. Crawling out of your warm makeshift sleeping bag at night to relieve yourself means less rest and more exposure to the cold.

Finding Food

Finding food in sub-zero terrain at any time of year will inevitably be a challenge. Life is tough and food is scarce for the animals that live in these environments, so inevitably it will be for you too. But that's not to say it will be impossible.

Your success in finding food will to a large part depend on where you find yourself in the first place and the time of year. Nearer the coast or by rivers or lakes you will be able to fish directly or even by cutting a hole in the ice. In many polar regions you will have a good chance of killing seals, penguins, or seabirds, while mosses and lichens have also been a staple diet of polar explorers over the years.

ICE-FISHING

In the mountains and near the sea, fish will be your best bet for food. In the mountains where there are running rivers you will be able to use the techniques we discussed in Chapter 2 (see pages 83–85), but in the depths of winter, when the rivers and lakes are frozen solid, you may need to make a hole in the ice in true Inuit style.

While it may sound romantic and intrepid – it will be, if you manage to catch something – this method of obtaining food is not without its challenges. Make sure you pick a spot where the ice is at least a foot thick. By making a hole in the ice, you will be weakening the whole structure surrounding it, so it is imperative it is thick enough. The converse of this is that the ice has to be thin enough to get through without specialist cutting tools!

Making the fishing hole in the first place is not easy. Melting your way through will probably be the easiest option. Build a fire on a platform of rocks (make sure they're not waterlogged as they may explode) and as they heat up they will gradually melt the ice beneath and fall through. Do this near a good supply of wood and stones so as to avoid the whole exercise becoming exercise!

The way I managed to get through a lake in the Alps once was by finding an area of thinner ice near a cusp of thick ice, and using my long stick to bash through the surface. Once you can get a small amount of ice broken, with some meltwater slushing around, it becomes easier to agitate this meltwater and to get through the remaining ice.

Your fishing gear should include the following: insulation under your feet and knees if you are digging through the ice (spruce branches are best and can be used to mark the hole if you leave it overnight); a sharpened stick, a rock or a knife for digging in the absence of a fire; two straight pieces of wood; some sort of fishing line; and some makeshift hooks and bait.

One stick will lie across the hole while the other, your "fishing rod," will be lashed to it at right angles so it can rotate freely with a line and

Ice fishing through a frozen lake.

Spruce branches stop the hole from refreezing over.

An inquisitive and hungry trout takes my line ...

... and becomes food.

the baited hooks attached off one end. The more hooks you can attach at different depths, the greater your chances of catching something. Generally, fish in frozen lakes are hungry and inquisitive in winter, and can be attracted by small flashing metallic baits used as lures. Make hooks from whatever wire you have handy, or use sharpened shards of animal bone or thorns.

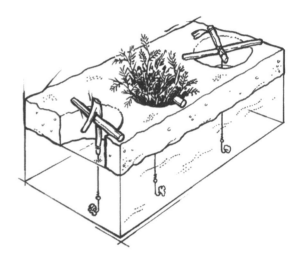

If you leave your ice holes overnight (definitely the preferred method if you want to avoid freezing to death), make sure you mark them by filling them in with plenty of the leafy tip ends of spruce branches stuffed as deep and tight as possible down the hole, which will stop the holes refreezing over, as well as make them easier to spot the next day if it snows overnight. Many a successful ice-fishing mission has been ruined by the hole refreezing. It's a waste of time and energy and can be easily counteracted with this technique.

Also attach some sort of flagging device to the reverse end of your fishing stick. If a fish bites, your line will tighten and pull the stick down so the other end, with its attached flag, will point directly up into the air and signal a catch.

ANIMALS

Trapping large animals like deer in the mountains in winter will be extremely difficult, so you will be better off trapping smaller mammals like squirrels, rabbits, foxes, marmots, mountain hares, beavers, mink, or weasels. It is always worth probing areas where avalanches have struck recently. Animals as well as humans fall prey to their devastating impact. In the Alps I once found a rotting chamois buried under a foot of avalanche debris. Despite the meat being putrid, the maggots were of course nutritious and fresh. I took a handful for bait and a handful for snacking on as I climbed.

In the polar regions, your options will be reduced mainly to seals and penguins, but as the seas are rich in plankton and krill, populations of both these creatures are often substantial. In extremis, seals and seal pups are easiest to catch – and at their most vulnerable – during the breeding season. (It is at this time that those sad news clips of seal pups being clubbed to death during the seal culls have been filmed.)

Out of the breeding season, however, they will be far more difficult to hunt and great skill will be needed to catch them by surprise. The best strategy is to spear them when they come up to breathe through breathing holes you might come across in the ice, or when they are asleep. The latter will not be easy either, though, as evolution has programmed them to open their eyes every minute or so and scan the horizon for polar bears and any other predator, like a man, who may be near.

The Inuit have perfected the art by keeping downwind as they approach and imitating the movements of the seal by crawling on the ice as they get nearer, but as an amateur you may well find the whole process quite a bit more difficult. Remember also that in the Arctic, seals will be hunted by polar bears, which will not be averse to a seal-hunter as a welcome change in their diet.

If you do make a seal kill, however, it will be invaluable, as the skin can be used for clothing or footwear and the blubber will burn on a fire. Seal meat should always be well cooked as it is vulnerable to *Trichinella spiralis*, a type of toxic worm that gets into muscle, causing trichinosis. Seal livers, along with those of polar bears, should be avoided as they can carry lethal quantities of vitamin A.

Use the guts of any catch as bait for your next meal.

Seal and penguin meat kept Shackleton's men alive at their camp on Cape Wild, Elephant Island, in 1916 after they had already taken the heartbreaking decision to eat their own beloved husky dogs. But for them it was just another episode in that remarkable tale of human heroism and endurance when all of the twenty-eight-man crew survived nearly two years in the Antarctic after their ship, the *Endurance*, had been trapped and then crushed by pack ice.

Seal livers, along with those of polar bears, should also be avoided as they can carry lethal quantities of vitamin A

Remember, in a survival situation, you will be called upon to leave your prejudices at home. Take Dougal Robertson, who with his twin sons found himself adrift in the Pacific after their schooner was hit by whales. At first he was careful to keep a sense of order and propriety. But as the situation became more desperate so did his tactics for getting food. Eventually he changed from passive victim to aggressive predator, and when a turtle became entangled in his sea anchor, he grabbed its beak and, with it thrashing on the floor, sliced its throat. Blood was spurting everywhere as he hacked its shell off and tore out its insides. He was covered from head to toe in warm blood when he distributed the raw meat to his boys, but from that one bloody moment he says he made the decision to survive. You might need to develop that same killer instinct to stay alive.

PLANTS

In some sub-zero terrain, including the mountains and the Arctic tundra, you may well be able to feed off trees, plants, and berries (see Chapter 2, pages 80–81), many of which are a good source of vitamin C. Spruce bark can also be boiled and tea made out of the needles, while the shoots, bark, leaves, and roots of Arctic willow can also be boiled and eaten. Spruce tree tea is absolutely delicious, nutritious, and warming, and has lifted my spirits many times.

Remember too that all lichens are edible and high in nutrients, but they will need to be soaked for at least twelve hours to allow the high acid content to leach out before being boiled in fresh water.

Edible lichens include:
- Iceland moss, which is common in the Arctic
- Rock tripe, an unlikely, leathery, very acidic specimen which grows on rocks with leaves that look a bit like lettuce
- "Old man's beard," which is better used as tinder, as it is often dry and found hanging off conifer branches, but can be a food candidate when things look desperate
- Reindeer moss, which looks like reindeer antlers and is considered a delicacy by the Inuit

If you come across a dead reindeer, don't hesitate to rip its stomach open, as it will more than likely be full of half-digested and hence edible lichen. And if it's good enough for the Inuit . . .

Eating lichen, though, should be a last resort. Generally speaking, it tastes pretty disgusting. Cardboard is tastier, but lacks the nutrients.

BIRDS

Penguins are very easy to catch because they are curious birds and congregate in huge colonies.

Shackleton's stranded crew kept themselves alive by eating seal and penguin meat.

In the Arctic, ptarmigans, which turn white in winter, are a good game bird but hard to see and harder to catch. During the summer months, all Arctic birds moult and cannot fly, so rich pickings are there for the taking during the three-week period of the moult.

In mountain ranges, you might well be able to catch crows or rooks as they are inquisitive birds and natural scavengers, but you will need bait and a trap (see Chapter 1). A secured, dry "fishing" line with a baited hook, left hanging from a branch or on a rock, can be very effective. Tie the other end to a stake or rock. Caves are excellent places to leave traps, but make sure you leave a good number in place (around ten or so) and reckon on around a 25 percent strike rate.

Penguins are very easy to catch because they are curious birds and congregate in huge colonies

Navigation and Movement

Navigation and movement through snow and ice will be hazardous whatever the environment. The terrain type and the season will determine the types of obstacles you will have to face. Not only will they be considerably more difficult to negotiate, but the basic skills of navigation and the ability to move quickly and easily will be considerably more challenging.

Cold itself will slow down the mental processes required to make effective decisions regarding direction, while the body itself may not function with the same efficiency as in warmer climes. Make sure that you have a well-thought-out plan before leaving a shelter and setting off through the mountains or across a featureless polar landscape.

GENERAL PRINCIPLES

SNOWSHOES

Attempting to travel across deep snow without some form of specialized footwear is a recipe for disaster. Long hours spent floundering through waist-deep snow is exhausting, unproductive, gets you soaked, plus it is dangerous – trust me, I have done it often! Survival is about thinking smart, not just sweating hard. Improvise a way to spread your weight over a larger area than just the sole of a boot.

Even using fairly basic materials, snowshoes can be easily improvised from lengths of whippy branches – willow is perfect for the job – bent back on themselves with the ends lashed together to form a shape like the head of a tennis racket and about 3 feet from tip to toe.

A layer of supporting mesh needs to be woven across this basic template (canvas,

> **Cold itself will slow the mental processes required to make effective decisions regarding direction**

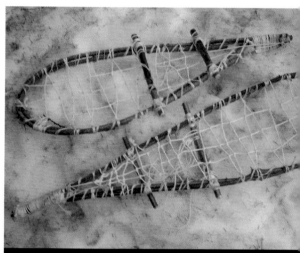

Snow shoes can be simple to construct ...

... and can save you from hours of floundering in waist-deep s

leather, reed cordage, or a thin layer of bark will do). This forms the base of the snowshoe. The central section needs to be strengthened with cross-struts to support the weight of the foot. Your design will be largely dictated by the materials available, but the guiding principle should be to find a balance between strength and weight.

If you have some paracord or string, you can easily tie this around the back of your heel and then back to the cross-strut. This keeps your boot nicely in place while allowing your heel to rise up and down.

For a quicker and easier makeshift design in forest terrain, break off two bushy evergreen branches about 3 feet long and lash the stem ends to the front of your boot. When you start walking, lift the leg from the knee and keep the bottom

of the foot horizontal through the stride so that the branch end of the snowshoe doesn't trip you as you put your foot down.

During the winter of 1846–7, a group of eighty-one American pioneers known as the Donner Party became trapped in the snow while crossing the Sierra Nevada. One of the group, F. W. Graves, was a native of Vermont and had spent his youth in the mountains. He was the only member of the party who knew how to construct snowshoes and was able to make fourteen pairs that were instrumental in saving those who did survive.

I have used this principle in the Alps and saved myself gallons of sweat by being able to cross deep snowed areas safely and swiftly. In total it took about three hours to make a pair of snowshoes, and I'm no shoemaker!

MOVEMENT OVER ICE

You are likely to find yourself crossing bodies of ice in all sub-zero terrains: across glaciers in the mountains and in Antarctica; across rivers and lakes in the mountains; and across sea ice in the Arctic. Ice, like snow, comes in many different forms and, more significantly when your life depends on it, many different thicknesses. However, crossing ice that may be only a few inches thick is common in the Arctic and may well be necessary in the mountains.

Learning to distinguish between different types of ice and its weight-bearing strength is a skill that must be learned. The penalty for making a misjudgment may be your life. Climbing out of an ice hole is always extremely difficult, especially if you are alone. In general, ice needs to be at least 2 inches thick before you should even consider walking on it. Dirty, dark ice is usually thin, whereas gray, light-colored ice is usually older and thicker. Ice covered by snow is often thinner than exposed ice, as the snow itself prevents it thickening and insulates it. Make sure you have a stick or a sharp knife with you before crossing ice. Prod it sharply three times before walking over it. If you do break through, the stick or knife will be crucial in giving you grip to climb back out.

Ice on rivers will be far stronger nearer the banks; and look out for any rocks or objects sticking up through the surface. These will cause the surrounding ice to be thinner because of the constant disturbance and eddies around the obstacle. Also be very careful if you suspect the river level has recently fallen. A gap between the surface of the river and the ice will make it far less stable and much more lethal if the ice breaks.

Survival is about thinking smart, not just sweating hard

MOVEMENT OVER MOUNTAINS IN WINTER

DOWNHILL
Walking downhill through deep snow requires a stride known as the "plunge step." Take large strides and keep your weight over your heel. Lean slightly forward, keeping your leg stiffer than normal, and the downward force of your weight will create footholds as you go. Increase your length of stride and hence your downward force if the footholds are too shallow; decrease it in slushy snow where you are sinking in too far. On very steep slopes, turn round, face the slope, and climb down backwards, kicking into the snow as you go.

UPHILL
Kick into the snowpack, letting the weight of your boot do the work, and keep your footholds angled downwards. Move upwards in a zigzag. The steeper the slope, the more extended the zigzag should be. A snow pole made from a tree branch can be used in much the same way as an ice axe. Move it to the next position before moving your feet so you have gained some grip on the snow face before shifting your body weight.

AVOIDING A FALL
Use the snow pole to support you as you go, and keep it attached to your wrist with a lanyard if possible. Always test the snow for firmness before you put all your weight on it. Be very wary of falling rocks and avalanches from above (see pages 130–131) and examine the shape, texture, and color of the snow ahead.

Hollows often betray crevasses below, and darker colors should be treated with suspicion. These slight depressions in the snow can be seen by the shadows they cast, so try to move in sunlight rather than overcast days, so these depressions show up. Also move as early in the day as possible, before the sun warms potential avalanche slopes and crevasse coverings.

Prevention is considerably better than cure, but if you do fall, grab your snow pole at the base with both hands and roll onto your stomach, plunging the pole into the snow and putting all your weight on it to arrest your momentum. Without a pole, spread-eagle your body and keep as much contact with the ground as possible.

POLAR NAVIGATION

USING THE SUN

While a working GPS would be gold dust, navigation, even using a simple compass, in the polar regions can be a frustrating process. The proximity of the magnetic poles can turn your precious navigational instrument into a twirling propeller of little practical use.

Instead the sun, when it shines, can be an extremely accurate navigational instrument. The basic principle of solar navigation is that the Earth takes twenty-four hours to revolve 360 degrees, one hour to revolve fifteen degrees, and four minutes to revolve 1 degree.

From "Principles of Celestial Navigation" (see Chapter 1, pages 34–35) we know that the sun will be roughly in the east at 6 A.M. and your shadow in the west. At noon in the Arctic the sun will be in the south and your shadow pointing directly north (reverse this for the Antarctic). At 6 P.M. the sun will be in the west and your shadow in the east.

Therefore, knowing that the sun moves at fifteen degrees an hour, you will always know your general direction. For example, at 3 P.M. your shadow will be pointing northeast in the Arctic (45 degrees) and southwest in the Antarctic. The only variation to be aware of is if you are at the extreme east or west of the polar regions, in which case some adjustment will be needed owing to your longitude.

MOVING IN A STRAIGHT LINE

Once you are oriented, try not to ruin it by deviating from your chosen direction. This means being sure you are walking in a straight line, which, in a whiteout or blank featureless ice vista, can be harder than you might think.

Wind blowing across snow or sand leaves behind telltale corrugated wrinkles called sastrugi patterns. As the prevailing wind is usually constant, these will harden into recognizable features. When you are sure you have orientated yourself correctly, note the angle at which you are walking relative to the sastrugi and keep that angle constant as you move forward.

ARCTIC VS. ANTARCTIC

It is usually easier to navigate in the Arctic than the Antarctic. This is due to the topography of the landscape, which often has more identifiable features due to the sea ice being constantly flexed and bowed into ice ridges and rubble heaps.

On the other hand, ice movement over the surface of the water is disorienting. Before you leave your shelter, orient yourself with any recognizable surrounding features from the highest viewpoint you can find. If a rubble pile is near, this may give you a vantage point which will be very useful. From here you will also be able to see hazards ahead. Once you have decided on a direction, use a feature to follow on the far horizon.

In the Antarctic, on the other hand, during the summer the sun shines around three out of four days, so solar navigation is actually a lot easier than using a compass.

You can also orient yourself from the way that rocks lie on glaciers. Their shadow shields

Move as early in the day as possible, before the sun warms potential avalanche slopes and crevasse coverings

Sometimes badly frostbitten feet are best left frozen until you reach safety. At least it means you will be able to walk on the frozen stumps

the ice from solar radiation, and over a period of time the ice around them melts, leaving the rock perched on its own little platform. In the Antarctic the sunlight comes predominantly from the north, so the rock will often fall that way. Don't make a decision based on the position of one fallen rock, but if others nearby have fallen the same way, it is likely they will all be pointing north.

Learn to read the mountain faces ahead of you for signs of avalanche danger and crevasses.

A FEW DOS AND DON'TS WHEN TRAVELING IN SUB-ZERO TERRAIN

DO:

- Move in the early morning or late in the afternoon if the snow is thawing during the day. At these times the temperature will be colder and the snow firmer. On the other hand, if the terrain is icy, move mid-afternoon, when it will be less slippery.

- Watch carefully for noticeable temperature changes that will make any climbing you have to do safer or, conversely, more dangerous.

- The threat of avalanches is very real in the mountains (see pages 130–131). To reduce your chances of being caught by one, move in the morning before the snow has been heated by the sun and when the threat of avalanches will be reduced.

- Use a snow stick to steady yourself over uneven terrain and, more importantly, to feel through the snow for hidden objects, weak ice, or hidden streams. If you do fall through ice, it may also save your life by giving you some grip as you try to haul yourself out.

- Watch the weather at all times. Dig yourself a snow hole or other shelter at the first sign of the weather deteriorating. Make camp earlier rather than later, especially during the short winter daylight hours. You'll only ever get this wrong once.

- Make every possible effort to stay dry. Cold is a killer in sub-zero temperatures, but its effect will be far greater if water and damp come into contact with your skin. Sodden clothes conduct heat away from the body as much as fifty times faster than dry clothes.

- Keep your feet dry. Even though the rest of your body may be dry, don't ignore your feet. If they get wet, dry them out at once. Frostbitten feet and toes are all too common among high-altitude climbers, and as they

"warm up" again the pain can be excruciating. Sometimes badly frostbitten feet are best left frozen until you reach safety. At least it means you will be able to walk on the frozen stumps.

- Be very careful of thin ice. Avoid it whenever possible and spread your weight by crouching low or crawling if it is unavoidable. The basic rule is: three good hard prods with your snow pole and it will probably be all right. If it goes through on the first or second strike, keep well away.

- Use rivers to navigate. In some regions of the world where the rivers freeze several feet thick in winter, they can be a viable route to salvation.

DON'T:

- Allow yourself to sweat heavily as you move. As well as costing you much-needed body fluid, if you allow your clothes to become damp, the water will later freeze and conduct heat rapidly away from you, hastening hypothermia.

- Walk on or under the lee side of a ridge in the mountains in winter. Cornices of snow are often blown by the wind into these huge, overhanging arches which are liable to collapse underfoot as the result of sound vibration.

- Try moving anywhere in a blizzard. Upwards and downwards, let alone the cardinal directions, are often impossible to distinguish in a whiteout. Your chances of falling into a crevasse or through the ice will be greatly increased and the nature of the terrain almost impossible to judge.

- Try crossing snow-covered streams.

- Hitchhike on an iceberg. Because most of their mass is submerged, they have a tendency to flip over when they start to melt.

Ice needs to be at least 2 inches thick before you should even consider walking on it

Natural Hazards - Mountains in Winter

AVALANCHES

Avalanches are often lethal. The secret to avoiding them is awareness of the conditions that make them likely to happen. Most avalanches occur on hillsides that slope at 30–50 degrees or more and are most likely to occur when more than 5 inches of snow has fallen within the last twenty-four hours. If caught high in the mountains during a severe snowfall, it may well be worth waiting a day before setting off – if that is an option.

Look out at all times for telltale signs of where avalanches have occurred in the past and where

SURVIVING AN AVALANCHE

If you are caught in an avalanche, do everything you can to reach the edge of the slide. Trying to outrun it will be futile. Cover your mouth. Many avalanche victims are killed by drowning from powder-snow inhalation. Try to keep your arms in front of your face to create as large an air space as possible before the snow freezes. Many victims have ended up digging the wrong way when upside down and disoriented. To find which way is up: spit or pee. Your dribble will be going downwards. Then dig upwards as fast as possible. Avalanched snow can quickly compact as hard as concrete after it settles.

I remember in the Alps seeing an avalanche debris site like nothing I had ever witnessed. Hundreds of acres of huge, thick, stout trees had been shredded into matchsticks, with the bark ripped off them and the snow all around as hard as rock. If caught in such an avalanche, you have little or no chance of survival, and it is often the air shock wave moving in front of avalanches that inflicts the initial violent damage.

On Everest, avalanches were a daily part of our existence, pouring off the high mountain ridges all around us. We narrowly missed being consumed by a huge avalanche, by only several minutes, on our final day of descent off the mountain. Having survived ninety-one days on the world's highest peak, the last morning we were struggling with a combination of frostbitten feet and exhausted bodies. We ended up leaving at 6.05 A.M. rather than 6 A.M., as we labored to get moving one last time towards base camp. Five minutes late – no big deal. A few hours into the descent, though, a huge avalanche swept across the glacier in front of us. If we had left on time and been a few hundred feet farther on, that avalanche would have devoured us. Instead we sat on our packs and watched this great white mass consuming the ground ahead of us.

There is an element of pure chance when moving through avalanche territory, but that element of chance is greatly reduced when you know the signs to watch out for and the correct time of day to be moving.

Remember, though, if you are caught out, the key reactions are: move sideways; move fast; cover your face; and if overtaken, use a swimming motion to dig out fast upwards – and say your prayers!

Avalanches destroy everything in their paths. Don't risk it — move early in the day before the sun hits the snow.

they are likely to happen in the future. Trees whose higher branches have been ripped away can indicate where avalanches have occurred before, and these areas should be avoided after a heavy snowfall. Cornices where snow has been blown into an overhang like a frozen wave on the lee of a ridge are also very dangerous. Deep snow that falls on convex slopes (like the outside of a contact lens) are the most likely to avalanche, as are steep gullies or slopes that have few or no rocks or trees to hold the snow in place. Beware of classic avalanche funnels on steep north-facing slopes. With fresh snowfall, these can avalanche daily.

If your footfall causes the snow to crack, it is likely that the snow mass is under tension and prone to avalanche. Avoid traveling when the heat of the sun is shining directly on likely avalanche sites in the afternoon. Wait until the area is in shade and keep to the high ground, where you will be less likely to be buried.

GLACIERS AND CREVASSES

The first rule of glacier travel as a sole survivor is to avoid crossing one unless your life depends on it. Glaciers are literally rivers of frozen ice. Like a normal unfrozen river, they "flow" downhill, albeit at a dramatically reduced speed. The huge pressures exerted on them by the uneven terrain beneath causes them to flex and bow, which makes them vulnerable to splits and cracks, called crevasses. These can sometimes be hundreds of feet deep.

Due to repeated snowfall and constant movement, crevasses are often disguised by bridges of snow which can easily collapse under the weight of a man. On mountaineering expeditions, climbers will always be roped together so that if someone falls into a crevasse they can be rescued by the others behind.

In the infamous Khumbu icefall on Everest — a giant, tumbling frozen cascade of ice blocks

Falling into a crevasse is often lethal – avoid it at all costs.

On mountaineering expeditions, climbers will always be roped together so that if someone falls into a crevasse they can be rescued by the others behind

the size of cathedrals riddled with giant crevasses – I had a crevasse give way under my feet. It was early in the morning, we were at 19,000 feet and I took a step on what looked like solid ice. As I put my weight forward, a crack appeared underneath my feet. There was a second's pause, then the whole area around me dropped away. I started to fall. The ice that I brought down with me knocked me out. I came to gently swinging on the end of the rope, with hundreds of feet of sheer black ice walls on both sides beneath me. My life was saved by being roped to my climbing buddies. Don't underestimate how dangerous, as well as terrifying, crevasses can be. Take detours!

If crossing a glacier is unavoidable, though, try to observe its overall shape and features before you begin. While all glaciers are different, there are areas which are more prone than others to crevasses. These include the edges (where drag and friction from the surrounding features increase these tears in the ice); the outside bend when a glacier snakes down a valley (maximum stretch and tension is found here); and humps from a concave hillside beneath (pressure from below). The top third or so of glaciers should also be avoided as this is where snow accumulates the most and where crevasses are likely to be hidden. Crevasses often form in parallel lines with smaller "splinters" radiating off, and are also often much bigger than they appear on the surface.

Seasonal and temperature variations and the quality of the light should all be taken into account when trying to judge the risk in using snow bridges to cross crevasses. In deep winter, temperatures will be lower and snow bridges will be more solid. On the other hand, in higher spring temperatures, crevasses will be more visible, but they will also be far more treacherous to cross.

CROSSING A CREVASSE

SNOW AND ICE BOLLARDS

If you have a rope, cut an ice or snow bollard. These are humps of tightly packed snow or ice which you should mold in the shape of a mushroom. These must be sufficiently densely packed to hold a rope with your weight should you fall into the crevasse. Typically a snow bollard will need to be about 5 feet across (double that if the snow is soft) and 18 inches deep, while an ice bollard should be at least a foot across and more than 1/2 foot deep.

If you have a strip of fabric, tuck it between the rope and the snow on the weight-bearing side of the bollard. This will help spread the pressure on the rope and stop it cutting through the ice or snow. Always err on the bigger size – better too safe than having the rope rip through the snow. You can also use several stout sticks sunk into the snow horizontally, with the rope wrapped around them, to act as an anchor. Use material again where possible to spread the load against the snow.

KNOTTED-ROPE TECHNIQUE

In the mountains, I have tested and used a technique that has only recently been pioneered by Alpine guides. This involves tying knots in a rope (in my case rigging lines scavenged from my reserve parachute), then dragging the rope behind you as you cross the glacier. On the end of this rope must be some sort of counterweight, which in my case was part of my parachute filled with some snow. When you are on solid, even ground, the knots and counterweight bobble and pull along the top of the snow behind you, but if you fall into a crevasse, they immediately bite into the snow and break your fall. I can confirm it's a technique that works.

CLIMBING OUT OF A CREVASSE

Be under no illusions. If you fall into a deep crevasse unroped and you are alone, your chances of getting out are very slim. If you survive the fall and there is no way to climb out, try to descend.

It is better than doing nothing and waiting for death. You may get lucky and find that the crevasse has a ramp farther down or to the side that leads out lower down the glacier. Frightening as it is to go down into the dark abyss, it may be your only choice. It worked for Joe Simpson during his famous escape from Siula Grande, documented in the film *Touching the Void*.

TIP: Be prepared. When moving through a crevasse area, either on a self-arrest system or with other climbers, always carry a few lengths of short rope to double as prusiks (see "Prusik Knot" in Chapter 1, page 43). These can aid you getting out if you fall. Trying to pull yourself up a thin rope is near impossible, but several prusiks might save your life, allowing you to make foot straps that can ascend the rope without sliding down. If you don't have such a length of rope, you can always use your bootlaces to do the same job as a prusik.

AND REMEMBER ...
- Never cross a crevasse unless you have to. It takes just one mistake to end your journey permanently.
- Travel, if possible, in the early morning, when the temperature will be colder. With the sun low in the sky, it will also be easier to spot the telltale signs of a crevasse, namely sagging depressions in the snow with a darker texture and color.
- If you find an ice bridge, make sure you probe it carefully with your stick first. If there is any sign of weakness, don't use it.
- Spread your weight as much as possible when crossing an ice bridge by crouching and crawling. Cross at 90 degrees to the main direction of the crevasse.
- Only jump across a crevasse if you are 100 percent certain of the location of its true edges on both sides.
- If you fall into a crevasse, spread your arms and legs and try to lock yourself between the walls to break your fall.

Surviving Patagonia, one of the coldest, windiest places on earth.

Natural Hazards - The Arctic

THIN ICE

The cautionary phrase "walking on thin ice" was not coined for nothing. As any husky dog musher will tell you, thin ice spells disaster. If you break through, your chances of getting back on dry land will be slim, and if you don't, you will be dead from hypothermia within minutes. Arctic ice in particular is variable in thickness and prone to breaking up. The gaps it leaves are known as "leads" and are potentially lethal should you fall into one.

If you do, swim to the edge where you fell in and maneuver your body onto the ice shelf like a seal. This means keeping a low center of gravity and spreading your weight. The ice on the edges of the hole will be thin and slippery and liable to fracture more as you exert more pressure trying to haul yourself out. If this happens, keep moving and breaking the ice back the way you originally came from, until the ice is thick enough to hold your weight as you clamber out.

I have had the misfortune of falling through the ice four times now. Frozen lakes in the high mountains of winter are killers. Rarely will there not be another way around, so find it and use it. The dangers of such sub-zero immersions are firstly the gasp reflex where the shock of the water means you gasp and breathe water into your lungs, and you subsequently drown; secondly, cardiac arrest, induced by the sheer shock of the water temperature; and finally the biggest killer of all, the all-consuming numbing effect of the cold, where after one or two minutes your body loses all sensation, robbing you of the coordination and strength to be able to haul yourself out.

The key to surviving such a fall into a frozen lake is to act fast while the adrenaline is working in your favor. Try to keep calm (easier said than done) and control your breathing. Remove any rucksack, turn around to exit the same way you went in – the only direction where you know for sure the ice will eventually be strong enough to hold your weight – then, using anything sharp (either a knife or the bottom of your ski-poles), reach out, dig it into the ice, and wriggle out, keeping a low center of gravity all the way until you are back to safety. I have used just bare hands before, but it is much harder.

Yes, it's as cold and nasty as it looks.

The priority then is to shed your wet clothes and get dry. If you have no other clothes, strip off, roll your clothes into the powder snow to absorb some of the moisture, wring them out, put them back on, and get moving to warm up. When you are warm, find shelter, then keep moving again until you dry out. These will be miserable long hours. When I did this in the Alps I had a fire prepared before I went in so I could dry my clothes straightaway afterwards. Alternatively you can "freeze-dry" clothes, where you remove them and allow them to freeze, then you can bash the ice out of them when they have gone stiff.

When one of Shackleton's crew slipped off the ice floe they were sleeping on one night, he had to walk round and round this small floe for twelve hours to avoid freezing to death. But he lived.

ICE RUBBLE AND RIDGES

The Arctic is prone to large areas of ice rubble which look like snow versions of abandoned building sites, with huge mounds of broken snow and ice. They are caused by giant ice floes crashing into each other and can appear out of a previously flat landscape without warning. Arctic explorers have often settled down for the night only to wake next morning to find their camp surrounded by huge mounds of rubble.

Ice ridges are much the same but caused by leads closing up and their edges riding over each other. The pressure of this pushes blocks of ice high into the air. Both are best avoided as they can lead to sprained ankles or worse if you attempt to cross the uneven terrain. Try to look for clear areas to cross instead. If you have no choice, be patient and proceed with caution.

FOG

Fog afflicts the Arctic, particularly in spring. This occurs when the leads near the edge of the ice pack get larger, and huge areas of open water cause a massive temperature gradient between the warmer air from the south and the surface sea temperature. This condenses into fog. Under these circumstances leads and thin ice are very hard to spot until you are on them. In foggy conditions proceed with even more caution.

Frozen lakes in the high mountains of winter are killers. Rarely will there not be another way around, so find it and use it

Natural Hazards - Antarctica

Many of the hazards of the Arctic and sub-zero mountain terrain are also a problem in Antarctica. However, there is one characteristic of travel in this part of the world that is a particular killer – the wind-chill factor. Topographical conditions in Antarctica mean that the continent can be divided into recognizable bands of weather, each with its own distinguishing characteristics. Apart from the interior, which has relatively calm weather, these areas are some of the windiest places on earth, including the windiest of all, Cape Dennison at Commonwealth Bay, which has an annual average wind speed of 50 miles per hour. Whenever you travel, this must be your main concern, being able to escape the wind quickly when needed.

Finally reaching the end of a glacier in Alaska.

Health Problems

One of the greatest enemies of survival in any environment is cold. Hypothermia occurs when the body progressively loses more heat than it can generate and the temperature in the body's core falls from its normal 37°C (98.6°F) to 35°C (95°F) or less. The effects of cold are greater at high altitude, so mountaineers are particularly vulnerable, but hypothermia can easily set in when the ambient temperature is well above zero. In permanent sub-zero temperatures, the hazard is magnified still further.

Cold is a mortal enemy and its effects need to be minimized before they take hold. This is the great key to survival in the cold: sorting out the problem before it is too late. Sometimes keeping warm is hard physical work, and frostbite only occurs when the climber or survivor loses that determination to keep wiggling his toes or flexing his hands. Keeping warm in such extremes is a battle of will, a resolution to keep limbs and extremities moving and working, resisting the temptation to give up and allow them to go numb.

Once again, I repeat, the key is recognizing the symptoms and acting before it is too late – before it becomes impossible to warm up. If your hands are beginning to get cold, stuff them down your trousers or under your armpits, or if you are with someone else, put your feet on their stomach. I have let someone use my stomach and it probably saved their toes. Do it soon and, most crucially, do it before you really need to.

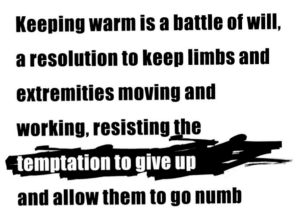

Keeping warm is a battle of will, a resolution to keep limbs and extremities moving and working, resisting the temptation to give up and allow them to go numb

HYPOTHERMIA

Retaining heat is always a far better strategy than losing it in the first place, so understanding the many ways the body loses heat is vital. There are five ways that it does. These are radiation, conduction, convection, evaporation, and respiration. In other words we lose heat like a heater trying to warm up its surroundings (radiation); by coming into direct contact with a cold surface like snow (conduction); by heat exchange with the surrounding element, which will usually be cold air (convection); by sweating (evaporation); and plain, ordinary breathing when cold air is sucked into the body and expired, taking heat and moisture with it (respiration).

While the ambient temperature is a significant cause of hypothermia, it is often the amplifying effects of water and wind chill that do the real damage. As we have seen, water conducts heat away from the body up to fifty times quicker than air, so by far the easiest way to avoid hypothermia is to stay dry. As well as avoiding river dunkings, sweat should be treated as a hazard to be taken equally seriously. When sweat cools and starts to freeze, it will conduct heat away from your body very rapidly. Remove layers as you warm up and reapply them as you cool down. Be aware of and manage your own body's temperature. This awareness is critical to success in the cold extremes.

Gathering driftwood in Patagonia, South America, in order to make a raft.

Heat drains from the body most quickly at the extremities where they come into direct contact with the surrounding environment and where the greatest volume of blood comes closest to the surface of the body. This is why around 30 percent of the body's heat is lost through the head and neck, owing to the large quantity of blood flowing through the brain. These areas must be kept well covered and protected.

When your core temperature drops, your own internal thermometer will allow your hands to get cold, as they are not vital to your survival, but it will not allow your head to get cold as the brain is critical to life. So you will continue to lose heat through your head until you eventually fall unconscious and die. So wear or make a covering for your head at all times.

The body's ability to keep itself warm will also be affected by dehydration, hunger, and lack of sleep, so all three need to be continually monitored. When you become dehydrated, the amount of blood available to warm your fingers and toes decreases, increasing the risk of frostbite.

and heart failure. A confused mental state is a reliable sign of the onset of hypothermia, but your brain will need to be operating properly in the first place to recognize this symptom in yourself if you are alone, which is why it is so important to respond quickly and learn to recognize these early signs.

FROSTBITE

Frostbite occurs when, in order to protect core heat, the body reduces the supply of blood to the extremities (starting with the feet and hands) and the tissue actually freezes. As well as initial numbness and tingling, the affected part will go white and waxy. This will be followed by the skin going red and becoming swollen, before breaking into dark spots and eventually going black. Blood poisoning can follow as the dead limb infects the rest of the body.

Minor frostbite on the outer tissue layers (frostnip) can be reversed without ill effect if caught early enough, but when the deeper tissues become frozen solid, the problem is more serious. If severe frostbite takes place in a survival situation, as stated, it is best to leave the limb frozen until help arrives. Survivors have been known to walk for days on frozen limbs, which they would never have managed to do if they had started to thaw out. They lost their limbs, sometimes their noses as well, but they lived.

SIGNS OF HYPOTHERMIA

Shivering is the first sign that the body is cooling too rapidly and is an automatic survival mechanism whereby the body tries to generate heat by contracting and releasing the muscles very quickly. If nothing is done to bring the body back into balance, the shivering will get worse, the skin will go blue, and your brain will become unable to think straight. A false feeling of warmth can sometimes ensue. This will be followed by loss of consciousness, coma,

Frostbite occurs when, in order to protect core heat, the body reduces the supply of blood to the extremities

Take the climber Beck Weathers, left for dead on Everest at 26,000 feet. As he sat there dying, he knew if he closed his eyes he would never wake up. Through swollen eyelids he saw a glimmer of light flickering. He knew that if he was to see his family again he had to get up and move. He staggered to his feet, both of them now stumps of frozen meat, and started to walk. He said he was going to keep walking until he either found the tents or walked off the side of the mountain. He found the tents. His will and spirit had overridden his frozen limbs. He lost his hands and feet and nose but regained his life.

AND HOW TO AVOID IT . . .

When wet, even the best clothing and footwear will conduct heat away from the body, so, above all, keep kit and clothing dry.

The feet are particularly vulnerable to cold and wet as boots are in constant contact with the snow, so every effort should be made to keep socks and the inside of your boots dry, even if this means changing and drying socks at regular intervals. In the SAS we used to put the wet socks down our trousers to dry out after we had changed them. Make sure your boots are not too tight as this will restrict circulation and your feet will freeze faster.

At night, don't leave your boots open to the elements. If you are not wearing them while you sleep, take them into your shelter and keep them next to your body. Wear gloves at all times and keep them dry. Keep bare hands away from all metal surfaces like mugs, crampons, or tent pegs, which will stick to raw flesh like glue.

Don't bring snow on your clothing into a shelter, because in the warmer air it will melt, making your clothes wet. Shake it off at the entrance. Use any grasses or undergrowth you can find to insulate your clothing and your shelter. Bracken, pine needles, and beech leaves are all good insulators.

Your overall objective, besides staying warm and dry, is to keep the blood circulating effectively. Anything that thins the blood will help it circulate better. These include Omega 3s, which are found in fish. Keep limbs moving every few minutes. Discipline yourself in extreme cold to do this religiously – include every moving part of your body.

SNOW BLINDNESS

The reflection of sun off the snow magnifies the damaging effects of the sun's rays and can cause snow blindness. This occurs because the UV light burns the corneas of the eye. Symptoms include red eyes, irritation and a yellow discharge, headaches, and blurred vision leading to temporary blindness. I witnessed a climber in the Himalayas, high up on Mount Lhotse, go totally blind when a mixture of snow blindness and the extreme cold both burned and froze his eyes simultaneously.

Snow goggles can easily be made from a strip of bark or cloth through which small slits can be cut. Also charcoal underneath the eyes will reduce glare. Don't remove these in overcast conditions when they may seem unnecessary – you still need protection. This is how snow blindness is often caused.

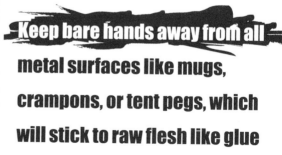

Keep bare hands away from all metal surfaces like mugs, crampons, or tent pegs, which will stick to raw flesh like glue

When reflected off the snow, the UV rays of the sun can cause snow blindness – always wear goggles.

The Bear Necessities: Surviving Sub-Zero Terrain

RULE 1: STAY WARM AND DRY

Hypothermia is the number-one killer in sub-zero terrain. It won't be the normal outside temperature that kills you, however, but the amplifying effects of the wind and the wet, so protect yourself from the wind and stay dry. Treat your limbs, head, and extremities like children – watch out and look after them.

RULE 2: BUILD A SNOW SHELTER

Use the environment to shelter yourself. Snow should become your greatest friend, not your worst enemy. The most basic snow shelters are quick and easy to make. Remember, snow is one of nature's best insulators. Bears hibernate in it, so it can't be all bad!

RULE 3: MAKE A SNOW STICK

Some sort of support, protection, and prodding device is a vital accessory in snowy and icy terrain. It will stop you falling through thin ice,
into a crevasse, or down a mountain, and help you move through the mountains with greater speed and ease.

RULE 4: MAKE SOME SNOWSHOES

You must spread your weight when moving over deep snow. Snowshoes can be made from any number of tough, flexible materials and strapped to the bottom of your feet. They are easier to make than you might think!

RULE 5: NEVER STOP BELIEVING

The temptation to curl up and give up must be resisted at all costs. Surviving in the extreme cold takes constant determination. But, deep down, you have what it takes. Remember that when you were conceived you won a race out of 500 million competitors, fighting a battle uphill and in the dark. You have always been a champion at heart. Believe, and you will survive.

"The greatest discovery of my generation
is that a human being can alter his life by
altering his attitude of mind."

WILLIAM JAMES

chapter 4

jungles

That's actually not a bad description of how it feels to be lost and alone in a real jungle. For far from being the creators and controllers of our own individual "comfort zone," we are suddenly thrown into one of the most complex ecosystems on earth.

Jungles can be defined as forests, sometimes untouched by man, located in the tropics. Different climatic conditions caused by varying latitudes, altitudes, and geological regions have created different types of tropical ecosystems. These range from equatorial rainforests, including the Amazon in South America and the Congo in Africa, to subtropical rainforests located in a 10-degree band north and south of the equator which includes Central and South America and large parts of Southeast Asia.

Life in these jungles is characterized by high temperatures, heavy rainfall, and oppressive humidity. When the rains come, they are often torrential and accompanied by thunder and lightning, which can cause heavy flooding. Instead of the seasonal variations of summer and winter familiar in temperate zones, jungle seasons alternate between the "wet" and the "dry." Even in the dry season there is rain, while the wet is like a monsoon. Storms and rainfall appear suddenly and then are gone. Day and night are of equal length. Darkness falls quickly and daybreak is just as sudden.

And owing to an ideal combination of all the primary catalysts of life (namely water, constant high temperatures, and sunlight), jungles contain more living organisms per square inch than any other wilderness terrain on earth. Which goes a long way to explaining why the jungle can be such an intimidating place. It is literally a hotbed for breeding every animal and insect you can imagine . . . whole lot more that man has not even discovered yet.

We must learn to live alongside this abundant nature if we are to have any chance of surviving in an environment which our ancestors turned their backs on many millennia ago. This is not our natural territory anymore and we must quickly learn to live by rules other than our own.

The great key to surviving in jungles is to adapt your mind-set: slow down and don't get easily troubled. Realize it is an abundance of wonderful, extraordinary life, and not, as you might feel when you first arrive and start sweating and getting bitten to death, a terrifying cesspit of mud and venomous monsters.

There is everything you need to survive in abundance in a jungle: food, shelter, water, fire, and tools. Flow with it, rather than fight it. You are part of the jungle food chain now, but remember that your brain and skills and strength, if used correctly, mean you can stay at the top of that food chain.

Even the nasty snakes of the jungle, or wild flesh-eating jaguars, tend to know what their staple diet is and stick to it. Snakes generally only attack if startled and cornered. You can be the king of the jungle if you learn to use it, enjoy it, and not fear it. And with this attitude you are most likely to survive it and get home again in one piece.

At first, the sheer scale, size, and intensity of the wildlife, creepy-crawlies, and huge, sap-oozing trees can be very intimidating – in fact, I have known soldiers to go mad from it. Consider then what it must have been like for seventeen-year-old Marcos Martínez Herrera, who became separated from his uncle in the Corcovado National Park in Costa Rica in 2003. He was then on his own, lost, for the next thirteen days.

When he was rescued, after covering more than 25 miles through the jungle, he described the terror of the nights, with the noises of wild animals keeping him awake. Even his Red Cross rescuers described it as a miracle he had survived. But something inside him kept his spirit alive and afterwards he described how he had continued to pray, followed his instincts, and refused to give up hope.

Although there were probably many things he could have done to make the ordeal less harrowing and uncomfortable, Marcos's experience vividly demonstrates how knowledge is ultimately not the most important ingredient in surviving extreme environments. While survival knowledge is of enormous benefit, at the end of it all it is your will to live and your ability to adapt your mental attitude that will make the critical difference.

Fear is a very common reaction for first-time jungle dwellers, as Marcos Martínez Herrera discovered. But fear won't help you; being alert and wary will. Think twice before you do anything. Before you sit down, check around that log. Before you lie down, clear the ground with a stick. Before you pee in a river, before you steady yourself against a branch, think. Look. One bite from the wrong creature can kill you. Every action in the jungle has a consequence to some animal, or plant, or to you.

They say you either hate the jungle or love it, but in a survival situation you have no choice. Be one of the ones who love it. Go with the flow and remember if you are smart and use all the techniques in this chapter, you will get out of there alive.

the jungle, you must learn to live by rules other than your own.

Fear is a very common reaction for first-time jungle dwellers, as Marcos Martínez Herrera discovered. But fear won't help you; being alert and wary will

Making a shelter will be the first tangible solution to your predicament. It will calm feelings of panic and help restore your morale. In an environment where the discomfort from the heat and humidity is intense, coupled with assaults on your body from biting, crawling, and slithering creatures of all descriptions, a shelter will help create the feeling that it is you in control of your situation, rather than the jungle.

A shelter will also go a long way to help you win the mental battle I talked about in Chapter 1 (see pages 16–19), to keep concentrating on the day-to-day tasks necessary for survival while holding firm to your determination to overcome whatever is thrown at you.

The jungle can provide everything you need to stay alive — food, water, and shelter.

STUDY THE TERRAIN

Night falls quickly and suddenly in tropical latitudes and it is important you use the hours of daylight to your advantage. Take time to study the terrain around you while you have the chance. Nothing will sap your energy and morale more than the realization that you have spent precious hours and strength constructing a shelter in the wrong location – and in the jungle, location is everything.

So think carefully about where you site your shelter, and use the topography of the jungle to the best advantage. Keep to higher ground and make sure you are a reasonable distance (a couple of hundred yards at least) from any water source. This will protect you from flooding caused by sudden and torrential downpours that could easily sweep both you and your shelter away. And when it rains in the "rainforest," it pours. Get used to this, plan for it, and let the rain soothe you rather than distress you.

Higher ground will also mean that you are less likely to find yourself blocking an animal's path to water. It will keep you clear of swamps and stagnant water, which are potent attractors of mosquitoes.

While a shelter will need to keep you dry, it also needs to protect you from ground assault, from all those crawling, slithering, marching, biting creatures, so your first task in shelter-making is to find a corner of the jungle floor that has as few potential hiding places for such beasties as you can find.

Keep away from grassy areas where ticks may be concentrated in large numbers, and make absolutely sure there are no ants on the move through your shelter site. Ants are the other kings of the jungle, along with you; in fact, without ants, a jungle would suffocate on its own leaves and die within six months. They work twenty-four hours of every day and night

of the year, and when a colony of ants is on the move they clear everything in their path – make sure it is not your camp.

When you're making camp, remember to look up into the jungle canopy, into those huge trees towering above you. Any number of objects can and do regularly drop down, including dead branches, coconuts, and leeches. Remember dead wood falling from above kills more people in the jungle than anything else. I did not used to believe this – until I first went to the jungle . . . Trust me, when you are moving around, the monkeys hear you; they then rush over to have a look at you, they swing on the vines, and the dead wood starts to rain down. Be careful of such loose falling logs above everything . . . it's such an unspectacular way to die! Finally, find a long stick and clear the floor of all the leaves and jungle debris.

> When it rains in the "rainforest," it pours. Get used to this, plan for it, and let the rain soothe you rather than distress you

MATERIALS

WOOD, VINES, AND BAMBOO

In the jungle, materials for making a shelter are plentiful. Young, pliable saplings are easily found and can be used to make the uprights for your shelter and bed. Bamboo can be found in most jungles and comes in every size from a handy headmaster's cane to 80-foot monsters towering above the jungle floor.

Also near to hand will be woody climbing vines, such as those Tarzan used to swing on, which you can use to lash your building materials into a frame structure, while the plentiful large leaves can be used as thatching material. Moss and plant life on the jungle floor will also make very effective padding for your bedding.

TIP: Owing to its strength, lightness, and flexibility, bamboo has always been prized as a construction material, but be careful when harvesting it. Bamboo often grows in clumps under tension. It can splinter suddenly and cause nasty wounds. It also has sharp hairs at the base which are a major skin irritant.

LEAVES

Leaves of every conceivable shape, size, and texture are also in infinite supply. These can be threaded between woven grids of saplings (always thatch from the bottom up) to make roofs or walls which will do an excellent job in keeping the rain at bay.

The Atap leaf – aka the "wait-a-while-vine," so named because it clings to the body with tiny barbs and slows you down whether you like it or not – is one of the most commonly used leaves for thatching by tribal communities. The atap has a long stalk with multiple long leaves on either side, a bit like a giant feather. Split the stalk in half from the tip end down,

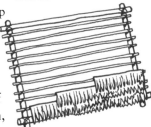

but handle with care as the leaf tips are very sharp. In this form the leaves can easily be woven into the wooden lattice of your roof or wall frame. It shouldn't take more than thirty minutes to cover the roof of your shelter, and the bigger the leaves you can find, the easier the job becomes.

ELEPHANT GRASS AND PALM LEAVES

Larger plants with long, broad leaves, like elephant grass, whose stems are like thin bamboo and grow up to 13 feet high, make excellent material for weaving into wooden frame lattices to make walls, roofs, and reflectors. Palm leaves with long stems are also good candidates, while the leaves of jungle plants that naturally divide into sections (like the cheese plants people often grow as houseplants) are very easy to weave into a lattice.

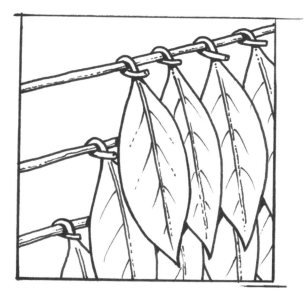

Slow down and become part of the jungle – never fight it, go with it.

TYPES OF SHELTER

The type of shelter you build will largely depend on how long you plan to stay and the materials that are available to you. Usually jungles are humid, so high winds are rare; therefore the primary form of protection you'll need will be against the wet.

Any materials you have been able to salvage will be helpful when building a shelter: a tarpaulin or a piece of plastic sheeting, or even just some cord and a knife. All of these are ideal materials for putting up an effective makeshift shelter that will keep off the rain and allow a breeze to circulate.

On several occasions I have chosen to go into the jungle with only a knife and a water bottle. No machete, no mosquito net, no hammock or tarpaulin – not even the steel and flint that I normally always carry. This made everything much harder, especially making fire, but I managed to make some pretty good shelters with just vines, branches, and leaves. Again, improvise, and remember in a jungle, above all other terrains, there is everything you need to hand, if you know where to look and get used to using your imagination.

While the detritus on the jungle floor may be soft, it will also be riddled with insects and alien life. With all shelters you must get yourself off the ground, away from the biting creatures that can make life a misery and sleep impossible.

A platform of wood or bamboo lined with softer palms or leaves on top is an easy first option for hasty shelters, but a raised bedding platform is much better and will provide protection from the jungle floor as well as allow the air to circulate more freely.

You must get yourself off the ground, away from the biting creatures that can make life a misery and sleep impossible

TEMPORARY SHELTERS: ONE-NIGHT B&Bs

Simple, easily constructed shelters can be made in minutes and will be far better than nothing at all. These can also give adequate protection against a tropical rainstorm. Remember: build before it gets dark – when the light starts to go, and you are 150 feet below the jungle canopy, it goes fast. Be prepared.

SHEET SHELTERS

Tie cord or vine between two trees or saplings or, if none can be found near each other, push some uprights into the ground about 6 feet apart and tie the cord between these. Drape a tarpaulin or sheet over the cord, extending a section onto the ground that can be used as under-bed protection. You then have a floor and a roof-shaped covering. Weight the side of the tarpaulin that is on the ground with heavy stones, and if the other side

doesn't reach the ground, attach cords to its corners and tie them to stakes pushed into the ground so they act like guy ropes. Finally, tie extra cords to both ends of the roof and attach them tightly to the uprights to keep the roof from sagging.

This simple structure will keep the rain at bay and allow fresh air to circulate in humid conditions. The Australian army still uses the "hootchie" – essentially exactly this construction – on jungle operations.

TIP: Make sure you keep your shelter sheet taut at all times and at an acute angle to the ground. The rain will then drain quickly and be less likely to penetrate the material.

FALLEN-TREE SHELTER

You can always clear the ground around a fallen, rotting tree trunk and sleep in the lee of this. Clear a small depression along the underside of the trunk and make sure rainwater won't run into it by making a simple, small runoff ditch around your new sleeping quarters.

Rotting wood of really large fallen trunks can be easily excavated to make a perfectly adequate shelter from the rain. In making both of these hasty shelters, be aware of snakes and scorpions, who love the shelter of fallen trees as well. At the start clear the area carefully with a stick, and keep a long-log fire (see page 28) going if possible. Further protection can be made by leaning branches against the trunk and covering with foliage.

TIP: With both these shelters, make sure the ground you are lying on is lined with palm branches interwoven for springiness and protection, or use bamboo with softer branches laid over the top to raise you even higher.

HOME SWEET HOME: SHELTERS BUILT TO LAST

A-FRAME POLE BED

The A-frame can be constructed quickly, but can also easily be adapted into a longer-term shelter. Lash together two poles into an upside-down V-shape. This, when placed on the ground with the pointy side up, makes one end of your frame. Then lash two more identical poles together to make the other end of your structure. Lash another pole between the upside-down Vs, joining the apex of each. Next create a sleeping platform by weaving a strong mesh webbing of plant material (bark and vines) between two more poles, like a hospital stretcher. When this is ready, lash each end halfway up the A-frames so the platform effectively supplies the missing cross-bar of the A.

A tarp can then be draped over the resulting structure to make both sides of a roof to protect against the rain. Alternatively lean branches against the A-frame and interlace as before with leaves.

TIP: Let the poles of the sleeping platform stick out beyond the frames at either end. These can then be used to hang your clothes or boots clear of the ground at night or as supports for a small table.

LEAN-TO

Lash a length of wood at shoulder height to a tree and let the other end lie on the ground. Six feet away on another tree, lash a second length parallel to the first. Between these two, place a cross-bar linking them together. Interlace smaller lengths of wood across and between the two main lean-to struts. Drape leaves, the biggest you can find, on top of this framework.

A raised bed can be made by laying bamboo or wood across the inside of the shelter and lining with softer palm or leaves. As with all lean-to constructions, this type of shelter works well with a heat reflector and a long-log fire (see Chapter 1, pages 22–28).

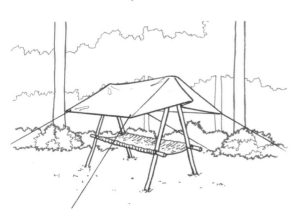

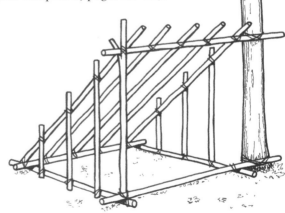

I have often used this type of shelter in the jungle and it is in my view the easiest type to construct. You can make it a temporary construction or a much more elaborate version. Either way, it is simple, and in the world of survival, simple wins every time. Remember KISS: Keep it simple, stupid!

TIP: If you have a ready source of bamboo, you can make a very effective roof by splitting the poles in half (longways) and linking them together curved side up and then curved side down like connecting roof tiles. This will create a natural guttering effect and the rain will run off easily.

JUNGLE SHELTER WISDOM

- Remove a layer of clothes before you start work. If it is humid or wet, this will mean you have something dry to wear when you are finished. (Although I had one experience in the jungle when it rained so much I had nothing dry and no spare clothes. After a few days I began to get quite bad sores, despite trying to dry out each night with my fire.) So, if you can, keep some articles of clothing dry as much for morale as health. (Soldiers are taught to keep their set of dry clothes dry at all costs, and always well waterproofed. These then get put on when their shelters are built and they are holed up for the night. Each morning you then climb into your wet kit and start the day again.)

- Keep some extra building materials for repairs and additions – for example a pile of roofing leaves – close to hand.

- Always check carefully for insects and snakes before you start work and never sleep directly on the jungle floor. If you haven't time to construct a raised bed, make sure you lay down some bamboo or branches which you can cover with moss or leaves for comfort.

- Ensure the jungle floor under you is dry and future water runoff will be directed away from your shelter.

- Avoid being close to animal tracks that may lead to frequently used watering holes.

- Look up. Make sure nothing in the forest canopy, from a dead branch to unwelcome slithery wildlife, will fall on you.

- Keep a fire smoldering at night by burning moss or other slow-burning materials on the embers of your fire. Keep a good supply of dead wood nearby.

- Termite mounds are perfect for burning at night. These saved my skin in the jungle when I had no mosquito net. Despite the fact that you are effectively burning termite crap, they burn for a long time and help keep biting insects at bay.

- Extend your shelter out over your fire. Your fire and tinder will need protecting from the rain as well. This is often overlooked, until you try to get a fire going in a thunderstorm!

- An effective way of tying vine or cord round a sheet or tarpaulin to stop it slipping is to wrap a small stone in the sheet first, then tie the cord around the stone. This stops the sheet slipping through your knot.

- The best dead wood to collect – as well as for making your tinder shavings – is found hanging from branches and bushes just off the ground. This will be drier than the damp wood on the jungle floor.

- Finally, unlike the sub-zero or desert terrains, one of the great things about the jungle is that the long twelve-hour nights mean as long as you have built your shelter correctly, you will at least get enough sleep. Make this work to your advantage: do the job well and enjoy the rest!

Finding Water

Whatever the season, rain and high humidity will be constant adversaries in the jungle. Torrential rain may ambush you at any time, and when the skies finally clear, a storm of sweat will be breaking out all over your body from the high humidity. Days typically have an 80 percent humidity count and during the night this can rise to 95 percent. It's not unusual for it to rain like clockwork at a set time each day, often at dusk, and often for a similar length of time. Learn to anticipate the local weather patterns, and travel or build shelters accordingly.

Your problem in the jungle will not so much be finding water, as getting it in a form that is useful to you. Life forms breed at a colossal speed in this environment, including all the toxins, viruses, cysts, bacteria, and parasites that play havoc with your guts. So just because there's lots of water around, don't fall into a false sense of security. The rule in the jungle is to assume that water is contaminated unless it is fresh rainwater or comes from a plant or tree that you have positively identified.

SIGNS OF WATER

Rivers and rainwater will be the main sources of water in the jungle, but they can't always be relied upon. Seasonal and geographical variations, and the type of jungle terrain you find yourself in, may mean that rain does not fall for several days or even weeks, and it could well be days before you find a running river or even a dried-up stream.

If this is the case, you will need to follow nature's signs. Remember, you are not the only one looking for water. In fact the whole ecosystem around you, from the largest trees to the smallest insects, will be doing precisely this, so use your eyes to see what your competitors are up to and the clues will be readily apparent.

Or alternatively just head downhill; you will eventually find a stream.

ANIMALS AND BIRDS

Animals and birds need regular supplies of water just as we do, so observing their movements in the morning or evening, when they generally like to drink, can often indicate where water is located. If you can't actively see or follow animals through the dense undergrowth, follow their trails and these will often lead to water. You will have an even better chance if you find two or more trails that converge.

INSECTS

All the flying, crawling, and creeping creatures of the jungle will have a source of water somewhere nearby that they use, so watch for ants marching up trees to a damp crevice, bees disappearing into a hole in a tree (make sure it's nowhere near their nest), or flies swarming. They will often lead in a promising direction.

Assume that water is contaminated unless it is fresh rainwater or comes from a plant or tree that you have positively identified

SOURCES OF WATER: RAINWATER TRAPS

TARPAULIN

Collecting rainwater is by far the easiest, quickest, and usually the purest way of attaining drinking water in the jungle. If you have a tarpaulin, tie it between trees so it makes a bowl shape, and large amounts can be trapped within a few minutes of a downpour that can be drained off into your water bottle or mug. If you are short of containers, with a bit of imagination, big leaves can easily be twisted into drinking vessels to store extra water for the night. Generally rainwater will be drinkable without purification.

TROPICAL LEAVES

Larger jungle leaves can be twisted into funnels that will guide water into containers. The more funnels you leave out, the more water you will be able to collect.

WATER HOLES

Ground where water has obviously been present in the past usually has water not far beneath the surface. When you find a spot that looks promising, dig down until the ground becomes damp or even wet and leave overnight so the water seeps in. Water collected in this way should be filtered and purified by boiling. If it is too wet to start a fire and boil the water, try straining through a sock laced with charcoal from a previous fire.

EVAPORATION STILL

An "evaporation" trap (see pages 78 and 202) can collect small quantities of water "breathed" out by the leaves of tropical plants.

SOURCES OF WATER: PLANTS

The foliage around you in the jungle, like every other living thing, including yourself, is largely made of water. Plants and trees can be a very useful source of water when the rains have temporarily dried up.

VINES

Many types of vine hold water, but caution is needed in deciding which are a good source and which are not. Vines have a capillary action which sucks water from the roots up into the climbing tips of the plant as it strains upwards towards the light. By making cuts at the top and bottom of the vine, the fluid in the capillaries is released. The greatest amount of water will be found in the heat of the day when the most fluid is needed at the growing end.

First make a deep cut near the top of the vine. Then chop it through completely at the bottom near the roots. This effectively cuts off the capillary action that sucks the water upwards and allows the downward pull of gravity to take over. Hold the vine above your mouth and, once you've made sure that the fluid released is pure and clear, let it drip into your mouth.

Make sure the vine doesn't come into contact with your mouth, as some can cause a skin irritation on contact. When the supply of water dries up, make another cut 2 inches or so up from the higher cut and proceed as before. Beware: if the sap is red, yellow, has a sticky, milky appearance, or tastes bitter, discard it at once. In the jungle I have often drunk from vines while on the move. I knew it was safe water, and it was easy to find, allowing me to keep hydrated as I kept walking.

Many types of vine hold water, but caution is needed in deciding which are a good source and which are not

BANANA, PLANTAIN, AND FIG

All of these are excellent sources of fluid. Banana and plantain can be tapped by cutting down the plant and making a hollow in the stump which will fill with water from the roots. You may want to discard the first few bowls as the water can be bitter, but the quality will improve and the stump can supply water for up to four days. Remember to keep the stump covered as insects will be on the prowl. Fig trees – which can supply literally gallons of fluid – need to be cut into and tapped with a tube. Thin tubes of bamboo do the job nicely.

BAMBOO

Bamboo, particularly large, old specimens which have mellowed from green to yellow, are often filled with water. Shake them or bang them and if you hear sloshing water, bore holes section by section to get at the fluids. You can also remove individual sections and carry them with you as you go.

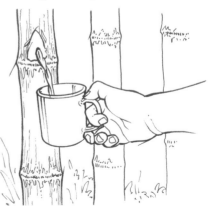

PITCHER PLANT

Southeast Asian jungles are known for their pitcher plants, whose leaves, often mistaken for flowers, form a natural jug shape that collects rainwater. The purpose of the leaves, as far as the plant is concerned, is to collect nutrients, including insects, so watch out for dead creepy-crawlies and boil the water.

ROOTS

When water is harder to find, remember that roots are the water reservoirs of all plant and tree life, so are always a good source of fluid, although it is more difficult to extract. Smash the roots into a pulp and collect the moisture. The stems of many plants also have water, so mash and drain in the same way.

ELEPHANT DUNG

Elephant dung is mostly still plant material, albeit semi-digested! In the jungle savannahs of Africa, or indeed places like the forests of Uganda, where there are still elephants that live in deep jungle, elephant dung can be a very useful water source. While in Kenya, I regularly drank the fluid squeezed from fresh elephant dung. Elephants have a very inefficient digestive system, and their dung, when fresh, is sterile enough to squeeze as a means of finding water. In very arid regions the dung can be quite dry, but often it is moist enough to squeeze the fluid from to drink. It might not taste that great, but elephant excrement can save your life. I found holding my nose helped it go down!

SOURCES OF WATER: TREES

PALMS

The buri and nipa palms contain a milky, sugary fluid that is good to drink. The secret is to cut a flowering stalk near the tip and bend it downwards so the juice drains out. This can be repeated twice a day; it's possible to collect as much as a quart in twenty-four hours. Depending on the tree, the flowering stalk may be at ground level or require some climbing to reach.

Coconuts are an excellent and tasty source of fluid and nutrients. Be careful to drink from green (unripe) coconuts as milk from the ripe nuts is a laxative, the effects of which will dehydrate you further and be counterproductive.

BAOBAB TREE

This distinctive tree is found on the sandy plains of northern Australia and Africa and collects water in its bottlelike trunk during the wet season. You can sometimes find clear, fresh water in these trees after weeks of dry weather.

PURIFICATION AND FILTRATION

Treat all water sources in the jungle with suspicion. Diarrhea is hard to avoid in the jungle however careful you are, as I found to my cost while in the Costa Rican rainforest. Despite being pretty careful about the water, I still got it badly and it wiped me out for twenty-four hours. You know it is bad when you get to the stage of not even having the strength to move when you have to go again! So always be scrupulous about where you drink from.

Boil water for at least ten minutes if there is any doubt in your mind about the source. This will kill virtually all known bugs.

To get at these unripe coconuts, my own nuts suffered!

Water can also be partially purified by letting it stand for twenty-four hours in sunlight. This will allow particulate matter to sink, while some bacteria will be killed by the ultraviolet in the sunlight. The purified water can then be poured through a filtration system which can be rigged up using any densely woven material like a T-shirt.

For an even more effective filtration technique, build a tripod structure from sticks and create platforms at three different levels. Layer the first platform with moss, the second with sand, and the third with charcoal from a fire. Pour water from above so it drips through each layer to a container below. Remember that while this can remove debris, improve taste, and reduce smell, it does not kill micro-organisms. Boiling is always the best and safest way without proper chemicals like chlorine or iodine.

Finding Food

Starving in a jungle should be no easy task, but it happens. I recently heard of an Amazonian tribe who discovered the bodies of several pilots of a plane that had crash-landed in the Amazon. It was discovered that they had lived off their own dwindling supply of rations on a small sandbank in the river. When these ran out, they resorted, in death-gripped desperation, to drinking aviation fuel and eating the seat cushioning. They were found dead, with an abundance of food and fresh water all around them – if only they had known where to look.

Food in a jungle should be a plentiful commodity. However, while hunting animals like rodents, birds, and monkeys for meat is routine procedure for many indigenous tribes, this should not be your first thought. They will be difficult to catch, and you will expend a lot of energy and time making snares and traps (see Chapter 1, pages 45–48) which would be better used seeking out more readily available sources of food, namely plants.

Animals will be difficult to catch and you will expend a lot of energy and time making snares and traps

While plants alone will not provide a balanced diet of proteins and carbohydrates, they will sustain you well in the short term. As we saw in the chapter on mountain terrain, most fruits, nuts, seeds, roots, leaves, and stems are extremely nutritious and there is an almost infinite number to choose from. Most can be harvested from the ground without the danger and difficulty of climbing tall trees or trying to cut them down, but be careful to scrape away rotting matter and insects.

Identification is the key, so if food stocks are getting low and you have no other choice, use the food safety test opposite. But always remember it doesn't work for mushrooms, which should be avoided. (The reason for this is that some deadly toxins from fungi do not take effect for up to forty-eight hours.)

In primary rainforest, most of the fruits will be high in the canopy, but some grow lower down or will have fallen in plentiful numbers, out of reach of the monkeys. The best places to forage are the banks of streams and rivers, which will be the most accessible areas. If you are picking fruit straight from a tree, don't pick more than you need. Food spoils rapidly in tropical conditions and is best left on the plant until you need it and it can be eaten fresh.

Unless you can positively identify lesser-known plants, it will be safer at first to begin with palms, bamboos, and common fruits. Watch out to see what other creatures of the forest, like the monkeys, are eating. Their food will not automatically be fine for you to eat, but most is – if in doubt, try the safety test on it.

PALMS

BANANAS AND PLANTAINS

These plants, which as we saw are also a good source of water, grow all over the tropics, reaching up to 30 feet tall. The fruits, buds, young stems, and inner parts are all edible.

RATTAN PALMS

These palms look more like vines and can be cut and hauled down to ground level. Remove the outer covering of the end stems and cut into lengths which can then be roasted.

BREADFRUITS

These are sometimes grown as domestic houseplants. The fruit is rich in starch and is edible raw after the skin has been removed.

BAMBOOS

New shoots are nutritious (ask any panda) but can only be digested properly when boiled.

FRUITS AND BERRIES

In tropical regions, the temperature remains fairly constant throughout the year, so fruits and berries are abundant. If in doubt, try the safety test below.

FIGS

Large numbers of varieties grow throughout many tropical and subtropical forests. They are straggly trees with aerial roots and leathery evergreen leaves rounded at the base. The pear-shaped fruits are edible raw.

Do not underestimate the value of the trees around you.

PALMS

Most parts of palm trees are edible, including the fruit, flowers, buds, and trunk meat, but cooking will almost always improve the taste. In the jungles of Costa Rica I often ate the soft center of Panama hat palms. The meat of a coconut is safe to eat as well, whether it comes from a green, unripe nut or a mature one.

FOOD SAFETY TEST

Jungles are often referred to as the "the world's pharmacy," but alongside substances that can relieve pain, heal infections, ease rheumatism, and cure diarrhea and stomach upsets, there are an equal number that can kill. The fruit of the manzanilla de la playa tree, which looks as if it would taste delicious, is in fact deadly

If you know where to look, you will always be able to find food in the jungle.

poisonous and the Indians use it to kill fish. Even the fire smoke from the wood is toxic and the sap will irritate the skin.

This is why you should never eat any kind of food unless you have made a positive identification. Safety testing an unknown jungle food is pointless (and potentially dangerous) unless done carefully and methodically. It takes time—up to thirty-six hours—as at each stage it is vital to discover whether or not any harmful substance has caused a reaction.

Always choose a potential food source which is available in large quantities and that you might be able to use as a staple, as there will be little point in discovering that an obscure fruit is edible if your chances of finding another source are small.

Break the plant down into constituent parts (fruit, stem, root, etc.) and test one piece at a time. Keep some hot drinking water close by to flush things through if a poisonous reaction takes place. Charcoal from your campfire is a powerful emetic if at any time you feel you have been poisoned. Swallow some and it will help you vomit the poison back up. White wood ash mixed to a paste can also relieve a stomach ache.

Don't try to eat or drink anything with a milky sap or that is diseased or old.

Charcoal from your campfire is a powerful emetic if you feel you have been poisoned. Swallow some and it will help you vomit the poison back up

SEVEN STEPS TO SAFE FOOD:

- Smell the plant part first, and if it smells bitter or of almonds or peaches, discard. For example, the strychnine tree, with its orange-like fruits, grows in the tropics. Avoid it.
- Crush the plant and smear the sappy oil onto the back of your wrist where your skin is tender. If any rash occurs or pain is felt, discard immediately.
- If all is well, do the same with a small amount of sap on the inside of your lips and gums. Leave for five minutes and again discard if there is any adverse effect.
- Next chew a very small amount of the plant and swallow the resulting liquid, but spit out the pulp. Wait eight hours and make sure you don't eat or drink anything else, as this will invalidate the test.
- If all is well, do the same with a larger amount and wait five hours.
- Finally, eat a handful of the plant and wait twenty-four hours.
- If all is still OK, the plant is safe to eat.

INSECTS

PALM GRUBS

These large white grubs with bloated bodies – a bit like giant maggots – can be found in the rotten bark of fallen sago and other palm types and are a delicacy for many indigenous peoples. I will never forget the first time I bit into one – oozing pus, it was the size of a small apple! To extract the grubs, cut into soft palm  wood and eat either raw or cooked. They are highly nutritious and are easily digested and

a great source of protein. Once you've eaten, take some for bait as well.

TERMITES

Weight for weight, termites are a better source of nutrition than vegetables, and a better source of protein and fat than beef or fish. They taste a bit like nutmeg, so don't pass up a termite mound if you're lucky enough to stumble upon one. I sat down once for an hour in the Costa Rican jungle and quietly ate hundreds of these as they poured out of the nest. They are so small you don't feel disgusted eating them like you do with the grubs!

FISHING

Fish can be a welcome change from a vegetarian diet, and many of the techniques for catching them are the same as those noted in the chapter on mountain terrain (see pages 83–85).

The way I have caught fish in the jungle is to lash my knife to a length of wood, make a burning torch with bark fibers soaked in the flammable resin from a meranti tree, then try to spear sleeping fish by night. In the shallows of rivers, crayfish and other fish lie facing upstream, resting. With a flaming torch to spot them lying just under the surface of 10-inch-deep shallows, you can strike them hard on the head with a blade and they will then float to the surface dead. A machete is best for this as the blade enters the water very fast, but I have managed to catch fish and crayfish like this.

One time I lost the fish after I had killed it, when I dropped it in the fast-flowing water and my torch flame died. Such is life. The crayfish I caught simply with my hands, bringing my fingers behind them from downstream and pinching them very fast. They tasted great!

Jungle navigation is a challenge. The thickness of the vegetation in general means that in the absence of distinctive landmarks, orientation is often difficult. Movement forward can be slow and laborious, while traveling in a straight line is often impossible. The thickness of the jungle canopy also means that because the stars are obscured for much of the time, using them to navigate (see Chapter 1, pages 34–37) is impractical.

So what can you do? As ever, it's the attitude you take to these problems which is most likely to offer up a solution. First of all, try to see the jungle as a friend with some annoying habits, rather than an enemy who is actively out to get you. As in all other wilderness terrain, think before you act. A water source and a shelter are far more important than moving immediately.

When you do decide to move, don't rush. The jungle has many ways of slowing you down, and the harder you push, the harder it tends to push back. After all, the myriad forms of life around you are involved in a slow-motion struggle for survival themselves. Plants and trees climb on one another in their relentless quest for light, strangling each other in the process.

To climb thus, evolution has equipped them with a working laboratory of thorns, hooks, anchors, and suckers that are just as happy to ensnare you as the competitor next door. Don't help them by stumbling into their defense mechanisms with great force. Your skin is your largest organ and, in the jungle, by far your most vulnerable. If the insects don't get to it, the undergrowth will. So protect it at all costs.

On my first forays into the jungle I ended up on numerous occasions doing battle with one small vine or root that had snared my foot, stopping me dead. I would yank and pull and try to rip my way through. The vines always held on tighter. One little vine or root is not worth a pitched battle over. Learn to conserve your energy in the jungle – you will need it all.

In the first instance, you must try to come to terms with the fact that few other wilderness environments are as disorienting as a tropical jungle. The first thing you should do is find yourself a stick both to support yourself and probe the way ahead. Learn to walk a bit like a blind man, gently moving the stick in front of you at ground level. This alerts resting snakes to your presence, and it is much better they strike the stick rather than your foot. Always move with this stick where you can, especially in dense undergrowth. Better safe than sorry.

Your skin is your largest organ and, in the jungle, by far your most vulnerable. If the insects don't get to it, the undergrowth will. So protect it at all costs

Also, always walk with a heavy footfall. This is the opposite of what soldiers are taught, but in the jungle it might save your life. Snakes work on vibrations: give them plenty of warning to move away from you. And you should always travel by day. Jungles at night are not only dangerous places where snakes and wild animals are on the move and hunting, but in such pitch-black darkness it is almost impossible to move

Vines can contain an ample supply of fresh water.

However, not every dip in the landscape leads to a stream or river, and the downside to this strategy is that you may find yourself in a deep valley and having to climb all the way out again. So, where possible, follow ridges or hill contours first, which will give you some height to see natural features and to spot a river course or a trail that might lead to safety.

One of the most remarkable stories of jungle survival illustrates this point precisely. On Christmas Eve 1971, a German teenager called Juliane Koepcke was flying across the Peruvian Amazon in a small plane with her mother en route to see her father for Christmas. During a freak electric storm, the wing caught fire and she awoke three hours later on the jungle floor still strapped into her seat. Of the ninety-two people on board, Koepcke was the sole survivor.

Although in shock and with a broken collarbone and no vision in one eye, she remembered her father's advice: *head downhill to a river, as a river will lead to civilization.* After eleven days in the jungle she was rescued by a group of Peruvian hunters. She survived with only a torn miniskirt, one sandal, and a big heart.

I copied her pattern while in a Central American jungle. After climbing a high tree to get the lay of the land, I then proceeded downhill towards where I had seen a large depression in the jungle trees that I suspected might signal a river. This river eventually led me out to the sea. In the jungle, rivers play the same role as roads in civilization – following one will normally lead you to a center of human activity. Think smart, get a view, make a plan, go for it!

effectively. You will only get lost, disoriented, and probably injured.

From first impressions, there may be very few clues indicating the most promising direction to travel. If this is the case, follow the line of least resistance in a downhill direction. The principle behind this is to descend until you find a stream. Streams will lead downhill to rivers, and all rivers will eventually lead to human habitation.

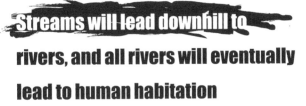

Streams will lead downhill to rivers, and all rivers will eventually lead to human habitation

LOOKING, SEEING, AND MOVING

Traveling through jungle terrain requires a sixth sense. The way you "see" the jungle will help or hinder you hugely. If you concentrate too much on the obstacles immediately in front of you, you will not be able to see the bigger picture; to see the proverbial "forest for the trees." The secret is to try to look *through* the undergrowth ahead and not straight at it. This will allow you to develop a sense of the contours of the land and the relative density of the undergrowth ahead of you. With this sort of lateral vision, you are also far more likely to spot animal trails that you can then follow.

Your body movements should be more like a slow-motion dancer than a bull in a china shop. Blundering through like a drunken legionnaire will leave you with cuts and gashes that will rapidly turn septic. Drop your shoulders, swivel your hips, bend your body, and shorten or lengthen your stride as necessary to slide through the undergrowth. It's perhaps hardly surprising that a snake's natural habitat is the jungle. Their slow, silent, slinky ways are nature's perfect example of how to make progress through this kind of environment.

Some days it feels as if all of nature is out to snare you — that's life though — just keep going.

Always wear long sleeves to avoid cuts and scratches. Your movements should be slow but firm. Do not slash indiscriminately ahead with your knife and stick, as you will end up exhausting yourself without having achieved very much. Try to be efficient in your movements. Don't use your bare hands to clutch at undergrowth or you will end up being stung or cut very quickly. Try to regulate your temperature and maintain a steady pace, resting up during the heat of the day. Constantly attend to your hands and feet, guarding against blisters and sores. Take responsibility for yourself and your own well-being.

OBSTACLES

THICK VEGETATION

Jungles tend to be split into primary jungle and secondary. Secondary jungle is the nightmare! It is the thickest type of jungle, formed where primary jungle has originally been cleared, maybe by nature in a landslide or fire, maybe by logging or for farmland. Whatever the original cause, suddenly now the sunlight can reach the jungle floor, and within a few years the undergrowth, weeds, roots, vines, and thorns have gone berserk – it is party time! With so much sunlight the jungle grows like wildfire.

It is hard to describe to someone what it can be like to fight your way through secondary jungle, but try to imagine the thickest, thorniest bush you have ever seen, then imagine hundreds of miles of such bush, full of snakes and mosquitoes. Such vegetation is almost impossible to move through – if your route turns into thicker secondary jungle, or an animal track leads you into it, retreat out, and get back into primary jungle that is less dense, so you can at least move somewhere.

Whether primary or secondary jungle, at first sight all jungles seem to be one long, seemingly unending obstacle course. The trick is to treat each and every obstacle as it comes and to have the patience to go around them and not over, under, or through them. You should always try to circumnavigate very dense vegetation, as well as swamps, lakes, and bogs.

Trying to hack through most types of jungle is extremely tiring. Even if traveling relatively quickly, you are unlikely to cover more than 3 miles a day, so keep your eyes peeled for trails and rivers that can speed up your progress.

BOGS, MARSHES, SWAMPS, AND QUICKSAND

All these obstacles are found near rivers and coastlines and anywhere where water mixes with the edge of the jungle. They are a strength-sapping mix of water, mud, vegetation, and sand. As well as posing a navigational hazard, they also pose a threat to life and limb as this is where crocodiles like to call home. Always go around them when you can and avoid getting wet unnecessarily.

If you do have to cross them, use whatever branches, logs, and foliage you can find to spread your weight. If you find yourself sinking, try to get in as horizontal a position as possible and swim breaststroke towards the nearest firm ground.

Don't use your bare hands to clutch at undergrowth or you will end up being stung or cut very quickly

I have spent many miserable hours wading through mangrove swamps in the jungle, trying to find a short cut towards the coast. It is hard, hard work. I ended up retreating. Think very carefully before trying to do battle with swamps. I saw many crocs, was up to my shoulders in gunk, and lost my sense of humor very quickly! Come up with a better plan. If you are stranded in a swamp, sleep above the water, among the tangled roots and vines.

RIVERS

Rivers can be either an obstacle or an opportunity, depending on whether you want to cross them or travel down them. In jungle terrain, rivers are often the quickest way to move as well as being a surefire navigational tool in that they will eventually lead to the sea. Rivers have been used for millennia as the primary source of travel, so it's not for nothing they are known as the "highways of the jungle."

CONSTRUCTING A RAFT

If you do decide to travel downstream, your options will be either to walk beside the river – which will be slow progress and require constant detours to avoid swamps and bogs – or you will need to build yourself a raft or boat. One of the advantages of being in a jungle is that the materials needed to keep you afloat are readily available all around you: bamboo (the perfect raft-making material), balsa, vines for lashing, leaves for sitting on, and branches for oars.

Constructing some sort of boat or canoe may be the first idea to spring to mind, but like igloos in the Arctic they are more difficult to make than first meets the eye and are best left to the experts. A raft, on the other hand, will have a greater surface area and is far less likely to capsize.

I've always enjoyed a spot of boating!

TYPES OF RAFT

The design of your raft will depend on the materials you have available. Don't waste energy dragging heavy logs through the forest. Search along the riverbank to find materials

BALSA RAFT

I have made rafts in the jungle out of balsa, and it's a great wood to use as it floats very well but is very light to move around, cut, and work with. The bark from the balsa tree also peels off easily in strips and makes very strong lashings.

Find and cut down around six neck-thick trunks about 10 feet in length and lay them on the ground side by side. Then find two thinner trunks and lay them at 90 degrees to the main structure, across each end. Then lash the main structure to these two cross-struts using as rope the bark of the trunks you have cut down.

BAMBOO RAFT

Bamboo's combination of flexibility, strength, and hollowness makes for another excellent raft-building material. The building technique is simple. Select the biggest bamboos you can find and cut them down. Then chop them at a point before they start to thin towards the top (10–11 feet long

Trying to escape a camera crew.

you can use and make sure they float well before you start to construct the raft. If you have a tarpaulin, you can wrap this around the logs for added air and flotation. Otherwise naturally occurring jungle materials should be enough.

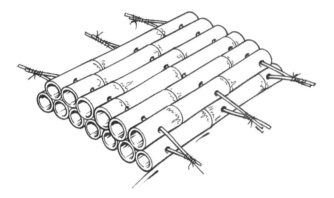

is perfect). Collect enough so that when laid out next to each other on the ground, they make a wide enough platform to carry you comfortably down the river. Next, use your knife or anything sharp to drill holes big enough for a vine to be pushed through at both ends of each individual bamboo with a third hole halfway along. Make sure that the holes are all lined up with each other when the bamboos are laid out side by side. Then push thick vines through the holes from one side of the raft to the other, lashing the bamboos together. You will need at least two layers of thick bamboo to be confident the raft is sturdy enough.

LOG/ARMCHAIR RAFT

This is one of the simplest – and most effective – flotation devices there is. Select two branches or the trunks of young trees. These should be as straight as possible and at least 18 inches thick. Lash them together with vines at both ends but leave about 2 feet of slack vine between them. Either cover this area with a tarp or sit

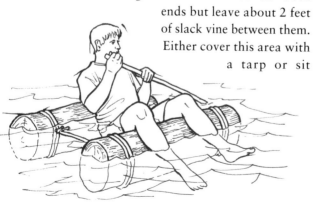

directly between the two trunks in armchair style and get ready to float downstream. A long straight pole can be used as an oar – either to pole along or to use like a canoe paddle.

RAFTING SKILLS

The best way to steer a raft is to equip it with a tiller. Start with an A-frame and attach this to the back of your raft. Then lash a long pole from the top of the A-frame down into the water. The movement of this pole will steer your raft. Wherever possible, drift downstream, but if the water is particularly still and shallow, use a pole to propel yourself, but don't use this in fast-running water, as it may yank you off the raft. Use a paddle in deeper water and try to remember the following top tips:

- Test your raft in the shallows first.
- Make sure it's sturdy. Sinking or breaking up is bad news. Tie more lengths of vine or bark than you think you might need, and tie one length around all the lashings as well, to tighten them and hold them in place.
- Attach yourself to the raft with a rope and bowline (see page 42). Do the same for your paddle.
- Don't leave anything dragging off the back.
- Stay near the inside edge on river bends, where the speed of the river will be less.
- Keep as near to the banks as you can, in case of emergency.
- Always listen out for the sound of rapids, waterfalls, and white water. Steer to the bank at once if a major hazard is suspected.
- Don't raft at night.
- Never run a rapid – if the raft gets turned over, you may end up crushed underneath it. If it is your only option, let the raft go through alone, and skirt round the rapid on foot to rejoin it.

CROSSING RIVERS

Rivers can be deceptively shallow but then turn deep, or slow with fast-moving undercurrents, as well as wide with narrow gorges round the next bend. Be ultra careful with big rivers, have a fallback plan in case you need a quick way out, and prepare for the river journey carefully by waterproofing your kit if possible and building effective equipment.

Before you even try to cross a river or stream, study it carefully. Estimate the speed and depth by looking at the surface and observing a stick thrown into the current. A high vantage point will help enormously. From here, you can look for the best place to cross and see possible obstructions.

Obstructions like rocks or fallen tree trunks will leave eddies and waves on the surface. Half-submerged tree trunks can cause "strainers." These are obstacles that allow the water to flow through – but not you. You will be pinned against them, and the force of the water will crush you. Keep well clear of these and look out for any debris being swept along by the river. When crossing, be very careful that you don't lose your footing upstream of a submerged object, as it is easy to become pinned against it or for your ankle to be trapped between boulders. Never underestimate the force of the current.

In the jungle, the water is usually murky and quite unlike the crystal-clear streams of the mountains. Mud and silt can be very dangerous if you sink into them. Take your trousers and socks off – you will be thankful for some dry clothes later and there will be less drag – and make sure your most important survival implements, like fire-lighting equipment, are kept as dry as possible. If you have any plastic bags or other waterproof materials, wrap them around your equipment and use it as a float. Keep your boots on to negotiate rocky riverbeds and protect your feet. If you are wet already, remove your trousers and use them as a makeshift flotation lifejacket, with the ankles tied and air trapped in the legs.

Make sure you use a pole for support as you go. This is called the tripod technique because between your two legs and the pole you always have two points of contact with the riverbed at any one time. The trick is to move sideways, facing upstream so you can see any debris that may be swept downstream towards you. Beware of shallow water, which can sometimes be more dangerous and rapid than deeper water.

To swim across a deep, swift river, swim downstream with the current at an angle; never fight it. Try to keep your body horizontal to the water. This will reduce the danger of being pulled under.

In fast, shallow rapids, lie on your back, feet pointing downstream, finning your hands alongside your hips. This action will increase buoyancy and help you steer away from obstacles. Keep your feet up to fend off any rocks and to avoid getting them caught by submerged trees or roots. Avoid crossing near eddies, which occur downstream of an obstacle like a boulder, where the force of the water going over and around the obstruction causes a suck-back effect that can easily pull you under. Even if the water is warm, build a fire and dry off quickly on the other side.

Crossing rivers in the wild is risky – take time to study the currents first and avoid the rapids

Natural Hazards

Jungles can be very uncomfortable. Conditions are frequently wet, humid, and fetid. If you are alone and lost, unfamiliar jungle sounds can be intimidating. You will be sharing your newly acquired home with more living creatures than anywhere else on the planet. Stinging and biting creatures, from ants, bees, and mosquitoes to centipedes and scorpions, will assault you from all sides, not to mention the bot fly eggs that can incubate and hatch under your skin.

And then there are snakes. Despite the fact that most snakes are not venomous and most will steer well clear of man, the fear of the creatures themselves can have a powerful effect on your sense of well-being. Hardly surprisingly, a sense of paranoia can easily set in. This paranoia, though, is simply due to a lack of knowledge. Snakes are generally very shy, and jungles are only scary because they are alien to the newcomer.

The truth is that the jungle is an eminently survivable environment. If you are aware of the threats and hazards of the jungle from the outset, you will have an excellent chance of survival. Most of the immediate threats to your well-being will be mental, not physical.

Small wounds, often caused by bites and stings, are the greatest long-term threat to your health, and prevention is far easier than cure. Death by a thousand cuts is far more likely than starvation, dehydration, or attacks from wild animals. So keep yourself covered at all times to minimize the assault on your skin. Jungles are fertile places and life grows everywhere. Your skin can quickly become host to the bacteria, fungi, and microbes that cause irritations and rashes. Keeping these at bay before they degenerate into infection will be half the battle. In the tropics, even the smallest scratch can quickly become dangerously infected.

INSECTS: WHEN SMALL IS NOT SO BEAUTIFUL

Very few insects have a toxic enough bite or sting to kill a healthy adult, but the long-term effects from parasites, infections, blood poisoning, and allergic reactions can be unpleasant, and potentially life-threatening. Prevention, therefore, is the key.

Death by a thousand cuts is far more likely than starvation, dehydration, or attacks from wild animals

CLOTHING

While various prophylactics, from pure DEET to citronella, will have varying degrees of success at keeping the insect hordes at bay, over time your sweat (owing to its body salts) will be a far more potent attracting agent than any chemical deterrent. So keep your skin covered both day and night. Remember to tuck your trousers in your socks and do your cuffs up tight, as insects will easily find your weakest line of defense, and don't forget to strip at least once a day to check for leeches and ticks (see page 180).

MAKING A HEAD NET

Some sort of head net can be a life-saver. Any form of clothing material will do, providing it is big enough to fit loosely over your head. First find some foliage or bark to provide a platform on top of your head so that the material flops around your face and is not in direct contact with your skin. Make some slits so you can see out. Tuck the material into your collar and you will now be well protected.

KEEPING THE CRITTERS AT BAY

- Always shake your clothes and boots out before you put them on. Any number of creatures may have used them as a nest. Make this "checking of boots" a habit.
- Smear unprotected skin in oil, mud, or fat. Smelly and unpleasant, but better than being bitten to death.
- Coconut oil (scratch the kernel with a knife, lay out in the sun, and the oil will collect on the surface) is a potent insect repellent. It can also help protect your skin against saltwater rashes.
- Use smoke from your fire to keep insects at bay and use the ash to spread a magic circle around your shelter. This will deter ground insects.
- The material from termite mounds (it looks like dried mud, but is actually digested wood) produces a smoke that burns all night and will keep biting insects at bay.
- Resist the temptation to scratch an insect bite. It might provide temporary relief from the itch, but the resulting wound could be serious.
- For itch relief, use a cold compress or a cooling paste of thick mud and ashes.

SNAKES

Most people are afraid of snakes; I certainly was until I became a bit more used to them and understood them a little better. This is the key to snakes: replacing the irrational fear with an understanding of how they operate.

More people are killed by falling coconuts than snakebites in much of the tropics, and while snakes may not be the cuddliest creatures on earth, they will on the whole try to avoid humans as long as they hear you coming. Exceptions to the rule include the king cobra of Southeast Asia; the bushmaster, fer-de-lance, and tropical rattlesnake of South and Central America; and the mamba of Africa, which have sometimes been known to attack man aggressively.

The chances of being bitten by a snake are smaller than you think, and if you are bitten, the chances are better than 50 percent that it will not be poisonous. And if it is poisonous, there is also a 25 percent chance that it won't have injected you with its poison (known as a "dry" bite). Snakes will only inject venom into a human as a last resort, as humans are not prey.

As a general rule, they like to find warm places when it's cold and cooler places when it's hot. Most species are also nocturnal hunters, another good reason not to travel after dark.

More people are killed by falling coconuts than snakebites in much of the tropics

TYPES OF POISONOUS SNAKE

Poisonous snakes have specialized glands that contain toxic venom and long hollow fangs to inject it. Most fall into two categories that can be distinguished by their fangs.

Those with fixed fangs (i.e., fangs that are permanently erect at the front of the upper jaw) are normally neurotoxic, which means their poison attacks the central nervous system, which can paralyze the lungs and suffocate the victim. This type is called proteroglypha.

The other type has folding fangs (i.e., fangs that usually lie flat but are raised in attack). These snakes have hemotoxins, which poison the blood and affect the circulatory system, destroying blood cells, damaging skin tissues, and causing internal hemorrhaging. This type is called solenoglypha.

In fact, most poisonous snakes have both neurotoxins and hemotoxins in their venom, although one is usually dominant. They also have digestive enzymes called cytotoxins which attack skin tissue and cause necrosis.

Basically toxin bites are bad news! So avoid getting bitten.

AVOIDING SNAKES

- Don't sleep next to brush, tall grass, large boulders, or large roots of trees. All these are great hiding places for snakes.
- Again, always check inside your boots and clothing before you put them on.
- Don't put your hands into dark places, such as rock crevices, heavy brush, or hollow logs, without first investigating with a pole or stick.
- Don't step over a fallen tree. Step on the log and look to see if there is a snake resting on the other side. (Watch out also for snakes camouflaged on the trunk!)

Never try to cut the bite or bleed the poison out

- Don't walk through heavy brush or tall grass without a stick, and always look down.
- Don't pick up a freshly killed snake without first severing the head. The nervous system may still be active and a dead snake can still deliver a bite.
- If you hear a snake, freeze until you are able to locate it. When you see it, back off slowly but never with your back to it, in case it moves to strike.

Don't take risks with snakes, and never handle unless you're an exp

The best way to kill a snake is with a heavy club or stick. Aim for its back, as near to the head as possible, and break its spine. Pin it down first with a stick, deliver the blows, then sever its head.

Once the head is removed, burn or bury it, then gut and cook the flesh as described in Chapter 2 (see page 86).

If you are bitten, try hard not to panic, as this will increase your heartbeat and the poison will be absorbed more quickly

DEALING WITH SNAKEBITE

The type of bite and whether or not it is poisonous can usually be identified by the pattern of the bite. Both poisonous and nonpoisonous snakes will leave an oval-shaped pattern of dots, but poisonous snakes will also leave large puncture marks from one to four fangs just above the oval. More obvious symptoms will be a severe swelling which can occur up to two hours after the attack.

If you are bitten, try hard not to panic, as this will increase your heartbeat and speed up the circulation of the blood, which will mean the poison will be absorbed more quickly. Remove all constricting items like watches, rings, and bracelets and try to apply some sort of constricting tourniquet between the wound and the heart. Trying to suck out the poison does not work as snake venom is very thick (plus you do not want that poison in your mouth, where capillaries absorb the venom much faster), and squeezing the bite runs the risk of pushing the venom further in.

Lie down and keep the wound lower than the heart. Drink as much fluid as possible. Never try to cut the bite or bleed the poison out. Creating an open blood flow means the toxin is absorbed even faster and directly into your bloodstream.

The most likely long-term problem, after the effects of the poison have worn off, is damage to the tissue surrounding the bite area. This can easily become infected from bacteria in the reptile's mouth, which is why bites from nonpoisonous snakes can also be dangerous.

SNAKES WELL WORTH AVOIDING ...

CENTRAL AND SOUTH AMERICA

Bushmaster: Large head and pinky-brown color with deep brown diamond shapes running down its back. Up to 8 feet long. Hemotoxic.

Fer-de-lance: Brown and light brown markings. Up to 6 feet long. Hemotoxic.

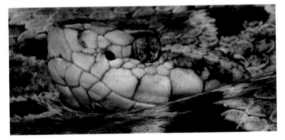

Tropical rattlesnake: Gold-colored with diamond markings and two dark stripes on the neck as well as its distinctive rattle. Up to 6 feet long. Hemotoxic.

AFRICA AND ASIA

Mamba: Slender and thin with a small head. Tree mambas are green while ground-living ones are black. Up to 6.5 feet long. Neurotoxic.

Cobra: Has a distinctive spread hood when alarmed. Up to 6 feet long. Neurotoxic.

Coral snake: Distinctive black and red bands with smaller yellow ones in between. Up to 3 feet long. Neurotoxic.

AUSTRALASIA

Taipan: Light to dark brown with a yellowy brown belly. Up to 9 feet long. Neurotoxic.

Tiger snake: Distinctive thick body with a large head and banded markings of browny-green and light brown. Very common and very fierce. Up to 6 feet long. Neurotoxic.

Australian brown snake: Slender and brown with a pale belly. Aggressive. Up to 6 feet long. Neurotoxic.

SPIDERS AND SCORPIONS

Some people are extremely allergic to spider venom. While it is unlikely that a spider will kill you, they are well worth avoiding. The worst are listed below.

TARANTULA

Location: Tropics of Central and South America.
Appearance: Large, hairy, and black.
Habitat: Generally they live in burrows or in trees.
Symptoms: Tarantulas have large fangs. If bitten, pain and bleeding are certain and infection is likely. Treat a tarantula bite as for any open wound (keep clean and cover), and try to prevent infection.

FUNNELWEB

Location: Australia.
Appearance: Large and brown or gray. Aggressive when disturbed.
Habitat: Woods, jungles, and brushy areas. Its web has a funnel-like opening, hence the name.

Symptoms: Pain, faintness, and fever. The only spider that can kill a healthy adult.

BLACK WIDOW

Location: Varied species worldwide. Black widow in United States, red widow in Middle East, and brown widow in Australia.
Appearance: Black in color with a red hourglass on the female's belly, which contains a neurotoxin.

Habitat: Under logs, rocks, and debris.
Symptoms: The initial pain is not severe, but severe local pain rapidly develops. The pain gradually spreads over the entire body and settles in the abdomen and legs. Weakness, tremors, sweating, and extreme salivation may occur.

SCORPIONS
(SEE CHAPTER 5, PAGES 214–215)

Location: Hot climates of all description.
Appearance: Instantly recognizable from its crablike claws and hooked tail ready to strike.
Habitat: Varies from rainforests to open plains to high-altitude mountains.
Symptoms: A scorpion sting is very painful, but rarely fatal in healthy adults. Swelling and numbness can last for several days.

Scorpions have crawled over me in the jungle at night. This is the time they are most active, being nocturnal hunters. Just crawling over me, though, they were harmless, going about their business, with no interest in stinging me unless provoked. As a general rule, the smaller the scorpion the deadlier the sting. I have caught scorpions using two fingers, one on either side of the sting in the tail. I broke off the pincers and ate the rest.

BEES, WASPS, AND HORNETS

Many people have been killed in jungles by accidentally disturbing a bees' nest and suffering a massive attack resulting in severe toxic shock. An aggressive swarm of bees can be very dangerous. The key to avoiding being mugged by a swarm of bees is to understand their behavior. Bees respond to movement, dark and bright colors, and carbon dioxide from exhaled breath. They build their nests in mounds and cavities, caves, hollowed-out cactus or tree trunks, and near water holes. Always be careful in these areas, and if you do accidentally surprise a swarm, don't panic and start swatting wildly as this will attract the whole swarm and before you know it they will be all over you. Instead, just retreat from the nest calmly and try to walk through some bushes to deter them from following you.

If stung by a bee, try to carefully remove the barbed stinger and venom sac by scraping it with a fingernail or knife blade. Avoid squeezing, for this will force more poison into the wound. Wash the sting site thoroughly to reduce the chances of infection.

Bee stings can be alleviated by any of the following: a cold compress; a paste of mud and ashes; sap from dandelions; coconut meat.

Bee stings can be alleviated by any of the following: a cold compress; a paste of mud and ashes; sap from dandelions; coconut meat

MOSQUITOES

Mosquitoes spread malaria, dengue fever, and can also carry bot fly eggs on their proboscis, so they are a definite threat to your long-term health. Symptoms of these fevers include a sudden onset of high temperature, headache, joint and muscle pains: not something you need with all the other problems you will be coping with. So keep well covered.

CATERPILLARS

Many are toxic to the skin and produce rashes and allergic reactions. If you find one on you, brush off in the direction of its head, which will make it release its spines more easily. They can be a surprising danger in jungles.

BOT FLIES

Bot fly larvae are carried by mosquitoes and burrow under the flesh, where they grow and form boils under the skin. They can be dug out or suffocated by blocking their breathing holes with tree sap or Vaseline. The German teenager Juliane Koepcke, whose remarkable survival story I referred to earlier, was riddled with bot flies burrowing under her skin. She related the terrifying feeling of waking in the night and feeling as if her skin was alive and moving around her. Watch out for bot flies, and in the jungle develop a guerrilla mentality of carefully checking every bit of your body whenever you have time.

TICKS

Ticks have eight legs and mouthparts that bite into the skin and suck on the blood beneath. Check yourself daily as they are clever at finding inaccessible parts of the body (especially the hairy parts!) and are often hard to locate. They can spread diseases like Lyme disease and should be promptly removed after they are found. The problem is removing them without leaving behind their mouthparts, which can fester and become infected.

Salt, alcohol, or the embers from a fire will force them to let go (but don't burn them too long as this will kill them with their body parts still attached to your skin). They can also be suffocated with tree sap or oil spread over them. Do not squeeze the tick's body, and wash your hands after removing. Wash the wound often.

LEECHES

In marshy ground, leeches are almost impossible to avoid, however well covered you may be. They are heat-seekers and have an uncanny ability to penetrate the smallest gaps in your clothing. Their bite wounds are not painful but do tend to itch. They can also cause heavy bleeding due to the natural anticoagulant they inject.

As with ticks, they will normally release their suckers if salt, alcohol, or heat is applied to them and can be suffocated with Vaseline or some types of tree sap. Do not pull off, as the wound will almost certainly turn septic.

CROCODILES

There are two types of crocodile: the saltwater variety and the freshwater variety. The former, "salties" as they are known, are bigger, stronger, and much more aggressive than their freshwater cousins. The problem is that saltwater crocs can also live in freshwater rivers and frequently do.

Fearsome predators, and among the world's leading survivors for a good reason.

There have been some monster specimens, some up to 20 feet long, among them a saltie called Sweetheart that terrorized the fishermen of Australia's Northern Territory in the 1970s; and more recently, in 2006, alligators were reported to have started attacking and eating humans in the Florida Everglades as a reaction to being fed and becoming used to human presence.

The favored feeding technique of crocs and alligators is to drown their prey and keep it under

Try to keep out of the water if you suspect crocodiles or alligators may be close by.

a rock or submerged log until it rots sufficiently to be torn apart and eaten. In the Everglade swamps I came across some healthy-sized alligators and even had to swim in an alligator-filled river. They can stay submerged for up to forty-five minutes so I had to sit and wait to check that all was clear. I then crossed by swimming underwater (yes, scary!), but this meant my body and head were less likely to be mistaken for a turtle or duck, which are the staple diet of alligators. The bottom line is, if there are crocs or alligators around, keep out of the water and always be careful when collecting water from a riverbank. Crocs hunt by observing where their prey comes down to the water to drink and they then wait patiently for the next visit. Don't let it be you.

ARMY ANTS

Army ants congregate in colonies of millions and keep moving all the time as they are too destructive to inhabit any one place for long. They are carnivores and will eat anything in their path, from insects to crocodiles, and carry it back to their queen in bite-sized chunks. Army ants will not change direction for you or for any living creature. Appropriate respect is advised.

POISONOUS FROGS

You will often see small frogs in jungle streams. If these are brightly colored, leave them alone. The colors indicate poison and have evolved as a deterrent to predators. The poison can be toxic and in some cases lethal, so if in doubt avoid brightly colored frogs as a source of food. The toxin is used by some indigenous Indians to make poison darts and even to stun fish in pools.

AND LAST, BUT NOT LEAST . . . THE CANDIRU

This Amazonian catfish is only about an inch long, the size and shape of a toothpick, and is transparent, so very hard to see. Most of the time it sucks blood from the gills of other fish, but it is also able to swim up a fountain of pee into the urethra (attracted by the salt in the human bladder). From here its barbed dorsal fin can only be removed by surgery. So it's probably worth avoiding peeing directly into jungle rivers.

The Bear Necessities: Surviving the Jungle

RULE 1: FRIEND NOT FOE
Adapting to such an alien environment is a mental battle that must be won. Think of the jungle as your friend, not your enemy. It can provide everything you need to survive.

RULE 2: SLOW DOWN
Speed is not the way of the jungle. The faster you go, the quicker you'll fall. Move slowly and deliberately around obstacles, checking the undergrowth as you go.

RULE 3: KEEP COVERED
The jungle's greatest danger is "death by a thousand cuts." Keep stings, bites, and scratches to a minimum from the outset and ensure your skin is covered.

RULE 4: SLEEP HIGH
The jungle floor is a repository of creepy-crawlies. Always try to sleep on a raised platform or A-frame bed.

RULE 5: RIVERS – HIGHWAYS OF THE JUNGLE
The sure way out of any jungle is by its rivers. Look for them, then follow them. They will eventually lead you to safety and civilization.

"If the creator had a purpose in equipping
us with a neck, he surely would have meant
for us to stick it out."

MARTIN LUTHER KING

deserts

I SPENT A CONSIDERABLE AMOUNT OF MY MILITARY TIME IN THE DESERTS OF NORTH AFRICA, BOTH WITH THE SAS, WHEN I WAS POSTED TWICE TO THE DESERT, AND LATER ON DOING BASIC TRAINING WITH FRENCH FOREIGN LEGIONNAIRES DOWN IN WESTERN SAHARA. THESE EXPERIENCES HAVE REINFORCED MY BELIEF THAT IT IS BEST NOT TO MESS WITH ANY ENVIRONMENT WHERE TEMPERATURES ARE THAT HARSH. BELIEVE ME, DESERTS ARE HOSTILE PLACES: PERHAPS THE MOST HOSTILE OF PLACES ON EARTH. THEIR PRIMARY DEFINING CHARACTERISTIC IS THE LACK OF THE ONE SUBSTANCE HUMANS NEED MORE THAN ANYTHING ELSE TO SURVIVE: WATER.

Deserts are defined by their lack of rainfall – an average of less than 10 inches a year is the accepted norm – with the Atacama Desert in northern Chile being the driest of them all. In the Atacama it rains on average less than a centimeter per year with some areas not having seen a single, solitary raindrop in living memory.

The other defining characteristic of the desert is the blistering heat. Deserts are prone to temperatures which in the summer months regularly rise above 122°F. What little water that does fall is quickly evaporated, producing landscapes which are vulnerable to erosion. And these landscapes, which were once seabeds and mountain ranges, over millions of years have been sculpted by the wind into some of the most sublime panoramas on earth.

Study a map of the world's deserts and you will see that in the northern hemisphere huge swathes of desert terrain occupy the area between the equator and the Tropic of Cancer. These include the Big Daddy of them all, the Sahara in North Africa, and its near neighbors the Arabian Desert and the deserts of the Middle East.

In the southern hemisphere, the Atacama Desert in northern Chile, the Namib and Kalahari Deserts of southern Africa, and the Australian deserts all lie on latitudes south of the Tropic of Capricorn. Finally there are the so-called "cold" deserts like the Gobi Desert of Central Asia and parts of the North American deserts which stretch up into northern latitudes and which, while subject to extreme heat in the summer, also experience extreme cold in the winter.

One-fifth of the earth's surface is defined as desert. While some of this is characterized by the endless rolling sand dunes of popular imagination, the rest is made up of a wide variety of contrasting terrain. Depending on location, latitude, and altitude, this can include everything from mountains, rocky plateaus, and canyons, to salt plains or sandy gravel flatlands punctuated by scattered vegetation and dried-up riverbeds.

While these differing terrain types have a profound impact on the way a traveler experiences the desert on an aesthetic and spiritual level, they also have a profound impact on his chances of coming through a survival situation unscathed. The basic principles remain the same, but nothing can substitute for the knowledge handed down over innumerable generations by desert dwellers like the Aborigines of Australia, the Tuareg of the Sahara, the Bedouin of the Arabian Desert, and the Native American Indians. Without the

Deserts are perhaps the most hostile of places on earth

benefit of their knowledge, and stripped of the modern-day technology on which we so often depend, no twenty-first-century adventurer could survive for long.

DESERT TERRAINS

SAND OR DUNE DESERT

This is the archetypal desert terrain of wind-etched sand dunes stretching to eternity and dwarfing the tiny, silhouetted figures of a camel train, immortalized in films like David Lean's *Lawrence of Arabia*. It includes large areas of the Sahara and Namib Deserts, the latter containing dunes as high as 1,200 feet and more than 18 miles long.

MOUNTAIN DESERT

Mountain desert is characterized by canyons, gullies, and ravines. This type of terrain occurs where mountain ranges have been eroded away over the millennia and the winds have sculpted them into surreal formations rising out of the desert floor. It includes large areas of the Great Basin Desert of Nevada and Utah in the USA. It was here, in the Moab Desert, that I filmed the desert program for the *Born Survivor* TV series, and the temperature often rose to a blistering 52°C (126°F). My shoes felt as if they were permanently on fire!

ROCKY PLATEAU DESERT

Such deserts are vast areas of relatively flat broken terrain interspersed by deep canyons where rivers

Not all deserts are flat and sandy!

Endless sand dunes, of the type I would march over with the French Foreign Legionnaires.

once flowed in the distant past. The Grand Canyon is one such and is characteristic of large areas of desert terrain in the American West.

SALT MARSH

Areas of salt marsh are among the most difficult and dangerous types of desert terrain in which to survive. They are characterized by a crust of alkaline salt left behind by water evaporation, which can be highly corrosive and makes any remaining water undrinkable. Many deserts in the Middle East include areas of salt-marsh terrain.

BROKEN DESERT

This is characterized by mazes of dried-up water courses twisting and turning through the landscape, leaving behind a desiccated and dissected landscape interspersed with ridges and furrows and a maze-like pattern in the soft sand. It is found all over the world and is characteristic of the borders of most deserts.

And here we are – desert marching in the Western Sahara.

Finding Shelter

The primary need for a shelter in desert environments, where the temperature differential between shade and direct sunlight can often be as much as 17°C (31°F), is protection from solar radiation. While most people fear the cold more than the heat, hyperthermia (overheating) can be just as lethal as hypothermia (freezing). Dehydration and sunburn are also potential killers and a rise of just 3.5°C (6°F) in the body's core temperature will lead to heat stroke.

To compound the problem, it will not be just finding shelter from the heat that will be the issue. It may also be necessary to protect yourself from the cold. While the temperature can sometimes soar as high as 65°C (149°F) during the day, at night it may drop well below freezing. Death from exposure in the desert is common.

The body gains heat through the same primary processes as it loses heat: namely conduction (direct contact) and convection (through the air). Any form of shelter should aim to reduce the effect of these wherever possible.

So the first task – as always in a survival situation – is to get your priorities right.

DESERT CLOTHING

Your first and most basic form of shelter is the clothes you stand up in. You must make sure that your head, neck, skin, and eyes are protected from the sun. You should ideally be wearing loose-fitting, long-sleeved shirts and trousers which allow air to circulate but prevent sweat from evaporating too quickly, thus allowing the body's natural cooling system to operate effectively, keeping dehydration to a minimum. Breathe through your nose and not your mouth, as this will reduce dehydration caused by evaporation from the large area of moist tissue in your mouth.

Never venture into the desert without a wide-brimmed hat or, to take a leaf out of the book of desert-dwellers the world over, a head scarf. It acts as a shield from the sun's heat and a screen to keep the wind and sand out. While it won't make you very popular, a trick I've used before is to pee onto my headscarf to cool my head. After a few days the smell can get pretty horrible, but the moisture will help combat the ferocious heat of the sun. Remember: in a survival situation, you should use any technique you can to help yourself, and there's nothing more important than keeping your brain cool – it is your most valuable survival tool!

If you have no sunscreen, smear charcoal from a fire or dirt from the desert floor to protect exposed skin on your face and hands. Smears of charcoal under the eyes will help prevent sun-blindness and also reduce the glare reflected onto your retinas. (This is why American footballers smear colored sun cream under their eyes: to deflect the glare.) If your sunglasses are lost or broken, keep your eyes covered as much as possible with that head scarf.

Camel (left!) and me in the Western Sahara. Camels are the ultimate desert survivors.

A tiny gap in the cloth will still be enough to see through.

One technique for substitute sunglasses, which I have also seen done, is to tie some bark from a cottonwood tree around the eyes, making slits through it so you can see. It's an old Inuit trick, and they use cord made from the leaves of yucca plants to tie the "sunglasses" on with.

There is much disagreement about whether predominantly dark- or light-colored clothing is better for desert conditions. The supporters of light clothing argue that this reflects the heat, while dark fabrics absorb it and heat the body more. The downside to this argument is that white clothing can let solar radiation through, which can both burn and heat the skin and cause sweat to evaporate quickly. Darker fabrics may hold more heat in the fabric but they will keep harmful ultraviolet radiation at bay, and if they are baggy will allow air to circulate so that the body's natural cooling system can work efficiently.

The ideal solution, favored by many long-term desert-dwellers, is to wear a layer of lightweight, white clothing over a layer of lightweight, darker clothing.

While the temperature can sometimes soar as high as 65°C (149°F) during the day, at night it may drop well below freezing

LOCATING A SHELTER

Look for simpler and easier forms of shelter before thinking of building one or digging into the ground. The end must justify the means, and building an elaborate shelter will sap your energy and you may lose copious quantities of body fluids and salts.

In deserts the key is finding shade, whether in the form of rocky outcrops, boulders, sand mounds, depressions in the ground, or even a giant cactus. But remember that not all shade provides protection from the sun in the same way.

During the day, shelter from vegetation (trees and bushes) will often be preferable to rocks, which store heat that radiates out like an oven. While in the Moab Desert, the rocks were so hot that I used one to fry a raven's egg I had found. It was sizzling within two seconds!

Vegetation will also keep the surrounding air more moist through evaporation. At night, on the other hand, the storage-heater effect of rocks can work to your advantage. If you have a survival blanket, poncho, or some parachute-type material, drape it over, around, or across these natural features.

If your vehicle has broken down, remember that staying near the vehicle is usually by far the safest option as you will have a greater chance of being spotted both from the air and on the ground. However, don't stay in the car, as you will cook during the day and freeze during the night. Use the shade from the main structure and dig down into the ground, which will be as much as 17°C (31°F) cooler 6 inches beneath the surface. Build sand barriers around the sides up to the chassis, which will keep out the wind and help cool your shelter.

The folly of leaving behind a vehicle, your one form of readily available shelter, is tragically exemplified by the 1989 case of an English couple, Andrew and Jane Hughes. On holiday in Tunisia on the edges of the Sahara, they headed out from their hotel on a day trip to the nearby market town of Duse with their two young children.

On the way, hindered by bad roads and worse signposting, their car broke down in the sand. Believing that the town was nearby, they set out to reach it on foot, but after an hour of walking, it was still nowhere in sight. At this point, Andrew sent his wife and the children back along the road to the car. He knew that they had just passed some water tanks farther back down the road, and they were also carrying 1.5 quarts of water. Meanwhile, he continued towards the town.

In the blistering heat and with no water, Andrew collapsed and spent the night on the desert floor. Next morning he was rescued by a passing farmer who took him back to the car, only to find that his wife and children had never made it. After further mishap when the farmer drove off without looking back, leaving Andrew with his car, which promptly broke down again, he was finally rescued by a patrol of Tunisian soldiers. They had tragic news for him. His wife and children, having never found the elusive water tanks or the car again, and with no water and no shade in the pitiless heat, had died within two days. How different things might have been had they all stayed, at least until nightfall, next to the car.

BUILDING A SHELTER

The end must justify the means, so any shelter construction that requires manual labor should be carried out during the early morning or early evening when there is enough light but the temperature is at its most manageable and dehydration will be kept to a minimum. The key in the desert is to use your imagination and improvise, using whatever materials you can find to maximum advantage.

A shelter will need a roof to protect you against the sun. In truth, no one should think of venturing into a desert in the first place without some kind of emergency sunshade in the form of a survival blanket, poncho, tarp, or even an umbrella; in terrain where alternatives like leaves and branches are in short supply, they may be the only option. If you do have some material for a sunshade, fold it in half, as two layers will protect you far more effectively than one. The outer layer will stop the direct layers of the sun, while the air space in between will help dissipate heat through convection.

TYPES OF SHELTER

VEGETATION

Depending on the type of desert terrain, small trees and bushes can provide very effective shade. If there is sufficient material available, lean-to and A-frame constructions (see Chapter 2, pages 70 and 72) will keep the sun off. A platform of vegetation made of roots and branches will also protect from the heat of the ground during the day and the cold during the night.

ROCK OVERHANGS AND CAVES

Potentially the perfect option, assuming you are in this kind of desert terrain, and they often have some depth to allow air to circulate and dissipate the radiation off the rocks. Be very wary of snakes, spiders, scorpions – even mountain lions – and any number of biting and stinging creatures that might have got there before you and had the same idea of seeking protection from the heat of the day. (By the way, a snake without shade in the heat of the day will die within an hour. All animals need shade as well as you.)

MAN-MADE SHADE

Man-made materials such as space blankets, ponchos, or tarpaulins will all provide shade against the sun, and the former have a reflective surface which will be invaluable in the

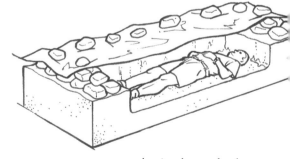

sweltering heat of a desert. In extremis, put it on the ground and wrap yourself in it, but if at all possible keep the air circulating by draping it over a rock or bush first. A two-layered roof leaving a space of 2–3 feet in between will reduce the temperature beneath considerably.

SCRAPE SHELTER

Find any natural feature above the level of the ground that is casting a shadow and dig a shallow scrape on the shaded side; it need be no more than about 2 feet wide. Use the material that has been dug out to make a sun wall around the sides of the scrape. Try to locate the shelter in a north/south axis as this will mean the sun will cast the maximum possible shadow during its daily trajectory from east to west. Use a tarpaulin or space blanket placed over the scrape, pinned down with rocks, for further shade if you have one. If not, and there are any flat rocks available,

lay them in a pyramid shape over the scrape. Scrapes require time and energy, so work when the sun is coolest in the early morning or evening.

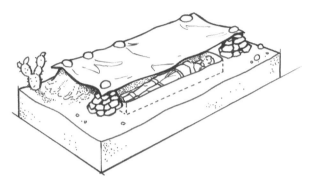

Fighting my way through the Sahara Desert.

Finding Water

In the desert, dehydration is public enemy number one. Not only will you lose bodily fluids at a frightening rate (around a quart an hour in the midday sun), but your chances of finding a series of reliable water sources to replace it are small. The human body can survive up to three weeks without food, but without water in a desert, as the Hughes family so tragically discovered, you will be lucky to survive two days. Search and rescue teams I have worked with in Utah have a motto for what happens when you are caught in the desert without water: "Down in twelve hours, dead in twenty-four." Don't let it be you!

In a desert, in temperatures over 29°C (84°F), experts advise that a realistic minimum water intake per person per day should be about 4.5 quarts

Because water is so bulky and heavy, anyone who ventures out into a desert without motorized transport or camels will not be able to carry enough water to survive more than a few days without resupply anyway. Which is why finding your way back to civilization or being rescued after getting lost in a desert is a far more urgent issue than in other wilderness environments.

Consider this. In a desert, in temperatures over 29°C (84°F), experts advise that a realistic minimum water intake per person per day should be about 4.5 quarts. And that's resting in the shade.

Increase the temperature to more than 50°C (122°F) and start hiking and the consumption level skyrockets to more than 13.5 quarts per day. Hence the figure: a quart an hour in the heat of the day.

In most deserts under normal desert conditions (i.e., with no rain and little vegetation), your chances of being able to find this amount of liquid are very limited. For this reason, water preservation is an immediate and very urgent priority. Remember: a panicky search for water without thought will almost certainly result in a greater loss through perspiration than you can reasonably hope to find by chance.

In any desert survival situation, you must find shade and minimize exertion. Only then will you have any chance of keeping your water account in credit.

If you do still have some water supplies, experts disagree on whether or not you should ration it. Common sense suggests that there is no point in gulping down your last remaining supplies if you are still urinating in any quantity. On the other hand, there is no point in conserving water if you are shortly going to pass out with heatstroke. Use your judgment – if you are already very dehydrated, drink, if not, rationing may be the best answer.

Significant amounts of body fluid are also lost through the simple act of breathing, as the hot desert air is sucked into the lungs and then exhaled, taking water vapor from the body along with it. Many desert peoples, including the Bedouin, keep their mouths covered for this reason and it is why you should breathe through your nose as much as possible.

I have tried a technique before used by a Mexican tribe called the Tarahumara, who can run 50 miles a day in the desert heat on only

River gullies like this save lives – learn to recognize signs that will lead you to water.

a tiny amount of water. This they achieve by holding a mouthful of water in their mouths without swallowing and only breathing through their noses. This means that the air they breathe in is constantly hydrated.

The technique works, although it requires an iron will to adhere to it without giving in to the urge to swallow. Think sugary doughnuts and licking of lips! I set myself a fifteen-minute target each time to keep the water in my mouth before swallowing, and this made the journey pass easier, as well as helping keep me hydrated.

TIP: Copy the camels. Their long legs keep the air circulating beneath them (so you should rest up on brushwood during the day to keep air circulating under you), and camels also orient themselves end on to the sun when resting so that the minimum amount of sunlight hits their bodies. (Do the same: minimize the power of the sun by hiding from it, covering up or finding shade.)

SIGNS OF WATER

Time out to scan the surrounding desert for signs of water before you set off in search of it will be time well spent. Remember, every step you take will dehydrate you still further. The trained eye can often locate signs of water from a distance. An educated guess is always far better than a blind stagger.

The following natural signs are all good indicators that water is present at, or near, the surface:

VEGETATION

In the parched landscape of a desert, concentrations of vegetation stand out from a

> **Animals usually drink in the early morning and the evening, so a large movement of animals at these times may well indicate a water source**

long way off. While a clump of bushes, cacti, or grass does not guarantee accessible water, it generally indicates that moisture is, or was, within 18 inches of the surface.

ANIMAL TRAILS INTERSECTING

Animals need water as much as humans, and are also creatures of habit who return to the same water source day after day. Animal trails will often intersect near a source of water, joining into a larger trail that may well lead to water. Animals usually drink in the early morning and the evening, so a large movement of animals at these times may well indicate a water source.

ANIMAL DROPPINGS

As with animal tracks, a concentration of animal poo indicates a place where animals regularly gather, and this will often be near a source of water.

BIRD FLIGHT

Birds also drink early and late, and a flock of birds flying overhead will often be heading towards water. If doves or pigeons are nearby, it almost certainly signifies water, and like other birds, they tend to fly high on the way to water and low on the way back. Remember, though, this does not apply to carnivores like vultures, eagles, or hawks, which get much of their fluids from the flesh of their prey.

BEES AND SWARMING INSECTS

Bees usually stay within 2,600 feet of water and will fly in a straight line to and from their source, but be wary not to disturb the swarm (see page 179). Flies also stay near to water, while the presence of mosquitoes almost certainly means you have found what you are looking for.

Finally finishing basic training with the Foreign Legionnaires.

COASTAL DUNES

Water often seeps inland into deserts on coastlines, leaving behind wetlands containing some water that may be of tolerable salinity on the surface or that can be distilled in a desert still (see pages 200–201). Sand dunes near the high tide mark also sometimes have shallow pools where the lighter surface water is drinkable.

SOURCES OF WATER

Water, like everything else on the planet, is subject to gravity, and wherever it falls, it will be flowing, dripping, or sinking downhill. For this reason you will have a far better chance of success in valleys, dried-up riverbeds, gullies, narrow canyons, and at the base of cliffs or rock formations than atop ridges or dunes. Springs in the desert can form when a porous band of rock is sandwiched between two nonporous bands, often at the base of a cliff or an outcrop. The water flows through the porous band and dribbles out as a spring.

Keep your eyes skinned wherever you are. Rain soaks very quickly into sand or soil, but it can lie in pools on a rocky surface for some time, and shaded sandstone hollows can hold water for months.

In deserts subject to seasonal rain or flash floods, dried-up water courses – these come in varying depths and widths – often contain water within a foot of the surface under damp sand. Where the water course follows a serpentine shape, your best chance will be at the lowest point on outside bends as this is where the water flows slowest in full flood and lingers longest when the waters dry up.

Water can be extracted from the damp sand or mud by soaking a rag or bandanna in soil and wringing out the water into a container or digging down to create a well or solar still (see pages 200–201). Always keep a wary eye on the weather if venturing into areas subject to flash flooding, as in extreme cases a dried-up riverbed can turn into raging torrent within a matter of minutes (see page 210). I have heard of flash-flood gullies filling up to 80 feet deep in seconds. Flash floods kill.

Owing to its scarcity and the lack of an ongoing supply to flush nasties away, desert water is particularly vulnerable to pollution. This is because much of the water is stagnant and often contains rotting small rodent carcasses. So filtering and purification techniques (see Chapter 4, pages 158–159) may be needed to avoid illness and further net loss in body fluid. When polluted water is suspected and boiling is not an option, distilling the water in a desert still can work, but will again require a physical effort that may well outweigh the potential gain.

NATURAL SOURCES OF WATER

CACTUS

Cactus is generally overrated as a source of water. Even desert dwellers only use their fluids as a last resort. One problem is identifying a cactus that isn't poisonous or so unpleasant to taste it makes you vomit; another is extracting the fluid. Nonetheless, in the American deserts, the fishhook barrel cactus – helpfully identifiable by its barrel shape and fishhook-shaped spines – is an excellent source of additional fluid in an emergency.

Cacti are generally overrated as good sources of water.

PRICKLY PEAR

Cactus fruit such as the prickly pear can be mashed into a pulp so that the fluid drains out. The stem is also full of water, but don't drink if it is a sappy, white color, as it won't be a prickly pear and will be poisonous. The organ pipe cactus of the lower Sonoran Desert in Mexico also has a fruit that is sweet and moist.

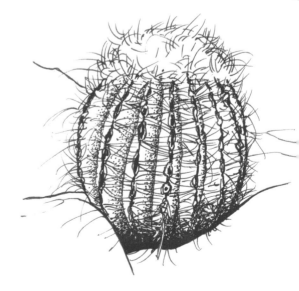

As a last resort, they can save your life.

AGAVES

Agaves have been cultivated in European tropical gardens for centuries and are easily recognizable from their long, floppy, spiky leaves which grow in a rosette formation around a flowering stalk. Water often collects at the bottom of the leaf stalks. The American century plant (large agave) has a huge stem that can grow up to 32 feet high and is recognizable from a long way off. Rainwater collects at its base, and moisture can be collected from its stem and leaves.

TREES, PLANTS, AND ROOTS

Many trees and plants in the world's deserts, including the trunk of the baobab tree in Africa and Australia, the roots of the needlewood tree in Australia, the shoots of the desert gourd of the Sahara, and various agaves and yuccas in the Atacama Desert in South America, are all useful sources of fluid in a crisis. In Australia, some trees, including the baobab, desert-oak, she-oak, and paperbark trees, collect water under the bark which can be siphoned off. The roots from trees such as the baobab, kurrajong,

wattle, and some gums can be cut into short lengths and stood end-up in a container so that their moisture slowly drips out.

TIP: While cacti can survive on tiny amounts of water each year, some bushes in the deserts, like tamarisks, suck up gallons of water from underwater reservoirs every day. If you can find these bushes, hunt around for salt deposits left on rocks that indicate water evaporation. Such deposits often come from a "seep," a small trickle of water oozing out from the rock. I found one of these in the Moab Desert and used the hollow stem of a trumpet flower as a straw to suck up tiny pools of fresh mineral-rich water. The pools would refill in seconds.

Nature often provides all you need to survive even in the parched, arid deserts. A classic example is the squawbush whose red berries are coated in a mineral salt. These can be eaten raw and are an excellent source of vitamin C and will help replace lost minerals. Native American Indians collect these by the basketful in the desert to use in cooking and as a salt replacement when on the move. A good indicator that you need more salt is if the sweat dripping into your eyes no longer stings. This means you are low in salt and need more minerals.

GYPSY WELL

If you are lucky enough to find some saturated ground near a dried-up water course, dig a small pit away from stagnant water and allow the surrounding water to flow in. If the water is murky, then drain and refill. The outside bends of dried-up riverbeds are best. Dig down at the lowest point no more than one and a half feet. Any more and you will be likely to be wasting your time.

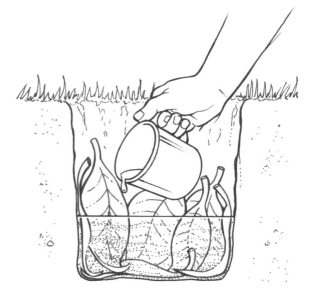

WATER BY CONDENSATION

Water is present in even the driest environments. You may never see it, but there will always be at least some water vapor in the air and moisture in the earth, as well as in the leaves and roots of plants and trees. Condensing it in quantities that are greater than the amount you lose through sweat while you're at it is the real challenge.

SOLAR OR DESERT STILL

Considerable debate surrounds the usefulness of the desert still. Its principle is to condense moisture trapped in the ground by means of a pit and a clear plastic sheet. The difference in temperature between the sheet and the surrounding ground causes the moisture to condense and drip into a waiting container.

Some survival experts claim to be able to produce as much as 0.5 quarts in twenty-four hours, but everything depends on the moisture content of the soil itself. The truth is that collecting half a quart of water is only really possible if the still is located in a damp riverbed, where you would probably be able to scoop the water out or squeeze it from a saturated bandanna anyway. The effort required to dig the still – even at night when the air is cooler – may not be worth the end result of possibly only a few sips of water.

For these reasons, solar stills are best seen as a supplement to other sources of water. Nonetheless, the technique is well worth knowing as it can also be used in areas of higher water availability to distill polluted or brackish water. If you have sufficient water containers and plastic sheeting, then setting multiple stills is more worthwhile if you are staying put in one base camp for sufficient time.

If the sweat dripping into your eyes no longer stings, take it as an indicator that you are low in salt and need more minerals

Dig into the soil in a bowl shape to a depth of between 2 and 4 feet, and between 3 feet and 4 feet wide. Make sure you keep the sides of the pit at an angle where the soil will not collapse inwards and keep the outer circumference at the same level all the way round, otherwise the still won't work properly. Next, dig a smaller hole in the center of the pit to take a container which will collect the water. If you have one, run a small tube from the container out of the pit. This will mean that you can later suck the water out without having to dismantle the still.

Next, scour one side of the plastic sheeting with sand – this will help the condensed water

run into the pot – and place it scoured side down over the pit, putting a stone in the center so it is weighed down to form a steep funnel shape. If the sun is so hot that the stone might melt the plastic, wrap it in fabric first. Finally, pin the edges of the sheet down firmly with soil and rocks around the edge of the pit so it forms an airproof seal. Make sure the plastic doesn't touch the insides of the pit as this will prevent the water running into the container.

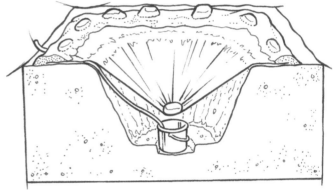

DEW TRAP

Dig a pit around 18 inches deep and line with any material which will stop water leaking through. Fill it with stones and lick off the dew before sunrise. This technique is a variation on a Bedouin method of turning over half-buried rocks just before sunup so that the colder surface condenses the dew.

TIP: To increase the amount of water gathered in stills, fill the bottom of the pits with rocks and cover with any nearby vegetation like leaves, cacti, or desert brush. Your urine or any polluted water you have will also be distilled if you add it to the mix. I have used urine in a still like this to add to the moisture available for distillation, and it works well – learn not to waste your pee. And if you have a rag, pee on it – urine will evaporate more effectively from a piece of saturated cloth than from vegetation.

EVAPORATION STILL

In areas of substantial vegetation, evaporation (often called transpiration) stills can be very effective and are far easier to rig up than a solar still. Place a clear bag over the leafy, fleshy parts of a suitable (nonpoisonous) plant or tree and secure it firmly so no air can get in, and make sure the bag is left in direct sunlight. Plants with pulpy roots usually contain more moisture than those with thin, spiky roots. The sun will then draw the moisture out of the leaves and it will collect in the bottom of the bag. Prick a hole in the bag when you are ready to drink and tie a knot to seal the bag afterwards. Don't leave it more than a couple of hours because after this time the leaves will stop producing water even if they still contain moisture. Drain the water and start again. Multiples of these stills work most efficiently.

Use your judgment – if you are already very dehydrated, drink; if not, rationing may be the best answer

Exhausted at the end of a large wadi climb in the Sahara Desert

Finding Food

Finding food should never be your first priority in the desert. In fact, if you are unable to find a water source but have access to food, you would do better not to eat it until you have found water. Digestion uses up precious reserves of the body's fluids and will accelerate dehydration, particularly if you are eating fatty or salty foods. Carbohydrates – like fruits, roots, and leaves – often contain moisture, while fats and proteins – meat and nuts, for example – need body fluids to be digested.

As a rule of thumb you should avoid eating even vegetables unless you have at least 0.5 quarts of water to go with it and avoid meat unless you have about 1.5 quarts. If you have any dehydrated survival rations, don't eat them without water.

Many desert regions support plant species whose fruit, roots, leaves, or stalks are safe to eat. Many will taste like cardboard but they may still contain valuable nutrition. Remember too that the meat of all mammals, reptiles, insects, grubs, and birds is edible when they have had their heads, guts, and any poison glands removed.

In the first instance, you should always search for sources of plant food and insect grubs before considering hunting animals for meat, as the loss to your water and energy account will very likely make hunting not worthwhile. Some reptiles, like lizards, may be an exception to the rule and can sometimes be caught by hand or with a snare, so the trapping techniques I described in Chapter 1 (see pages 45–48) can come in useful in desert terrain.

"Bush tucker," as outback desert food is known in Australia, has now even become mainstream, with popular aboriginal staples like ants, lizards, locusts, and snakes appearing on menus in the top city restaurants. And so while food may appear to be in short supply and

> **If you are unable to find a water source but have access to food, you would do better not to eat it until you have found water**

certainly will be in the harshest, dune-ridden areas of deserts like the Sahara and the Atacama, many other deserts have a more reliable food source than is at first apparent.

PLANTS AND TREES

Desert plants mostly fall into two types: ephemerals, which come to life once a year during the annual rains; and perennials, which have evolved to survive long periods of drought by retaining water in their root systems, leaves, and stems. Many types of desert support trees, bushes, and plants that are edible, but a great number of them have to be cooked first, which may not be a realistic option owing to lack of water. Avoid anything with a milky sap as it will almost certainly be poisonous. If in doubt, don't eat it, or apply the food safety test described in Chapter 4 (see pages 161–163).

PALMS

Most parts of palm trees are edible, including the fruit, flowers, buds, and trunk meat, but cooking will almost always improve the taste. Nipa palms have leaves that are about 20 feet long and seeds, gathered around the bottom of the leaf stalks, that are edible. Sugar palms, capable of reaching a height of 50 feet when fully grown, have edible nuts. Date palms grow all over the Middle East and are considered the desert's greatest luxury. The leaves are also edible if cooked. The meat of a coconut is of course edible and nutritious and is safe to eat whether it comes in either a green, unripe, or mature nut. The juice within, however, should only be consumed from green nuts, as milk from ripe ones has laxative effects.

PRICKLY PEARS

The fruit of the prickly pear, known as "tuna," grows around the flat pads of the main plant and goes bright red when ripe.

Knock these tuna off with a stick to avoid getting pricked by the tiny hairs, roll the fruit in the sand to remove the spines, then split the fruit and suck the moisture out and eat the flesh. They can be eaten unripe and green if that is all that is available. To get at the main body of the cactus flesh, remove the sharp larger spines by burning or peeling.

The organ pipe cactus and the distinctive and huge saguaro cactus, instantly recognizable from cowboy comics, also have edible fruits, but these cacti only grow in the Sonoran Desert in the southwestern USA.

MESQUITE BUSH

Several species of mesquite bushes are to be found in the deserts of the USA, some of which grow up to 30 feet tall. The seed pods of all these varieties are edible and were a favorite of the Native American Indians. The mesquite is abundant in many areas and can also be a good source of shade.

ACACIAS

There are around 1,300 species worldwide, with most being native to Australia. Acacias are medium-sized scrubby trees with small leaves which can be boiled and eaten. Acacia roots are also a good source of water. The seeds can be roasted.

BAOBABS

The pulpy fruits (up to 10 inches long) of these unmistakable trees with their bulging, ridged trunks are found all over Africa and Australia and are edible raw, including the seeds.

INSECTS

Insects, especially larvae, are an excellent source of nutrition – they contain valuable fat, protein, and carbohydrates – and many have a high fluid content which makes them easy to digest. Do not eat furry grubs or any that have black showing through the skin.

TERMITES AND ANTS' EGGS

Termites and ants' eggs are the most reliable, nutritious (and tasty) variety of insect bush tucker. Stick a twig in a termite mound, twirl it around, and their natural biting reflex will cause them to grab the stick and cling on, providing you with a healthy meal. Another method is to dig a hole in the top of a termite mound or ants' nest and line it with a plastic bag to catch them as they fall in. Termites are more nutritious eaten raw, but people often say they taste better fried. Raw termites, however, are a favorite of mine (when there are only insects on the menu that is!).

WICHETY GRUBS

These grubs – the large, white, wood-eating larvae of the ghost moth – live on the sugary sap of the witchety bush, a type of acacia, and other gum trees. They are packed full of protein and high in calcium and have been a staple food of the Australian aborigines, who have eaten them – either raw or barbecued – for thousands of years. Raw grubs have a liquid center, taste slightly sweet, and when cooked have been compared to chicken or shrimp in peanut sauce. Their presence can be detected from the bore holes they leave in dead trees, stumps, and roots.

LOCUSTS AND GRASSHOPPERS

Edible when cooked, locusts and grasshoppers have an exoskeleton which helps them retain moisture, but this along with head, legs, and wings must be removed before eating.

CRICKETS

Crickets tend to seek shady corners behind scrub or rocks to escape the heat of the day. Then in the early evening they come out to feed on plants or grasses. Their distinctive cricket sound can give their locations away. Make use of this: remove the rock and swat at them with your hand. I have managed to catch plenty of these in this way. Remove their legs, which tend to get stuck in your throat, then eat them raw and whole – head and all. They look horrible and alienlike, but pound for pound they are one of the most protein-rich bugs around.

SCORPIONS

Scorpions are technically arachnids rather than insects – they have eight legs rather than six. They can be eaten raw as long as you pick them up quickly and safely by their tail stinger – one finger either side of the ball of venom on its end, ensuring the pincer can't get at you – then the rest of the scorpion is fine to eat. Remember: often the smaller the scorpion, the more potent its venom, so weigh this up when selecting which to eat. I ate one alive in Kenya after some deliberation as to whether to eat the clawlike pincers first to stop them biting me. In the end I just crunched and it was surprisingly good, as well as being packed full of protein and nutrients. But proceed cautiously.

Crickets look horrible and alienlike, but pound for pound they are one of the most protein-rich bugs around

MAMMALS AND REPTILES

Marsupials, wild goats, pigs, rabbits, snakes, lizards, and cattle all inhabit the world's deserts. All reptiles are edible, including venomous snakes – but remove the head and venom glands first.

LIZARDS

Lizards like sunny areas on rocks and can sometimes be caught by hand or by stabbing with a stick or throwing a heavy stone. There is an old Native American trick where you make a snare from some yucca plant cord and an old bootlace and then catch them as you entice or poke them out of their holes. Avoid the glands, which can sometimes be poisonous. Goannas are fatty and oily, so cook them well, but they have white flesh and are good to eat.

SNAKES

All land snakes are edible. They are best killed by throwing a heavy rock at the back of the head from a safe distance or, even better, by doing so after pinning the head down with a flat-ended stick. If you can pin the head down, an alternative and very effective way of killing snakes I have seen is then to grab the tail (above the anus) and swing the snake fast over your head, smashing its head into the ground. This kills it instantly.

The key with snakes is to learn the poisonous ones of the area you are in (they often tend to have larger, triangular heads, and rounded tails). Using this technique, indentifying the others doesn't matter so much, as they will tend to be non-venomous. These you can confidently pursue, pin down, and kill. A snake is a steak! But be extra careful hunting poisonous ones.

Remove the head, but remember some snakes can bite after the head has been chopped off, owing to the still active nerve endings. Split the skin lengthwise along the underbelly and peel off before gutting it and cooking the meat.

Scorpions are edible apart from the venom sac in the tip of their tails.

Navigation and Movement

Navigating successfully across all types of wilderness terrain, with or without a map, is a major challenge. It's getting lost that's the easy bit. Of all the wildernesses I have been exposed to, feeling disoriented in the desert was the most unnerving because the stakes are so high. Whereas in a jungle or in the mountains, I know that if I keep my cool and observe the basic rules of survival I will have a good chance of coming through, in the desert I know that time is against me. Even if I do find water, it may not be enough to sustain me for long. Remember: "Down in twelve hours, dead in twenty-four."

Deserts are peculiarly disorienting places to be. One moment you feel as if you know exactly where you are and you have a firm fix on a distant object on the horizon, the next you can be utterly confused when the same landmark has dipped out of sight or inexplicably morphed into another similar object that seems to be beckoning you in a completely different direction.

The effects of the heat both inside and outside your head undoubtedly have a lot to do with it. The air close to the ground, up to a height of about 10 feet, is super-heated and can often shimmer and refract light so that a mirage effect builds up and objects on the horizon appear and disappear, bend and refract, and no matter how many hours you keep walking towards them, they never seem to get any closer. And that's when you're well hydrated and protected against the sun! Imagine how tough things would be if your brain started to fry and your grip on your mental faculties began to slip.

So, once again, the lesson is to make sure you don't let this state develop in the first place. More than in any other type of wilderness, it pays to think first and make every drop of energy and water count in the desert.

Rising panic at the first realization that you are alone and lost in a desert often causes people to grab at straws and make an all-or-nothing bid for a way out. It may be a water hole that they are sure is directly due south – but which can so easily be missed or has dried up – or a desperate gamble on a hunch that a road or town is definitely this way or that.

The trouble with this strategy is that the chances of success are very poor, and in just a few hours in the heat of the sun, you may easily put yourself beyond help with no gain whatever. If you decide to move, do so late or early when the sun is not so fierce and when you will be able to orient yourself better and see objects on the horizon more easily.

The air close to the ground, up to a height of about 10 feet, is super-heated and can often shimmer and refract light so that a mirage effect builds up

As we saw in the first chapter (pages 32–37), there are many ways to use the sun, the moon, and the stars to get your bearings. These include the shadow-stick method using the moving shadow of the sun or the hands of a wristwatch or a crescent moon to find a rough north and south. It also means that in the northern hemisphere – in the Sahara, for example, or the Gobi Desert in Mongolia and China – Polaris, the North Star, will be easily visible in clear desert night skies. In the southern hemisphere, including the huge deserts that occupy much of Australia, south can easily be identified by the Southern Cross.

Another trick is to observe which way clumps of barrel cactus (aka the compass cactus) lean. These compass cacti tend to grow and lean south towards the sun. One on its own is not enough to rely on, but if you notice clumps of them leaning the same way, they'll probably be pointing south. The principle believed to be at work here is that the flowering plants grow towards the south to protect their flowers from the heat of the sun – i.e., they turn side on to the sun's main power, in the same way a camel orients its body end on to the sun when resting.

In sand deserts, the shape of dunes can also be a useful indication of direction – assuming you already know the direction of the prevailing wind. The windward side is usually less steep than the side in the lee of the wind.

But while orientation to the cardinal points may be no great problem, deciding on the best direction to go can often be more a matter of luck than judgment. Crossing large expanses of desert of any type on foot is a major undertaking, so the pros and cons of moving at all should be carefully weighed up.

Moving at night is sometimes possible if the moon or the stars are bright enough, but be very careful as injuries in desert terrain are very common, and even something as simple as a sprained ankle may mean that all chances of further progress have gone. Moving at night with little moonlight, when it is very hard to see, is unwise as there will be a real risk of losing orientation or being unable to see hazardous features like ravines and gullies.

Remember that you will be able to see objects far more clearly by looking just above them or to one side rather than by looking directly at them. This phenomenon occurs because the rod cells in our eyes – concentrated around the outer edges of the retina – are much more light-sensitive than the cone cells in the center, which are more sensitive to color.

MOVING ACROSS DESERT TERRAIN

The best way to move across desert terrain is to orient yourself using the methods discussed above and to fix on an object on the horizon which is in the general direction you want to go. To ensure that you are traveling in a straight line, keep checking your tracks as you go or leave small piles of stones behind that you can look back at and confirm your course.

If you are walking across sand embedded with sastrugi patterns – where the prevailing wind has blown the sand into corrugated wrinkles – note the angle at which you are walking relative to the sastrugi and keep that angle constant as you move forwards.

In the Sahara Desert in 125-degree heat. Rubbing charcoal under your eyes can minimize glare from the sun and help prevent sun blindness.

Look after your feet at all times, as they are your sole form of transport. Make sure sand does not get into your boots, and stop at once and adjust them if you feel even the slightest chafing. This is liable to get worse very quickly and is far more easily prevented than cured. In the Moab, my feet swelled considerably with all the heat and slip-sliding up and down dunes. Take time to nurse them better, rub them, and remove shoes and socks when you are resting in the shade.

Walk steadily, resting for a few minutes every half hour while sipping whatever water you have. Where there are sand dunes, always follow the line of the valleys between the dunes, where the sand will be harder.

Stony riverbeds are more likely to flood than sandy ones, and be very wary when vegetation is present and the surrounding area is completely parched. This usually indicates a flood river.

In 1997 a group of twelve tourists ignored weather warnings before descending into Antelope Canyon in Arizona. They were only 325 feet into the canyon when they were swept away by a flash flood. Only the guide survived.

QUICKSAND

Quicksand occurs in deserts all over the world and is actually sand mixed with water bubbling up from an unseen water source beneath. The surface can sometimes be covered by a layer of dry sand, which is why it can often be hard to see. Quicksand is not usually very deep, so your feet will often find the bottom, but if you are in danger of sinking, think of the sand as being like normal water (in fact it's more dense than water) and float on your back or "swim," keeping your body as horizontal as possible.

In Moab, I sank in quicksand on a riverbank to show how cattle can die so quickly in the stuff. The danger of it is that the more you struggle the more the suction pulls you in. Never fight it, conserve your energy, manipulate your body onto the surface and monkey-crawl out.

OBSTACLES

FLASH FLOODS

Always be wary of the sudden appearance of running water in a dried-up river basin and move to higher ground at the first sign of rain. Flash flooding can occur with little or no warning even when there is apparently no rain in the vicinity. Rain that has fallen on distant high ground up to 90 miles away will quickly find its way down into the valleys over the rock-hard ground. Small gullies that you might be walking along or resting in can suddenly turn into raging torrents that will kill you. Never linger in such flash flood–prone gullies.

Look out for clumps of vegetation in the desert – they indicate the presence of underground water sources.

SANDSTORMS

Owing to the mixing of air masses of different temperatures, deserts are prone to high winds kicking up sandstorms, which can sometimes blow at up to 80 miles per hour. Unlike snow, which can potentially bury a static object like a human, sand will be blown away as fast as it accumulates, so getting buried is usually not a concern. The main danger in a sandstorm is either getting lost or not being able to reorient yourself when it has died down. If you can, find some sort of natural protection and lie downwind out of it with your head or feet in the direction of travel so that when the storm has blown out, you will know in which direction to continue. Protect your eyes, face, and mouth with some material and sit it out.

MIRAGES

Desert mirages are a natural phenomenon where light is refracted by the super-heated air just above the desert floor. This shimmering blanket of air can make distant objects like mountain ranges rise over the horizon, giving the impression that they are much closer than they actually are. A clearer view of the surrounding landscape will be possible either by finding a vantage point more than 10 feet above the desert floor or by waiting until the evening, when the temperature will have fallen once again.

JUDGING DISTANCE

Judging the distance of far-off objects is notoriously difficult in the desert, and the lack of any sense of scale and the refraction of light in the heated air compounds this effect. Practical experience shows that people usually underestimate distance by as much as a factor of three to one, making a rock outcrop that is actually 2 miles away appear as if it is just 1/2 mile away. This can lead to catastrophic errors of judgment.

Natural Hazards

There are many ways of coming a cropper in the desert – including dangers from snakes, scorpions, bees, venomous spiders, sandstorms, and flash floods to name but a few – but it is heat, and the effects of heat, that is the number-one killer.

In terrain where ground temperatures can sometimes reach 65°C (149°F), prolonged direct exposure to infrared and ultraviolet solar rays will rapidly damage skin and eyes, cause swift dehydration, and an uncontrollable rise in the body's core heat, resulting in cramps, exhaustion, stroke, and ultimately death.

As we have already seen, reducing the dehydrating effects of direct sunlight and heat should be the first objective in a survival situation. Always seek out shade during the heat of the day and travel in the early morning or evening or by night if there is sufficient moonlight. Always resist any desire to remove your clothes. Clothing is your only form of portable shade and your first line of resistance against the effects of the heat.

EFFECTS OF SOLAR RADIATION

Heat is absorbed into the body through radiation from direct sunlight, conduction from the ground, and convection from the air. Without protection, the human body will quickly be unable to cool itself through perspiration. Just a few degrees' rise in the body's normal core temperature will trigger a series of progressively severe conditions in excessively hot environments.

Clothing is your only form of portable shade and your first line of resistance against the effects of the heat

PRICKLY HEAT

This condition is usually associated with the period of acclimatization to a hotter environment. Irritation and prickliness on the surface of the skin is caused by the sweat glands becoming blocked when the body is suddenly exposed to high temperatures.

HEAT CRAMPS

Severe muscle cramps can occur after sweating heavily in excessive heat conditions and are caused by a loss of body salts or electrolytes. As much as 2 grams of salt per 16 ounces sweated may be lost, reducing the ability of the muscles to absorb water.

HYPONATREMIA

When a supply of water is not the problem and an individual continues to drink larger and larger quantities of water but stops eating because of the very high desert temperatures, the loss of sodium, potassium, and other electrolytes through sweating can result in a form of water intoxication known as hyponatremia. The symptoms include nausea, dizziness, and faintness. If you have no other form of salt, you may be able to lick some off the side of rocks or cliff faces where water with a high mineral content has evaporated, or seek out the squawbush berries discussed earlier.

HEAT EXHAUSTION

A pale face, sweating skin, exhaustion, weakness, dizziness, bad temper, and an inability to think straight are all signs of heat exhaustion caused by progressive dehydration and the increasing rise in the body's core temperature.

HEAT STROKE

Hyperthermia, when the body has lost the ability to regulate its core heat through sweating, finally results in heatstroke when the core temperature rises above 40.5°C (105°F). In sufficiently extreme conditions, heat stroke can occur without any warning symptoms of muscle cramps or heat exhaustion. Symptoms include a severe headache, burning skin with no sweating, a pulse that can reach 160, reddened whites of the eyes, beetroot-red face, weakness, fatigue, dizziness, shivering, nausea, diarrhea, and vomiting.

SAND OR SUN BLINDNESS

This is caused by the reflection of the sun off the sand and rocks in much the same way as snow blindness in cold terrain. Makeshift eye protection from bark or covering the eyes with clothing or a head scarf is the best protection in the absence of sunglasses. Charcoal rubbed under the eyes helps reduce the glare as well. Reapply every few hours and carry a coal from your fire with you for this purpose.

There is only one effective treatment for all these conditions of heat stress, which is to find shade and water as quickly as possible and to slowly cool and rehydrate the body.

Remember, as a sole survivor in a desert situation, your mental state can be quickly affected by the sun and you may soon be unable to help yourself. Prevention is always better than cure.

SNAKES

As in the jungle, venomous snakes are a potential hazard in the desert, so it always pays to be cautious where you tread and where you put your hands. As in the jungle, a stick or walking staff is as valuable for checking the way ahead as it is as a support. Most snakes will avoid a human if they hear one coming, but can be very aggressive if surprised. In the heat of the day they will seek out shade, so be careful when sitting down under a bush or in the lee of a rock. If you're scrambling up a hillside, look before you clamber onto a ledge as something unwelcome may have arrived before you.

Snakes are masters of camouflage – beware!

Boots should be shaken out in the morning and all other clothing checked. Never go barefoot in the desert, night or day. For information on the different types of snake bite toxin and what to do if you are bitten, see Chapter 4 (pages 173–177).

DESERT SNAKES WELL WORTH AVOIDING . . .

Coral Snake: Thin body with brightly colored bands of red, yellow, and black. Found in the American deserts and south into Mexico. Up to 2 feet long. Neurotoxic.

Egyptian Cobra: The culprit who did away with Cleopatra, otherwise known as an asp. Short fangs with a small head and trademark cobra hood. Up to 6 feet long. Neurotoxic.

Death Adder: A native of Australia, one of the world's most deadly snakes. Grayish-brown with dark bands, a broad body with a thin tail. Nocturnal and buries itself during the day. Up to 3 feet long. Neurotoxic.

Sand Viper: A denizen of the Sahara and deserts of the Middle East, known for its distinctive sideways movement through the sand. Light, yellow-brown color with darker patches and a triangular head. Up to 2 feet long. Hemotoxic.

SCORPIONS AND SPIDERS

While most of the 800 species of scorpion worldwide are not lethal, they can give a nasty sting, which will only add to your woes in a survival situation, so they should be avoided, unless you know what you're doing and are planning to eat it, of course. The general rule about scorpions, though, is that the bigger the claws, the weaker the sting. And vice versa. They are mostly nocturnal and hide in cool, moist, shady places during the day, so all terrain of this type should be approached with caution.

Filming in the USA, I came across a giant hairy scorpion which was quite an impressive beast, but the one you really want to look out for is the bark scorpion, which is actually quite small and translucent yellow in color. It injects a neurotoxin which is incredibly painful and causes muscle spasms and difficulty breathing. Remember it is the tail that contains the venom.

The most deadly desert scorpions are to be found in the African deserts and the Middle East, where they grow up to 6 inches long and have a powerful neurotoxic sting that can be fatal and cause symptoms that include body spasms, double vision, blindness, and involuntary rapid movement of the eyeballs. So: well worth checking those boots in the morning.

Venomous desert spiders are restricted to the black widow and the fiddleback spider.

Crossing large expanses of desert of any type on foot is a major undertaking. Move in the early morning, at dusk, or at night under a full moon

probably because its natural habitat and hunting range have come under increasing pressure from human activity.

COUGARS

The mountain lion, or cougar, can be found in all four deserts of the American Southwest. They are rarely seen and don't usually attack humans, but you should always be careful entering caves where they often sleep or at water holes where they hunt their prey. Attacks on humans have increased in recent years,

BEES

Although bees are not primarily associated with the desert, in certain desert regions of the world, like the Sonoran Desert of North America, they are prolific. See Chapter 4 (page 179) for more information.

The Bear Necessities: Surviving the Desert

RULE 1: THINK WATER
In the desert, dehydration is Public Enemy Number One. Don't waste a drop of water and make it your first priority to find.

RULE 2: KEEP YOUR HEAD COVERED
In extreme heat, your head and neck will gain heat as fast as they lose it in freezing weather. Always keep them loosely covered.

RULE 3: FIND SHADE
Nothing will make you dehydrate faster than direct exposure to the sun. Keep well covered

and out of the sun and use the terrain and surrounding foliage to keep in the shade.

RULE 4: DON'T WASTE ENERGY
Any vigorous activity will make you sweat. In the heat of the day, don't exert yourself unless you are certain there is something to gain.

RULE 5: MOVE EARLY OR LATE
If you are sure that moving on will help and you are confident of finding water, do so early or late, when the sun is less fierce, or under a full moon.

"Paddle your own canoe."

AMERICAN PROVERB

chapter 6

the sea

Paddling my little boat back to safety through the giant Alaskan ice floes.

ART AND LITERATURE ARE AWASH WITH SHIPWRECKS AND CASTAWAYS. SHAKESPEARE'S LAST AND GREATEST OF PLAYS, *THE TEMPEST*, BEGINS WITH A SHIPWRECK; COLERIDGE'S *THE RIME OF THE ANCIENT MARINER* TELLS THE STORY OF A SURVIVOR ABOARD A PRISON SHIP CREWED ENTIRELY BY GHOSTS; GÉRICAULT'S *RAFT OF THE MEDUSA,* AN EPIC SHIPWRECK CANVAS WITH UNDERCURRENTS OF CANNIBALISM, SHOCKED NINETEENTH-CENTURY FRANCE.

And then, of course, there are the many classic novels of sea survival, both real and imagined: Herman Melville's *Moby-Dick,* Defoe's *Robinson Crusoe,* Henri Charrière's autobiographical *Papillon,* and William Golding's *Lord of the Flies.* The list goes ever on, and man's obsession with terror at being lost on the high seas seems unquenchable – and with good reason.

In these days of sophisticated modern technology, you would be forgiven for thinking that ocean odysseys following a disaster at sea have been consigned to history. While the numbers have certainly diminished hugely from their peak during the Second World War, the fact is that every year, someone somewhere will embark on a voyage which he or she thinks will be just a short trip, only to find themselves a few hours later drifting away from land with meager rations.

The problem is that despite all our modern technology – EPIRBs (Emergency Position Indicating Radio Beacons), survival suits, GPSs, satellite phones, VHF radios, reverse-osmosis pumps that produce fresh water from sea water – not everybody has access to it when it is really needed. Nor is everyone sufficiently prepared for a situation which can arise very quickly and unexpectedly – and often out of a clear blue sky.

While on the vast majority of occasions safety procedures work well and survivors are picked up from well-equipped life rafts within hours, there will always be some – lone yachtsmen, fleeing refugees, or explorers stranded in a distant land after a boating accident – who are not so lucky. You might well find yourself in a fight for survival, alone at sea with a minimum of safety devices, signaling aids, and survival equipment. The British Special Forces teach their men, above everything, to prepare for the unexpected.

The sheer vastness of the sea and its many faces can strip even the strongest men of all hope. Life-giving water is all around but is unobtainable; nourishing food so near and yet so difficult to bring aboard; ships pass by on the horizon ignorant of the castaway's desperate cries for help. Redemption is always so tantalizingly close and yet continuously slipping beyond your gasp as you wait day after day in enforced captivity, powerless to help yourself, adrift in a cage with invisible bars.

The sea is on a different scale to every other wilderness on the planet. The oceans cover three-quarters of the earth's surface, filled by an estimated third of a billion cubic miles of seawater. This is made up of five oceans, with the Atlantic, Indian, and Pacific Oceans separating the world's major land masses, flanked by the freezing waters of the Arctic Ocean in the north and the Southern Ocean in the south. The main surface currents of the central oceans circulate warm and cooler water around the world like a giant pumping heart, controlling the world's climate in the process.

The sea's lack of surface features and landmarks is the very definition of what land is not. On land, it is virtually impossible to stand and see nothing to disturb the horizontal line

My 2003 Arctic crew and I head into a North Atlantic storm.

where the sky meets the earth in an unbroken 360-degree circle. But at sea, alone in a life raft, this is an everyday reality. The solitude is more than profound. It can penetrate the mind more than any other wilderness on earth.

To be shipwrecked, both literally and metaphorically, means the stripping away of any security blanket you may once have had. Whatever your status, it is of no relevance in the face of this immensity. The sea will both humble and reduce you. How you react to this will determine your fate.

The will to live is under its greatest threat when confronted with enforced passivity. Perhaps of all the environments we have considered in this book, surviving for a sustained period at sea requires a greater effort of will than any other.

The sea is on a different scale to every other wilderness on the planet

Which probably explains why many of *the* most remarkable stories of survival have occurred at sea. Chief among them is perhaps the most remarkable survival story of all time, Ernest Shackleton's famous 1916 crossing of 800 miles of Antarctic waters in an open boat, from Elephant Island to South Georgia, to find help for the rest of his stranded crew.

And the record for the longest survival at sea is an incredible four and a half months. Poon Lim was a Chinese sailor serving on a British cargo ship, the *Ben Lomond,* when it was torpedoed by a U-boat off the coast of Brazil during the Second World War. Although he was a poor swimmer, Lim was wearing a lifejacket and was able to stay afloat for two hours before he finally clambered aboard a life raft whose rations included a ten-gallon canister of water, some chocolate, sugar, biscuits, and a flashlight.

For the next 133 days, Poon Lim's unbreakable spirit was his only lifeline. His limitless ingenuity in the face of everything the sea could throw at him is an object lesson in how to survive against incredible odds. His will to live allowed his imagination to remain active so that he was able to find ways of collecting fresh water and harvesting food from the sea when his rations ran out.

Without any prior knowledge, Poon Lim discovered for himself many of the survival techniques described in this chapter and earlier in the book: he used the canvas cover of his lifejacket as a tarpaulin to collect rainwater; he used the hemp rope which had been used to tie down the rations on the raft as a fishing line; he made fishing hooks from the spring of his flashlight and the nails from the wooden boards of the raft; he fashioned a knife from a biscuit tin which he then used to gut the fish he had caught and cut them into strips so they could be dried in the sun, keeping the leftovers as bait; and he caught a seagull by making a bird's nest from seaweed dragged from the bottom of the boat and baiting it with fish, and he drank its blood, ate its liver, and sucked on its bones for water. Amazingly, he also caught a shark and brought it on board, wrapping his hand in canvas to protect himself from rope burn.

Like so many other survivors at sea, he also endured the torture of seeing ships pass by and planes pass overhead which failed to spot him, an experience that hardened his resolve to reach land. When he was finally picked up by a passing ship after 133 days alone at sea, the crew decided he was in good enough condition (he had not even lost weight!) for them to continue their three-day fishing trip before taking him to hospital.

In the face of the bare facts of this extraordinary story, it is hardly surprising that the British navy used Poon Lim's account as a case history in their survival manuals for decades afterwards.

Sir Ernest Shackleton – a born survivor of the sea.

At sea, the survivor and his shelter are one. While your raft may be able to travel without you, you can go nowhere without it. The raft you scrambled into when you abandoned ship, ditched your plane, or – like the autobiographical hero of *Papillon* – constructed it out of coconuts, will be your only shelter from the elements until you reach land. And unless you sink, freeze, fry, or are eaten before you get there, reaching land will eventually be inevitable. It may take months or even years, but the currents and winds of the world's oceans will eventually toss you ashore. The only issue is whether you will be alive to enjoy it when you get there.

If you are to survive, much will depend on the state of your mind and body, the raft, and whatever equipment and rations you have in the initial aftermath of the disaster. Analysis of how people have survived sea disasters has shown that preparation beforehand for an event that you hope will never happen improves the chances of survival immeasurably.

Sea disasters, by their very nature, often happen very quickly. Steve Callahan in his book *Adrift*, the harrowing story of his seventy-six days drifting 2,000 miles across the Atlantic, described how he became an "aquatic caveman" in his quest for survival. While making a solo crossing of the Atlantic, his yacht collided with a whale and within seconds the boat began to sink. Although he nearly drowned in the process, he somehow managed to retrieve the survival bag which he had initially been unable to cut free as the boat began to sink.

Aboard his life raft was enough food and water to last two weeks, but he knew it would take about three months to reach the Caribbean, where the trade winds from the Sahara were blowing

him. Without the contents of his survival bag and the ability to generate fresh water from a still, as well as being able to catch fish with the line and spear gun, he would almost certainly have died.

There are many other examples where people did not survive who almost certainly would have done if safety procedures had been followed and the crews had familiarized themselves with the safety equipment beforehand, keeping it well maintained and easy to deploy in an emergency. Sometimes, too, the makers of safety equipment do not think through the likely physical and mental condition of someone struggling to use it. Instructions are too complicated to follow or the necessary actions too fiddly for someone whose fingers are frozen.

> **Unless you sink, freeze, fry, or are eaten before you get there, reaching land will eventually be inevitable**

Every action that needs to be performed when a boat goes down (from the moment you wake in the middle of the night to find freezing water pouring into your cabin) *must* be carried out without having to think. If you need time to gather your thoughts and start remembering where you have put things, or whether indeed you have them with you at all, you may well be fighting your final battle.

By the time you find yourself aboard a life raft and facing a sea-survival situation, the mantra

Left alone on a South Pacific island, I contemplate my escape.

of all sea-survival courses – "*Cut, stream, close, maintain*" – should be indelibly engraved on your mind. Cut the rope attaching the raft to the sinking vessel so that it does not take you down with it; *stream* the sea anchor (see pages 238–9), which will aid stability and keep you in the vicinity of the sinking vessel so that the rescue services can locate you; *close* the canopy entrance to retain heat and keep yourself protected from the sea, the rain, the cold, and the sun; *maintain* your raft, equipment, rations, hygiene, and morale to the very best of your ability.

Whereas on terra firma there may be much that you can do to improve your shelter, at sea it will be only a matter of maximizing the efficiency of what you already have. There will be nothing else. When refugees put to sea in unseaworthy vessels trying to escape from war or economic collapse, they often do not make even the most basic preparations and pay the price with their lives.

The moment you find yourself alone in your raft, throw out your sea anchor (see pages 238–9) or improvise one from a bucket or any large container that will act as a drag on the current. This will help keep you in the vicinity of the wreck and make it easier for a rescuer to find you if you have been able to send out a Mayday. The sea anchor will also help keep the boat or

Every action that needs to be performed when a boat goes down *must* be carried out without having to think

raft heading into, and not side on to, the wind and waves. Being turned side on to the waves is generally the classic first step before a capsize; keep the bow pointing into the sea by deploying your sea anchor early and before the seas get up.

If it is sunny, stay under the sun canopy at all times to reduce dehydration, and if it is stormy, deploy any covering the raft may have and make sure leaks are kept to a minimum. Try to keep the floor of the raft dry and cover it with canvas or a tarp for insulation. Unless the accident has taken place in the tropics, once the initial hazards of drowning or being injured have been overcome, exposure to cold is by far the most likely killer, followed by dehydration and, only then, lack of food.

Now make a mental list of all the equipment and rations you have at your disposal and work out a rationing plan that will eke out your dwindling supplies as long as possible. Leave out tarps to collect rainwater and rig up some fishing apparatus (see page 232–234). Catching something will be sure to try your patience, but now is the time to start as you will need plenty of time to practice.

Keep a constant check on the raft for inflation and make sure the buoyancy is firm but not skintight, remembering that tubes will expand in the heat and contract as the nights cool the air inside them. Look for anything that causes chafing and might cause a future

leak and fix it now rather than later. "A stitch in time saves nine" is never more relevant than at sea.

SHELTER FROM THE STORM . . .

Protecting yourself against exposure to the elements as a survivor at sea is a constant battle. Much will depend on the equipment you have on board, but many examples exist of people who have survived a sinking only to fall into fatal listlessness when there was much they could have done to protect themselves. Getting warm when you are cold is always far more difficult than staying warm in the first place.

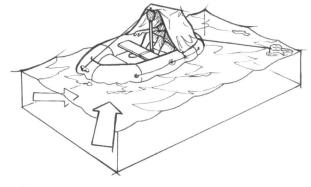

TIP: You can use your sea anchor (see page 238) to orient the raft at an angle to the wind so it catches the cooling breeze.

> Keep a constant check on the raft: look for anything that might cause a future leak and fix it now rather than later. A stitch in time saves nine

COLD

After drowning, hypothermia is the main cause of death in incidents at sea. The cold can be a serious problem in temperate as well as polar latitudes, owing to the constant wet conditions. A survival suit, if you have one, should always be worn. Continued exposure to cold water must be avoided, so bail water out quickly rather than

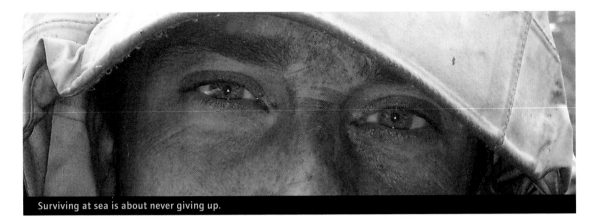
Surviving at sea is about never giving up.

leaving it sloshing around, because it will get colder at night when the sun goes down. As with the ground in a shelter on land, you should insulate yourself from the cold bottom of the raft as best you can. Garbage bags are a very effective improvised protection against the wet and cold.

SUN

Do everything you can to protect yourself from the sun as burning will both severely dehydrate you and result in blistering that can fester. Most modern rafts have a canopy under which you should shelter, while making sure there is sufficient ventilation. If not, use tarps or canvas sails to rig up some protection. If you have a hat, wear it or cover your head and neck with clothing soaked in seawater. The reflected glare of the sea can be particularly damaging to the eyes, and areas like your chin can easily burn and chafe. If necessary, improvise by wrapping a strip of fabric around your eyes and making slits to see through. Fish-liver oil, which you can collect by drying fish livers in the sun and collecting the oil as it oozes out, is an effective sunscreen. Any form of grease or fat, including that of birds, will also help keep your skin's moisture in and provide some protection against the sun and salt.

SALT

Long-term immersion in salt water can do serious damage to the skin and will rapidly result in sores and boils, which can easily swell and become infected. Pressure sores, like bedsores, compound the problem as in the narrow confines of a raft it is difficult to shift around and take the pressure off vulnerable areas. Hands, elbows, and buttocks are particularly susceptible. Salt water sucks away the skin's natural moisturizers and speeds up its deterioration. Wash all salt from your body and your clothes whenever it rains.

STORMS

In heavy weather make sure you take down any makeshift sails and deploy the sea anchor (see page 238). If the waves are coming from behind (a following sea), maneuver the sea anchor so the door is away from the waves and doesn't ship water. Sit on the side nearest the oncoming wind to keep the raft stable and stay low in the boat. If the raft feels like it may be blown over, let a little air out. This will make it floppier and ride lower in the water so it is less likely to capsize. But don't overdo it!

Survivors of sea disasters, both real and fictional, invariably describe the bitter irony of being surrounded entirely by water when they have nothing to drink. What looks like an ocean of plenty is in practical terms a parched desert.

If you arrive in a survival raft in one piece, your thoughts will quickly turn to water. Owing to its weight and volume, it is impractical to store huge quantities of water on a liferaft, so they are often equipped with the next best thing: a solar still or reverse osmosis pump (see pages 229–230). These use, in a smaller and more designed form, the same condensation principle as the solar still we saw in Chapter 5 (pages 200–201). The more of these stills you carry or can make, the better.

PRESERVING WATER

As in each and every wilderness, the importance of preserving water both in and outside the body cannot be overstated. To remain reasonably well hydrated, you will need to drink at the very least a quart a day, although in temperate latitudes it has been shown that survival is possible for a short period of time on as little as 2–6 ounces, which is between a quarter and half a glass of water a day.

Even with a solar still and a good prospect of being able to collect rainwater, rationing of the water you have aboard is a sensible precaution as you may have no idea how long it will be before

In Antartica you must survive two of the world's great wildernesses – sea and ice.

you are rescued or reach land. On the first day of any survival ordeal, it usually makes sense to restrict water consumption if you are already reasonably well hydrated, as the body needs to adapt quickly to a lack of water and there is no point in wasting water that will otherwise simply be jettisoned in urine.

Every drop of water should be treated like gold. Use every container you have to collect water, even if it is only a garbage bag, and keep them all well sealed and attached to the raft. If you build up a healthy supply, make sure you rotate the containers and drink the oldest first.

Take every possible precaution to stop the water being contaminated with seawater, and make sure when taking a drink that you gargle and moisten your lips before swallowing as this will help to keep your mouth and throat moist and remove symptoms of acute thirst. As well as staying under the sun canopy during the heat of the day, drench your clothes with seawater if you are sweating excessively, as this will cool your body down. Remember, though, that this should be used only in very extreme heat, as skin sores caused by the salt can become an uncomfortable side effect. It's better if you use urine to soak clothing, because it acts as an antiseptic for the skin.

Cooling down by swimming alongside the raft is also an option, but be extremely cautious. Don't even think of doing so without tying yourself to the raft, and keep a very close eye out for sharks. I once tried to cool off by jumping off my boat and was almost attacked by a 16-foot tiger shark! Many a fatality has been caused by currents or winds blowing rafts away from survivors having a cool-down dip. Rafts can often travel faster than a man can swim. The speed of currents can be deceptively fast. Beware! Try to avoid unneccesary risks and always check the sea before jumping in.

SEASICKNESS: A WARNING

While the problem of seasickness might normally be addressed in the hazards section of this chapter, it is so central to the issue of dehydration that it is important to cover it early on. No one is immune to this miserable affliction, and the symptoms are not hard to recognize: the prickly sensation of sweat on the brow followed by dizziness, queasiness in the very pit of the stomach, and the sudden realization that you might not make it to the side of the boat in time.

Like altitude sickness to the mountaineer, seasickness is a hazard to anyone who finds themselves on the high seas. It is caused by the temporary confusion of the sense organs. On the sea, everything is moving, and the senses we normally use to locate ourselves in three-dimensional space are easily muddled. Our eyes, the fluid in our inner ears, and the sensors in our bones can usually make sense of spinning and turning by locating a static surface like the ground or the horizon. When these are moving too, the senses have no static resting point with which to orient themselves, and the reflex response is to throw up.

Generally, seasickness is something we can tolerate and eventually adapt to and accept. Funny when it's over, if not at the time. Alone in a raft it is less funny. The actual sensation

Every drop of water should be treated like gold. Use every container you have to collect water, even if it is only a garbage bag

of feeling sick and then being sick is the least of your problems. There is a small chance that the remains of your stomach contents may attract sharks, but the real risk is that you will lose more precious bodily fluids and salts than you can easily replace, and this is a serious issue when water is at a premium.

Most rafts are equipped with seasickness pills, and you should take them at the first hint of queasiness. Keep looking at the horizon, which gives the senses at least one steady object to fix on. Otherwise putting pressure on the center of the wrist is an acupuncture technique which stimulates the nerves in the arm and helps the brain ignore the contradictory messages it is receiving from elsewhere.

I remember being told by an old Greenland fisherman before setting out into what turned out to be one of the worst storms I have ever encountered at sea, that seasickness has two phases. The first phase is when you feel so sick you think you are going to die; the second phase is when you are so sick you hope you will die. I laughed it off until 500 miles later, on the edge of the Arctic Circle, in Force 9 gales and sub-zero temperatures in our small open boat, where we were all throwing up, facing the reality of an ever-diminishing chance of survival. But that's another story!

Finally completing our 3,000-mile crossing of the freezing North

The first phase is when you feel so sick you think you are going to die; the second phase is when you are so sick you hope you will die

The first phase is when you feel so sick you think you are going to die; the second phase is when you are so sick you hope you will die

COLLECTING DRINKING FLUIDS

RAINWATER

The key to the effective collection of rainwater is to be prepared. Watch the skies for cloud changes (see Chapter 1, pages 37–38). Spread whatever tarpaulin, sheet, or canvas you have available in a bowl shape over the maximum surface area possible. Keep it in place overnight as it will be

SOLAR STILL

If one or more solar stills have been stored in the life raft, read the instructions carefully as there are many different designs. Set them up immediately you are cast adrift. They are usually inflatable and spherical or conical in shape but only work on flat, calm seas. Water droplets which have evaporated from a black cloth heated in the sun condense on the edges of the still and collect in a reservoir. But they are unlikely to be able to produce enough water to be depended upon in a survival situation, around 16 ounces per day if you are really lucky.

A solar still based on the design described in Chapter 5 (see pages 200–201) can also be constructed if the right materials are available. Place a weighted-down cup in the bottom of a larger container and surround with any absorbent material you have to hand. Pour about an inch of seawater into the large container so it surrounds the cup. Cover the outer container with a sheet of plastic weighted down in the center so that the plastic makes a funnel shape over the cup. Leave in bright sunlight and the seawater will condense and drip into the cup. This type of construction will only work in calm weather.

very hard to set up in a hurry in the dark and rain often brings with it wind and an increased swell, which will make it harder still.

DEW

Dew still forms in the morning at sea and can often be worth the effort of collecting. Leave a tarp out at night even if rain does not seem likely.

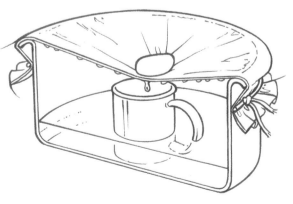

REVERSE OSMOSIS PUMPS

These devices have been one of the biggest breakthroughs in the problem of providing the survivors of sea disasters with fresh water. They pump seawater at a very high pressure through a membrane that filters out the salt. Nonetheless, they should not be relied on as the only supply of fresh water in a survival situation.

FISH AND TURTLES

Fish contain a useful source of fluid in their spines and eyes. You can harvest the latter by cutting the spine and the vertebrae in half or by covering the fish in a cloth and twisting as if you are wringing them out. As for the eyes, I always try to swallow them whole so I don't have to taste what's inside! Fish blood is also potable but should be drunk immediately or it will spoil. The blood of turtles has a concentration of salt similar to humans (see page 235) and is an excellent source of fluid which can be easily collected by slitting the turtle's throat.

REHYDRATION ENEMA

Enemas are a very effective way of rehydrating the body as the rectum is designed to absorb fluid. If some of your water has become contaminated by dirt or the plastic residue of your raft and you are unable to purify it, you can still benefit from its rehydration potential through an enema. Taking in the water rectally means the potentially contaminated fluids bypass your stomach. This technique was used to great effect by Dougal and Lynn Robertson who with their three sons and the son of some friends were cast adrift in a raft when their schooner was attacked and

Sea water is actually toxic because it contains a concentration of salt that is three times higher than the blood and leads inevitably to kidney failure

sunk by a killer whale west of the Galapagos Islands in 1972.

Lubricate a hose or tube with fish oil or fat and insert it a maximum of about 3 inches. Pour in about 16 ounces of the water and stay lying down for ten minutes. Repeat twice a day.

THE PERILS OF DRINKING SEAWATER

It may require an iron will, but avoid drinking seawater at all costs. Throughout history castaways at sea have weakened and tried to drink seawater only to be driven mad by hallucinations and delirium. Some start by swilling their mouths out, but the residue of salt leads inexorably to an even greater thirst and the inevitable temptation to swallow. Seawater is also actually toxic because it contains a concentration of salt that is three times higher than the blood and leads inevitably to kidney failure.

There are some cases where drinking small amounts of urine or seawater along with large amounts of fresh water to supplement it has had a sustaining effect on the body over time – but this has been shown to be the case only when there is a stable and reliable supply of fresh water to dilute the salt or urine by a large margin.

Without an ample supply of fresh water, never resort to this method. Instead, think smart, be inventive, get fishing, make stills, catch rain, collect dew, but *don't drink salt water*.

On top of the dehydration it will cause, the further depletion of body fluids will make you even more desperate. It is thought that the madness brought on by drinking seawater is caused by high concentrations of salt reducing the fluid passing between brain cells.

This is why people end up eating each other – out of mad desperation. Your body doesn't need meat, it needs water. The crew from the real story behind the tale of *Moby-Dick* were reportedly found adrift with the last two survivors deliriously fighting over the gnawed bones of the comrades they had eaten. This is quite a bad stage to get to!

DRINKING SEAWATER: STRANGE BUT TRUE

There still remains some controversy around the subject of drinking seawater. It centers on the voyage of Frenchman Alain Bombard, who in 1951 voluntarily crossed the Atlantic in a raft without food and water. For the first seven days he drank nothing but small amounts of seawater, later alternating this with whatever fresh water he could find from fish and rainwater. After sixty-five days at sea, he arrived in Barbados having lost almost half his body weight and with diarrhea, skin rashes, and lost toenails, but still alive.

While Bombard's experiment is a fascinating story of one brave man's attempt to defy the elements, it does not stand up to rigorous scientific analysis. Bombard did not record the relative amounts of seawater and fresh water consumed and made light of the fact that he was twice picked up by passing ships during the voyage, eating a meal and almost certainly consuming fresh water.

The fact remains that while drinking seawater may not kill you immediately, your life will be on a very short line. If you do not go mad first, without fresh water your kidneys will shut down in less than a week.

When escaping a deserted island, the surf is often your first hurdle.

TIP: Never celebrate what you think will be an imminent rescue by going on a water binge. Rescuers sometimes cannot see you or lose track of you, so you may have to endure many more days at sea before finally being picked up. Only celebrate when you are actually aboard the rescue vessel!

Finding Food

As with the vast expanse of water that is all around but cannot be drunk, the tantalizingly close presence of such a fertile food as the oceans' fish is another torturous irony sent to test the endurance of those cast away at sea. But while dragging fish from the deep has often proved far more difficult for sea survivors than they would have hoped, your chances will become progressively easier as the inevitable buildup of barnacles and weed on the bottom of the raft begins to create its own little ecosystem that will attract fish big enough to eat.

While in times gone by the British navy fed its sailors limes to keep scurvy at bay on their long sea voyages, this is probably not something you would need to worry about as scurvy takes at least three months to develop. Most of the vitamins required to keep you healthy are actually present in fish. As well as protein, vitamins A and D both reside in fish flesh, while vitamins B1 and B2 can be found in their livers.

FISHING FOR FOOD AT SEA

There will almost always be something aboard a serviceable raft that can be adapted into a fishing apparatus. The only variable ingredient is the ingenuity of the survivor himself. Fishing lines can be fashioned from bootlaces as well as the threads of clothing, sails, and tarpaulins, while hooks can be made from metal, plastic, bones, or safety pins. Spears can be made by lashing a blade to the end of an oar.

Bait presents the classic catch-22 situation (i.e., needing to catch something before you can use it). So use any lures your raft may contain in the first instance. But once you have caught something, you will be up and running – keep using lures as well as bait to increase your chances.

Fish are attracted to focused points of light, so nighttime, especially under a full moon, can be a very productive time to fish. If you have a mirror or reflective surface, use it to reflect

TO EAT OR NOT TO EAT?

When your water sources are unreliable, it is always unwise to eat anything unless you have enough water to digest it. Proteins, in the form of fish, turtles, birds, or seaweed, require much more water than carbohydrates to digest. But this protein makes up the mass of what you can potentially harvest from the sea. So if you have any carbohydrates in your survival rations, it is best to eat these first as they need less water to be digested.

In fact, you will almost certainly be using up your survival rations first anyway as catching fish from a raft without specialist fishing equipment is quite a challenge.

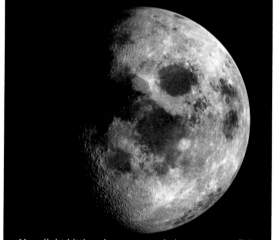
Moonlight hitting the water can help you attract fish.

Fish are attracted to focused points of light, so nighttime, especially under a full moon, can be a very productive time to fish

moonlight into the water. An artificial form of light like a flashlight will also attract fish. Conversely, during the day, fish like the shade, so drop your line over the side of the raft that is in shadow. Also, remember that water refracts light and you will have a much better chance of spearing a fish with a spear gun (if you have one) if you aim closer to the raft than the fish appears to be. When Steve Callahan was adrift in the Atlantic, it took him nearly two weeks before he finally succeeded in spearing a fish. In the end he also realized that if he aimed at fish that were almost under the boat, so he was aiming straight down, the distance and the refraction would be minimized and his aim would be truer.

If you catch a fish but have no cooking equipment, eat it raw. I have often done this when I have caught fish; it is the freshest way.

These days, with the arrival of sushi as a delicacy from Japan, the idea of eating fish raw is not as alien as it once was in the West, and I doubt such squeamishness will cross your mind when your survival depends on it. Although reef fish can be toxic (see opposite), any fish caught in deep sea is unlikely to be a problem.

TIGHT LINES

Tight lines are every fisherman's dream, but have an added significance for the castaway at sea. A taut line is the beginning of a fight for survival for both you and the fish. Think Ernest Hemingway. So while you're locked in this titanic struggle, don't forget the damage the fishing line can do to the raft and your hands, both of which are fundamentally important to your survival. Find some protective canvas for your hands and the boat.

SHARP POINTS

Hooks are designed to be sharp, but don't forget they can potentially damage you and your raft as well as the fish. Watch your hands and don't puncture your home. (Ditto when spearing fish!)

SCHOOL'S OUT

Anyone who has ever dropped a line of feathered hooks into a school of fish will know how exquisite it is to feel the line almost leap out of the water as a feeding frenzy breaks out below and within seconds every hook has a fish attached. If you see a school of fish approaching, get that line overboard at once.

SMALL IS BEAUTIFUL

Despite the fact that Poon Lim hooked a shark (see page 221), if you happen to hook a large fish, cut the line at once. If it gets anywhere near your raft, it may sink it and there may well be no way you will be able to do anything with all that fish unless you are quickly able to dry it, as it will spoil within half a day. Cut the line and pick on someone your own size.

REEF FISH AND CIGUATERA POISONING

Don't eat any fish that looks in any way suspicious. If close to land in the tropics, be extremely careful when eating reef fish as many are poisonous and carry an illness called ciguatera, a toxin that accumulates in the systems of fish that feed on tropical marine reefs. Spikes, livid colors, sunken eyes, spotting, wrinkled flesh, or a nasty smell are all signs that the fish may be either diseased or poisonous. Eating a poisoned fish will kill you far faster than another night without food.

ENJOYING THE SPOILS

Almost every part of a fish apart from the head and tail can be eaten, including the guts. While it may seem unpalatable, the guts of fish can be cooked and eaten while the bones contain marrow which can be sucked dry. In the tropics fish will spoil within just a few hours, so cut up into slices any meat you don't eat immediately, dry it in the sun, and keep it aside for later use, as it will keep almost indefinitely. Turn the strips regularly to make sure they don't start growing mold, and cut them as small and thin as possible to reduce the drying time.

FLYING FISH

Few yachtsmen who have crossed an ocean have not experienced the magical sight of schools of flying fish skimming across the water as they try to evade a predator. Sometimes they can be heard thudding onto the deck at night followed by a brief scurry and then silence. Next morning your breakfast is waiting for you. If you do see them at night, shine a flashlight in their direction, as they are attracted by bright lights. If you set up a white sail, they will often fly straight into it and fall stunned onto the deck. Flying fish also make excellent dorado bait.

BIRDS

Once they have been gutted and plucked, all birds are edible – raw as well as cooked – so don't be squeamish about trying to hook or snare them. A bird may sometimes land on your raft, in which case you can either try and club it with an oar, spear it, or smother it. A simple noose snare (see Chapter 1, page 47) may also work, with a piece of bait to attract the bird to stand in it, so you can trap its legs. Birds can also be hooked by throwing out a fishing line with a hook and some bait, or by simply leaving three or four safety pins baited and attached to lines on the roof of your canopy. The quickest way to kill a bird is to grab its wings and break its neck.

SEA TURTLES

Sea turtles are very nutritious, and many indigenous people still feed on them in Central America. They are an excellent source of blood, meat, and eggs and a better source of nourishment than fish. If you have an option, catch female turtles above males as they contain the eggs, which are full of protein and fat. You can tell the difference as male turtles have a longer tail and concave lower shell.

Be careful when you hook or spear a turtle, and don't try tangling with large ones as their claws and beak can do a lot of damage to both you and the raft. As a sole survivor with no help, your best bet is to drown the turtle before bringing it aboard. Do this by holding its head underwater until it stops moving.

If a flying fish lands in your raft, thank God – then eat it!

Don't forget to drink the blood while it is still fresh as it is an excellent source of fluid.

Practicing what I preach in the Everglade swamps.

PLANKTON

If it's good enough for whales, it's good enough for you. Plankton are found in all the world's oceans (but prefer the colder ones) and can be caught by dragging any sort of small mesh net, like a pair of women's panty hose or a tightly woven article of clothing, behind the boat. During the day plankton remain near the surface, but they sink lower at night. The result of your labors may be a foul-smelling soup, but it will be rich in vitamin C and sugars.

SEAWEED

Don't ignore the fruit and veg of the sea. In addition to sometimes being very tasty, seaweed is rich in proteins, carbohydrates, vitamins, and minerals. Seaweed rarely tastes that great raw and is better boiled. However, if you're lacking fresh water and can't rinse the seaweed, it's probably better not to eat it at all. The best way to catch seaweed is to drag a line with a hook over the back of the boat, but make sure it is a hook you can afford to lose.

FOOD BY THE SEASHORE

If you do make it to shore but find yourself stranded on a desert island, your chances of finding seafood and shellfish will usually be greatly increased. It's more plentiful, there is greater variety, and it is easier to catch.

CRABS, LOBSTERS, AND SEA URCHINS

Crustaceans like crabs and lobsters are plentiful on coastlines all over the world, as are octopus and squid, shellfish and sea urchins, which are considered a delicacy in many parts of the world. Break the urchins open and eat the innards. I know from experience that they look and taste like baby poop, but they're very nutritious!

Mussels, limpets, barnacles, clams, sea snails, and sea slugs are all also edible.

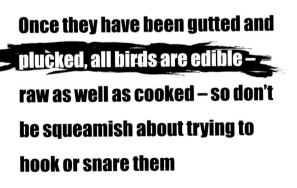

Once they have been gutted and plucked, all birds are edible – raw as well as cooked – so don't be squeamish about trying to hook or snare them

During our world-record-breaking expedition across the Arctic Ocean, we spent weeks traveling through frozen spray.

CONCH

Conch is found in sea grass on sandy sea bottoms all over the tropics. The white meat of the creature inside can best be extracted by smashing the end of the shell. This breaks the vacuum protecting it so it can be extracted. Remove the surrounding dark skin first and only eat the white meat.

SEA CUCUMBERS

Sea cucumbers live on sandy seabeds all over the world. They ooze white sticky threads of mucus when picked up and squeezed. This mucus is an irritant, so clean and gut the sea cucumbers thoroughly before you eat them.

Sea cucumbers are very easy to recognize!

Navigation and Movement

Stripped of a keel, sails, and a source of power, a castaway at sea is at the mercy of the winds and the currents that patrol the world's oceans. In no other wilderness environment is the choice of movement and direction so severely limited. As a sole survivor stranded on a raft at sea, you are at the mercy of a force that is impossible to resist, let alone to control over long distances. Besides, inflatable rafts do not sail well, and most are designed only to drift. While some limited form of steerage and propulsion may be available to you in the form of oars and a sea anchor (see overleaf), ultimately the sea will take you where it chooses.

A map of the epic long-distance voyages made by survivors at sea reveals that a significant percentage started within 50 miles of land and drifted many hundreds of kilometres in the opposite direction before being rescued. The lesson in all these cases is that to resist the elements is futile. The only worthwhile long-distance navigational strategy is to try to use the techniques described below to estimate your position using the sun and stars, and to have some idea where you are being taken so that you will know when you are likely to be approaching land.

CHECKING YOUR POSITION

In a featureless landscape like the sea, the celestial navigation techniques we discussed in Chapter 1 (pages 34–37) are particularly relevant. As we saw, establishing the cardinal points of the compass can easily be achieved by observing Ursa Major and Polaris in the northern hemisphere and the Southern Cross in the southern hemisphere.

You should keep your raft upwind of any landmass so that as you get closer you can drift with the wind towards it. If you allow yourself to be blown downwind, you may well miss your target altogether

The direction your raft takes will depend on the prevailing winds and currents, although the former will have a greater effect on your direction than the latter. Rafts also usually drift at 30 degrees to the right of the wind in the northern hemisphere, and 30 degrees to the left in the southern hemisphere. Near the equator both winds and currents tend to be in a westerly direction. Currents in the northern hemisphere tend to go clockwise and those in the southern hemisphere anticlockwise. With this knowledge and with confirmation of your direction from the stars, you should be able to calculate on which landmass you are most likely to make landfall.

With what little directional capability you do have, and depending on what charts you have, it will be worth aiming for shipping lanes, where you will have more chance of rescue, and areas of higher rainfall, where you can collect fresh water. You should also keep the raft upwind of any landmass, so that as you get closer you can drift with the wind towards it. If you allow yourself to be blown downwind, you may well miss your target altogether.

METHODS OF STEERING

Even the most sophisticated life rafts do not have keels, an essential feature of any craft if it is to be successfully sailed into the wind. Without a keel, the effects of wind and current can be exploited by:

- Adjusting the inflation of the raft. When the raft is rigid and well inflated, the wind will propel it faster over the surface of the water, but with no wind the current will have more effect if there is slightly less air in the raft and it is sitting lower in the water.
- Deploying or hauling in the sea anchor (see below).
- Turning the doorway into the wind.
- Rigging a makeshift sail (see below).
- Using an oar as a rudder.

There is no point in actively trying to steer and propel a modern life raft for long periods of time as they are only really designed to drift. What limited maneuverability you can rig up in the form of a makeshift sail should only be used in sight of land when you are scanning the coastline for the best position to make landfall.

rope, you can secure this mast from the top down to different points of your raft. Your makeshift mast can then be covered by a tarpaulin or shade cover or any other form of fabric that is big enough and strong enough to catch the wind.

Once you have the basic structure in place, don't make the mistake of attaching the sail directly to the raft at its foot, as a strong wind could easily overturn the raft. Instead, tie any available lengths of rope to the corners of the "sail" and attach them to the side of the raft so they can be released in a strong wind.

> When the raft is rigid and well inflated, the wind will propel it faster over the surface of the water. With no wind the current will have more effect if there is less air in the raft

MAKESHIFT SAILS

Rigging a sail, like so much in a survival situation at sea, needs imagination and innovative use of the available materials. Lashing oars together in the basic cruciform structure of a mast and then in turn lashing this structure to the cross-seat and to the sides and back of the boat (see diagram) will make the basic rigging structure. If you have further

SEA ANCHOR

Unlike a conventional anchor that claws the seabed and digs in so the movement of a boat is restricted to a circle around the anchor, a sea anchor uses drag to minimize rotation and movement in the wind and acts as a kind of brake if you are being dragged by an ocean current. It is best used in foul weather to stabilize the boat and can be pulled in when the weather is calm so the raft can reap the maximum benefit from the current.

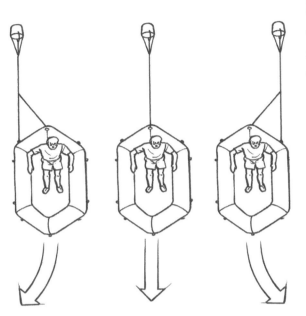

There are many different designs of sea anchor, but most have a parachute or cone structure on the end of a long rope. If your raft is not equipped with one, use a bucket with holes in the bottom attached to a rope, or even a piece of fabric tied to the end of a rope that will produce resistance as the sea inflates it.

For maximum efficiency, make sure you adjust the length of the rope so that when the raft is on the crest of wave, the sea anchor is in the trough. This will help keep the raft steady in very rough weather. When the winds are blowing with the current, don't deploy the sea anchor, as it will act as a brake. But when the winds are against the current (so-called "paradoxical winds"), deploy the sea anchor, as it will help keep you aligned to the direction of the current.

Sea anchors can also be used to a limited extent to control direction by drag-steering. Keeping it directly behind the raft will keep you in the line of the current; to the left will turn you left of the current; and to the right will turn you right of the current. This may seem counterintuitive, but is exactly the same principle as a rudder.

SIGNS OF LAND

The knowledge that land is near will give an immediate boost to morale as well as a confirmation that you are moving in the right direction. It is also quite possible that you will see, smell, or hear other signs of land long before you see terra firma itself. The change in smell can be very distinct when you have been at sea for some time. I can remember many occasions of smelling land long before seeing it. The smell of rich pasture or grass or heather is a wonderful sensation after long days of spray and salt water.

BIRD MOVEMENT

The presence of flocks of birds is usually a reliable indication that land is relatively close unless they are migrating and far from land. Note their movement as they will probably be heading away from land in the morning and back towards land to roost in the evening. Seagulls, ducks, and geese are a sure sign that land is near.

Seagulls indicate that land is nearby, and they are edible too!

CUMULUS CLOUDS

If you see a fixed cumulus cloud (see Chapter 1, page 38) in the distance when others around it are moving, or a single cumulus cloud in an otherwise clear sky, there is a good chance that land may be near. Cumulus clouds often form over islands, sometimes shaping and molding into the shape of the island itself. Also look out for unusual coloration on the underside of clouds, in particular a green tinge if you are in the tropics: this is caused by the green of jungle vegetation being reflected upwards.

CHANGES IN SEA AND SKY COLOR

The sea will often start to change color near to land as it either becomes shallower (turning a lighter blue in temperate waters or light green in the tropics) or even brown from the silt of a river mouth. The brown silt of the Amazon off the coast of South America spreads hundreds of miles into the Atlantic. In the tropics the sky, like the clouds, can gain a greenish tint from reflected vegetation. Lightning in the early morning may indicate a mountain range. In polar regions, the dark gray of the underside of clouds, so familiar when in open water, will begin to lighten near land.

WAVE PATTERNS

Wave patterns are liable to change as you come near to land. Currents and the pattern of the swell will be disturbed by a nearby landmass, and the effects of the wind will be reduced if you are approaching in the wind shadow of an island. If the swell is decreasing but the wind remains constant, it indicates that an island is blocking the wind and you will be approaching in the wind shadow of the island.

DRIFTWOOD AND VEGETATION

An increase in the amount of driftwood or vegetation in the water often indicates that land is near.

WIND DIRECTION

The wind generally blows towards land during the day and away from it in the evening. (This happens because the land heats up faster than the sea. The hot air then rises and cold air from the sea races to fill the void; hence the wind blowing towards land during the day. The opposite occurs at night.) If you detect this pattern, combined with other signs, it is a good indication of nearby land.

MAKING LANDFALL

Even near land that is well populated, search-and-rescue planes do not always see life rafts and you may need actually to reach terra firma before you can be rescued. As long as you can land safely, survival on an island or the coastline of the mainland will usually be far easier than at sea, and fresh water and food in greater supply.

Your joy at finding land may later be dissipated by the difficulties of getting ashore and the unknown hazards that may await you when you do. When Shackleton reached South Georgia with his men after crossing 800 miles of the roughest seas on earth, he

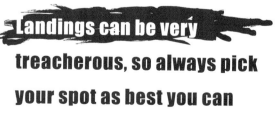

Landings can be very treacherous, so always pick your spot as best you can

Survival on a desert island requires patience, mental resolve and imagination.

Islands are often surrounded by treacherous reefs and rocks – learn how to approach a shoreline carefully.

was forced to land on the west side of the island. This meant he had still to cross a treacherous mountain range with minimal equipment to reach the whaling station on the east coast. Only then could he launch the rescue mission for the rest of the men he had left behind on Elephant Island. Landings can be very treacherous, so always pick your spot as best you can.

CHOOSING A LANDING SITE

Having crossed thousands of miles of ocean, nothing would be so careless as to drown while trying to get ashore. But that is what can easily happen. This is the point where the energy passing through the sea explodes with frightening force against the solid mass of the land. One has only to see what happens when a tsunami hits land to know that in hostile conditions, the sea will always come out on top, especially when after many days adrift your muscles may be severely weakened.

When approaching land, look for calm and gently shelving beaches away from rocks and cliffs where the breaking surf will be at its most violent. In the tropics avoid coral reefs which are very dangerous and in rough weather can easily rip a raft and its crew apart. There are no coral reefs where rivers meet the sea, but beware instead of dangerous currents.

PROTECT YOURSELF

Tie everything down that you can, either to yourself or the raft, and make sure you are wearing shoes and protective clothing. Do not tie yourself to the boat as you risk being dragged under. If you are wearing a lifejacket, make sure it is properly inflated. Swim on your back as it will be much easier. Remove anything above the level of the raft that might catch the wind or obscure your view of the shore, such as a shade canopy. If you are thrown out of the boat and find yourself being launched towards the rocks, keep your legs raised in front of you so that your feet and knees will absorb some of the impact.

OBSERVE THE SURF AND THE TIDES

The safest place to land will be where the wind and the currents are whipping up the least surf approaching the shoreline. This is likely to be in the lee of a landmass and not where the prevailing wind is blowing you towards land. In tidal areas, try to work out the rhythms of the tide and whether it is in or out. It will be far better to land on an incoming tide and be taken far up the beach than on an outgoing one that may have serious undertow.

USE THE SEA ANCHOR

Deploy a sea anchor (see page 238) as you approach land as this will help stabilize the erratic movement of the raft, keep the bows at 90 degrees to the waves, and stop the boat being swept uncontrollably ashore on the crest of the waves. Attach something buoyant like an inflated plastic bag to the sea anchor as this will keep it near the surface and stop it snagging on debris on the sea floor. Use the oars or paddles to keep the raft pointed towards the shore and constantly adjust the sea anchor to keep a strain on the line.

KEEP PERPENDICULAR TO THE WAVES

Avoid letting the boat swing side on to the waves as it will rapidly become unstable and be in grave danger of being capsized by the waves. Use oars to help propulsion and as a rudder.

RULE OF SEVEN

As Papillon observed when making plans to escape Devil's Island on his raft of coconuts, sea surf often approaches land in a series of seven waves, building progressively. In rough weather, try to approach the beach after one cycle of waves has finished and another is beginning to build.

AVOID SURFING

If the wind and surf are strong, make sure you are not caught by the waves and carried to the shore like a surfer on the crest of the waves. A surfer can turn sideways on and leave the wave when he chooses, but you may be jackknifed onto the beach or the rocks. The best technique is to paddle forwards and backwards to keep the raft in the trough between the waves. The same technique applies if you have been thrown out of the raft and are swimming ashore – stay in the troughs.

DON'T FIGHT THE CURRENT

If you find yourself being dragged back out to sea, or parallel to the shore, don't fight the current. Let it take you where it will, or steer the raft perpendicular to it until you find the edge. Swim diagonally with the current towards shore and pace yourself.

WAIT UNTIL THE BOAT IS GROUNDED

As you approach land and the force of the surf begins to die down, you can afford to allow yourself to catch a wave and be propelled towards the beach, especially if there is the danger of a strong undertow. Ride up the beach as far as you can and wait until the boat has grounded before jumping out and dragging the raft as far up the beach as possible.

Swim diagonally with the current towards shore and pace yourself

Natural Hazards

Of all the hazards confronting the castaway adrift on the high seas, few cast such a long shadow as the creatures that patrol the waters beneath the raft. While their actual threat to life and limb may not be as great as the perils of exposure, dehydration, and lack of food, Jaws and his friends will still be waiting.

SHARKS

Fear of sharks is one of the most primeval of instincts. It seems to awaken that part of the collective unconscious that comes from a time before man reached the top of the food chain and became the king of the jungle. The shark is the predator that attacks silently and unseen from the depths of an alien world.

Sharks live in all the oceans of the world, from the tropics to the coldest Arctic waters. There are more than 375 shark species, but only about a dozen are considered dangerous to humans and three are particularly so: the great white, the tiger shark, and the bull shark.

Sharks are attracted from miles away by noise, vibration, and the smell of blood or rotting food. They are particularly sensitive to any abnormal noise or vibrations which suggest a wounded prey – whether it be a human, fish, or a fellow shark – and they are capable of detecting one part of blood per ten billion parts of water, which means they can sniff out one drop of blood in an area the size of an Olympic swimming pool. They are also able to sense electrical fields which help them both navigate and detect their prey.

Sharks can attack at speeds of up to 40 miles per hour, and their mouths are filled with rows of razor-sharp triangular teeth inside a jaw that can close with the force of a steam hammer.

Shark attacks on rafts have been known, but they are rare. Around the world there are between fifty and seventy shark attacks a year, resulting in on average ten deaths while – according to the Florida Museum of Natural History's International Shark Attack File – fishermen kill anything between 20 and 100 million of them. Based on these figures, a revenge ratio of 1 of us for between 2 and 10 million of them makes them seem rather forgiving creatures.

Nonetheless, it's worth being careful. So when you think sharks may be in the vicinity:

- Do not fish. If you have hooked a fish, let it go.
- Do not clean or gut fish in the water.
- Do not throw rubbish or any waste overboard. When you do, throw it behind the raft all in one go to avoid forming a trail, and do it at night and when the raft is moving.
- Do not let your arms, legs, or equipment hang in the water.
- Keep quiet and do not move around.
- Do not attack the shark unless you are certain it is about to attack you.

- When you pee or poo, empty it from the raft in one go to avoid forming a trail, and try to do so at night and when the raft is moving.
- In the event of being attacked, stab at the shark repeatedly with a knife or a club, or even your fists, aiming for its eyes, nose, gills, or the nerve center on its head directly above its eyes.

WHALES

Although there are many stories of whales attacking yachts, including the two examples I mentioned earlier of Steve Callahan and the Robertson family, not to mention *Moby-Dick*, whales do not usually attack liferafts. If a whale does come near, stop any activity you may be doing, including fishing, and keep quiet. Make sure nothing is trailing over the side of the boat. Normally the whale will quickly lose interest and move on.

BARRACUDA

Barracuda are long, thin carnivores that can grow up to 6 feet long but are usually 3 to 4 feet in length. They have a mouthful of fiendishly sharp teeth and a fearsome bite and will mutilate both each other and their prey very efficiently. They are generally not a problem. They have been known to attack humans, but this is usually in murky water or at night when the victim is wearing jewelry or something bright that attracts the attack. Barracudas are often found in large schools.

JELLYFISH

Jellyfish catch their prey with nematocysts, small stinging organs in the tentacles like miniature harpoons with barbs on the end that inject poison to paralyze their prey. Human fatalities have occurred, but usually victims survive after suffering excruciating pain. If you do get stung, you should pee on the wound, as the acid in your urine will help to neutralize the proteins in the poison.

Of the 2,000 species of jellyfish, about 70 are a threat to humans. The following are the most common and the most deadly:

BOX JELLYFISH

Found in the Pacific and Indian Oceans near northern Australia and the Philippines, usually between November and April. Also known as the sea wasp, it is the most venomous creature in the sea, perhaps even on the entire planet – its tentacles contain enough poison to kill three adults. It is instantly recognizable from its white box-shaped "body," which is often as large as a basketball. It has a bundle of ten to sixty stinging tentacles which can be up to 30 feet long.

PORTUGUESE MAN-OF-WAR

Portuguese men-of-war are common in the Gulf of Mexico and the Caribbean Sea, but they are sometimes carried by the Gulf Stream as far north as Europe and found as far south as Australia.

Commonly referred to as a jellyfish, it is actually a colony of four sorts of polyps. Its tentacles normally reach around 40 feet in length but its sting is rarely fatal. The man-of-war's body consists of a gas-filled, bladderlike float usually tinted pink, blue, or violet, which may be up to a foot long and rise up to 6 inches above the waterline. Beneath the float hang tentacles which can actually grow up to 160 feet long.

In any survival situation, the key is not to fight the terrain, but to go with the flow, adapt to it, and use it to get you back to safety.

The Bear Necessities: Surviving the Sea

RULE 1: BE PREPARED
Nothing will improve your chances of surviving at sea more than thorough preparation for the unthinkable. Rehearse your survival drills and make sure all equipment is maintained and is easy and quick to deploy in an emergency.

RULE 2: PROTECT YOURSELF FROM THE ELEMENTS
The cold and the wet will quickly cause hypothermia, and the sun will dehydrate and burn you, unless you are well protected.

RULE 3: PRESERVE WATER
Only drink water in large quantities during heavy rainfall. The rest of the time fill every container and never waste a drop. Take a seasickness pill (kept on all modern liferafts) at the first hint of queasiness. Nothing will dehydrate and weaken you more than sickness.

RULE 4: DON'T DRINK SEAWATER
Just one gulp can be the thin end of the wedge. The relief will be extremely short-lived and delirium and kidney failure will inevitably follow.

RULE 5: NEVER GIVE UP
Mental strength is vital at sea as enforced passivity in a floating prison can drain your spirit unless you are prepared for it. Be the strong one. You're a born champion and, if you look for it, you have the heart to survive.

Four Elements of a Survivor

1) SKILLS

The skills within this book, if absorbed well enough and practiced sufficiently often, will give you a life-gaining advantage if you find yourself alone and stranded in any of these hostile worlds. Take this book with you on expeditions or use it as part of a survival grab bag. Keep it by your bed or in your downstairs bathroom and read it in small bites but regularly. Try to learn something new every day. That's a good discipline in itself. Remember: knowledge is power, and these skills are the basics on which you need to add the following layers to become an effective all-round survivor.

2) PHYSICAL FITNESS

Without the conditioning to be able to implement these skills and then actually have the strength to keep moving and walking to safety, the skills become purely academic. Keep yourself fit. Make physical training a habit, do something every other day for at least thirty minutes. Walk briskly, or run, do some simple strength circuits like push-ups and sit-ups, and stretch as well. These three elements – running, strength training, and stretching – form the basis of good physical fitness, and will give you a vital advantage in a life-and-death situation. Plus they will ensure your brain and concentration function at their most efficient level – and you will need both of these in spades.

3) GOOD FORTUNE

Luck will always play a part in any great survival escape. But luck is not as random as you might think. Learn to expect good things in your life; assume you'll get lucky. Why does the girl who's always dreaded marrying an overweight banker inevitably marry one? Our minds are magnets. It is a law of the universe: we attract what we expect. The luckiest people I have known are excited, positive, luck-presuming guys. Become one yourself. To paraphrase Napoleon: "I don't want good generals, I want lucky generals."

4) FINALLY: THE WILL TO SURVIVE

Ultimately your survival depends on this. How much do you want it? How deep is your well of determination or, more pertinently, how deep are you prepared to dig inside that well that you already possess? One of my favorite stories is of the two mice dropped into an urn of milk. The first mouse figured there was no hope of escape. The urn walls were too high, too slippery: insurmountable. As far as he could see, death was inevitable. He rolled over into the milk, hoping the end would be swift. The second mouse didn't see just a vat of milk, he saw the milk's potential. He started to tread water (or milk!). Then he trod faster; then faster. Slowly the milk began to curdle and thicken. He kept treading and kept swimming. The milk soon became cream, then slowly it turned into solid butter. That plucky mouse then crawled his way out of that urn. And therein, I guess, lies the final ingredient to being a survivor.

Conclusion

There is a huge amount of information in this book, more than you will ever probably need, but the key is to know by heart a few of the basic techniques for each of the essentials (i.e., a good shelter and a simple way to make fire, trap animals, and collect water). The rest will give you a good understanding of how the world of survival works, and as you learn more, that can then be added to this base knowledge. In time you will adapt a lot of it and find quirky little techniques that work for you. That's great.

I found as a kid, when I was learning a lot of this for the first time, that the best way to absorb such information was to keep the books close at hand when I was in the bath, on the john, or bored at train stations. I still do the same thing, and my bathroom is full of many of the great survival manuals of our time.

In this book I have tried to compile the most practical, easy-to-remember, and efficient of the methods I have learned. Some of the snares I have seen suggested by "experts" need an awful lot of time to make! When you are cold and wet and alone, you want to be able get food and water quickly and simply. The aim of this book has always been to keep you alive, not get you a medal in woodwork!

The bottom line is that contained here is everything that you need to survive in some of the world's most inhospitable terrains. These techniques are tried and proven and have worked for me time and time again.

I want to finish with one extra thing, which is that it is always good to have a "survival" party trick up your sleeve! Mine is to be able to put a chicken to sleep . . .

I did this for a bet in a bar once, while with the French Foreign Legion. A cockerel had been keeping us all up night after night, and we had been forbidden to kill it by the sergeants. I bet the other recruits I could put it to sleep and lie it down asleep on the bar within sixty seconds. That I did this successfully strangely won me more kudos than any mountain I have climbed or regiment I have belonged to!

The technique is very simple, and the hardest part is to catch the ruddy thing. Corner it, dive on it, throw a sheet over it, do whatever you need to do to catch it, but once you have it squawking wildly in your arms, this is the time to take the bets. No one will believe this wild, crazed chicken can be put to sleep in under a minute. When you're happy with the money on the table, grab the chicken's neck (no, don't

worry, I'm not going to wring it), then fold its head and tuck it under its wing and gently hold it there in place. Keep quiet, hold it nice and still, and within a minute it will be asleep, tricked into thinking it is nighttime. (Chickens aren't the smartest of creatures.) When you feel it still and relaxed, you can unfurl it again and place it slumped on the table . . . fast asleep. It's then time to call in your winnings.

Good luck, I hope you enjoyed the book, and if I see a chicken comatose on a bar somewhere, I'll know you at least read this page!

ISBN 978-1-4013-2293-9

Note to Readers: This book is intended to provide useful information and instructions to assist you in exploring natural and wilderness environments. Nevertheless, the author cannot anticipate all conditions, your experience, and your physical and psychological condition. For your safety, you should have the appropriate experience and resources before attempting to undergo wilderness adventures of the sort the author describes. You should use caution, care, and good judgment when following any of the advice described in this book. Consider your own skill level and safety precautions associated with such outdoor adventures. The reader assumes his or her own risk in undertaking such outdoor adventures. Neither the author nor the publisher can assume any responsibility for any injury, loss, damage to persons or property of a reader undertaking an outdoor adventure. The author and publisher are not advocating the reader undertake such an adventure, and the author and publisher expressly disclaim any liability arising directly or indirectly from the use of this book.

First published in Great Britain in 2007 by Channel 4 Books, a division of Transworld Publishers

Design by Bobby Birchall at Bobby&Co.
All line illustrations © Patrick Mulrey

Richard Morrison quote © The Times/NI Syndication

Hyperion books are available for special promotions and premiums. For details contact the HarperCollins Special Markets Department in the New York office at 212-207-7528, fax 212-207-7222, or email spsales@harpercollins.com.

FIRST U.S. EDITION

10 9 8 7 6 5 4 3

PICTURE CREDITS: Eric Baccega 59 (rattan palm); Hal Beral 236 (bottom); Bettmann/Corbis 18, 221; Brandon D. Cole/Corbis 234; Michael & Patricia Fogden/Corbis 178 (coral snake), 214 (coral snake); Laurent Gillieron/epa/Corbis 107; Bear Grylls 4 (left), 220, 228-229, 236 (top), 254 (all); Eric Guinther 59 (nipa palm); Wolfgang Kaehler/Corbis 57 (arctic willow); Belinda Kirk 4 (right), 46, 51, 53, 63, 66, 74, 84, 92-93, 109, 113, 117, 119, 120 (all), 121, 124 (both), 128, 132, 136-137, 138, 166, 172-173, 174, 187, 193, 195, 198-199, 206, 211, 213, 218-219, 225, 246; Kit Kittle 226; Neil Laughton 104; Pete Lee 8-9, 22; Danny Lehman/Corbis 55 (cat's tail); Emanuelle Maclean 2, 4 (left), 5 (left), 5 (right), 10, 31, 39, 78-79, 86-87, 151, 159, 161, 168-169, 181, 182, 223, 231, 236 (top), 241, 248-249; Simon Reay 12-14, 98-99; Chris Richards 165; Rupert Smith 5 (middle), 176, 188 (bottom), 190, 197; Robert Spoenlein/zefa/Corbis 64-65; Underwood & Underwood/Corbis 17; Juliet Wide 4 (middle), 7, 14, 20, 21, 68, 72, 88-89, 148, 162, 235. Endpapers © David Evans/Discovery Channel.

Acknowledgments

To the TV series production and camera team ... you know who you are. We've had countless long journeys in and out of countries, endless long days and nights filming, too many mosquito bites and a lot of laughs along the way. Simon Reay and Paul Ritz especially – thank you.

To Sarah Emsley and Doug Young at Transworld Publishers, Chlöe and Simon at Cunningham Management and Michael Foster and Liberty at ARG. For your constant energy and support. To Richard Madden, for burning the midnight oil with me. You're a giant of a man in so many ways.

To Rob MacIver at Diverse Bristol, Mary Donahue at Discovery Channel, and Ralph Lee at Channel Four TV, for your faith in me from the start. Thank you so much.

And above all, to my love Shara and my two little boys, for having been right beside me all the way through this long year, in spirit, if not always in person. I am home now for a bit, I promise.

Index

The heart of survival, as all the epic stories confirm, is hope. The hope that keeps you moving when everything inside you is screaming "give up." For me, that hope, through so many adventures and expeditions, is found in these pictures. It is really very simple. To be surrounded by my family – Shara, Jesse, and Marmaduke – my great joy and the pride of my life.

Thank you.

I can't imagine a person becoming a success who doesn't give this game of life everything he's got. The same is true in the world of survival; the survivors are always the men or women who give everything they have to the purpose of getting out alive. In life and survival, if you are tentative you lose your power. Bear Grylls, 2006.